Encounters in the Victorian Press

Palgrave Studies in Nineteenth-Century Writing and Culture

General Editor: **Joseph Bristow**, Professor of English, UCLA

Editorial Advisory Board: **Hilary Fraser**, Birkbeck College, University of London; **Josephine McDonagh**, Linacre College, University of Oxford; **Yopie Prins**, University of Michigan; **Lindsay Smith**, University of Sussex; **Margaret D. Stetz**, University of Delaware; **Jenny Bourne Taylor**, University of Sussex

Palgrave Studies in Nineteenth-Century Writing and Culture is a new monograph series that aims to represent the most innovative research on literary works that were produced in the English-speaking world from the time of the Napoleonic Wars to the *fin de siècle*. Attentive to the historical continuities between 'Romantic' and 'Victorian', the series will feature studies that help scholarship to reassess the meaning of these terms during a century marked by diverse cultural, literary, and political movements. The main aim of the series is to look at the increasing influence of types of historicism on our understanding of literary forms and genres. It reflects the shift from critical theory to cultural history that has affected not only the period 1800–1900 but also every field within the discipline of English literature. All titles in the series seek to offer fresh critical perspectives and challenging readings of both canonical and non-canonical writings of this era.

Titles include:

Laurel Brake and Julie F. Codell (*editors*)
ENCOUNTERS IN THE VICTORIAN PRESS
Editors, Authors, Readers

Dennis Denisoff
SEXUAL VISUALITY FROM LITERATURE TO FILM, 1850–1950

Laura E. Franey
VICTORIAN TRAVEL WRITING AND IMPERIAL VIOLENCE

Lawrence Frank
VICTORIAN DETECTIVE FICTION AND THE NATURE OF EVIDENCE
The Scientific Investigations of Poe, Dickens and Doyle

Encounters in the Victorian Press

Editors, Authors, Readers

Edited by

Laurel Brake

and

Julie F. Codell

First published 2005 by
PALGRAVE MACMILLAN
Houndmills, Basingstoke, Hampshire RG21 6XS and 175 Fifth Avenue, New
York, N.Y. 10010
Companies and representatives throughout the world

PALGRAVE MACMILLAN is the global academic imprint of the Palgrave
Macmillan division of St. Martin's Press, LLC and of Palgrave Macmillan
Ltd. Macmillan® is a registered trademark in the United States, United
Kingdom and other countries. Palgrave is a registered trademark in the
European Union and other countries.

ISBN 1–4039–4177–7 hardback

This book is printed on paper suitable for recycling and made from fully
managed and sustained forest sources.

A catalogue record for this book is available from the British Library.

Library of Congress Cataloging-in-Publication Data
Encounters in the Victorian press: editors, authors, readers / edited by
Laurel Brake & Julie F. Codell.
        p. cm. – (Palgrave studies in nineteenth-century writing and
culture)
        Includes bibliographical references and index.
        ISBN 1–4039–4177–7
        1. English literature – 19th century – History and criticism.
    2. Periodicals – Publishing – Great Britain – History – 19th century.
    3. Authors and publishers – Great Britain – History – 19th century.
    4. Literature publishing – Great Britain – History – 19th century.
    5. Authors and readers – Great Britain – History – 19th century.
    6. Books and reading – Great Britain – History – 19th century.
    7. Great Britain – Intellectual life – 19th century.   8. Press – Great
Britain – History – 19th century.   9. English periodicals – History –
19th century.   10. Editing – History – 19th century.   I. Brake,
Laurel, 1941–   II. Codell, Julie F.   III. Series.
        PR463.F56   2004
                                                        2004050894

Printed and bound in Great Britain by
Antony Rowe Ltd, Chippenham and Eastbourne

In Memory
of
Josef Altholz
and
Barbara Quinn Schmidt

Contents

List of Illustrations

List of Tables

Acknowledgements

We would like to thank members of the Research Society for Victorian Periodicals (RSVP), and participants in RSVP conferences over the years in which debates about the Victorian press have inspired us, as well as to acknowledge the stimulation of articles in RSVP's publication, *Victorian Periodicals Review*. The essays in our volume are expanded and revised versions of a selection of papers presented at the RSVP conference, 'Encounters: Readers, Authors, Editors', in London, 2000.

We also thank our editor, Paula Kennedy, and the staff at Palgrave Macmillan for their assistance in preparing this manuscript, and to the anonymous reader for helpful suggestions on all the essays.

We thank the following editors and publishers for giving us permission to re-use earlier versions of some of the essays in this volume:

William Scheuerle, editor, *Victorian Periodicals Review*, for permission to publish Aled Jones, 'The *Dart* and the Damning of the Sylvan Stream: Journalism and Political Culture in the Late-Victorian City', *Victorian Periodicals Review*, 35 (Spring 2002), 2–17.

Elizabeth Prochaska, Oxford University Press, for permission to publish John Plunkett, 'Civic publicness: the creation of Queen Victoria's royal role 1837–1861', which contains some material from a chapter in his book *Queen Victoria, First Media Monarch* (Oxford University Press, 2003).

Notes on Contributors

Laurel Brake is Professor of Literature and Print Culture at Birkbeck, University of London, where she lectures in English, specializing in Victorian Studies. Her research interests include nineteenth-century press, gender and culture, and Walter Pater. She has published widely on these topics, including *Print in Transition* (Palgrave 2001), *Subjugated Knowledges* (1994), and *Walter Pater* (1994), co-edited collections – with Ian Small *Pater in the 1990s* (1991), and with Bill Bell and David Finkelstein *Nineteeth-Century Media and the Construction of Identities* – and wrote recently 'On Print Culture: the State We're In', *Journal of Victorian Culture*, 6 (2001). She is currently at work on a biography of Pater called *Ink Work* for Oxford University Press.

Julie F. Codell is Professor of Art History and English at Arizona State University. Her numerous articles and reviews on Victorian art and culture have appeared in many scholarly journals, anthologies of collected essays, and encyclopedias. She wrote *The Victorian Artist: Artists' Lifewritings in Britain, c. 1870–1910* (2003), edited *Imperial Co-Histories: National Identities and the British and Colonial Press* (2003), and co-edited *Orientalism Transposed: The Impact of the Colonies on British Culture* (1998). She is currently preparing a book on visuality and imperial cultures in the Delhi coronation durbars and their exhibitions of Indian art, 1877–1911, and is editing a special issue of *Victorian Periodicals Review* on the press in nineteenth-century India.

Patricia de Montfort is British Academy Research Fellow at the Centre for Whistler Studies, University of Glasgow, Scotland. Her research interests focus on Whistler's writings, aesthetic ideas and journalistic connections. She has lectured and published on the Victorian art press, Whistler's *Gentle Art of Making Enemies*, and his connections with the publishing world of the 1890s. She is currently completing the final phase of work on a major electronic publication 'The Correspondence of James McNeill Whistler, 1855–1903', first published in 2003, and has recently started a study of Victorian exhibition culture.

Ian Haywood is Reader in English at Roehampton University in London. He has edited a three-volume series of Chartist fiction for

Ashgate and has published articles and essays on the nineteenth-century radical and popular press. His most recent book is *The Revolution in Popular Literature: Print, Politics and the People 1790–1860* (2004).

Aled Jones is Sir John Williams Professor of Welsh History and Head of the Department of History and Welsh History at the University of Wales, Aberystwyth. His publications include *Press, politics and society* (1993) and *Powers of the Press: Newspapers, power and the public in nineteenth-century England* (1996). He is currently working on a study of missions, empire and national identity in Wales and Bengal, 1840–1939.

Graham Law is Professor in Media Studies at the International College, Waseda University, Tokyo. In addition to a wide range of articles on nineteenth-century literary and publishing history, he is the author of *Serializing Fiction in the Victorian Press* (2000) and the compiler of *Indexes to Fiction in 'The Illustrated London News' and 'The Graphic'* (2001). He has also produced editions of a number of Victorian novels, including David Pae's *Lucy, the Factory Girl* (2001) and Dora Russell's *Beneath the Wave* (2004). He is co-editor both of the *Wilkie Collins Society Journal* and of a forthcoming collected edition of the letters of Wilkie Collins (2005). He is currently working on a history of the newspaper novel in its global context.

Patricia O'Hara is Professor of English at Franklin and Marshall College. From 1995 to 2000 she served as editor of *Nineteenth Century Studies*. She has authored scholarly essays on Victorian literature and anthropology and on the Blue Willow pattern of china (*Victorian Studies* 1994). Her personal essays have appeared in *Newsweek* and the *Sycamore Review*. She is presently writing a book of literary essays.

Barbara Onslow lectures in the English Department, University of Reading, England, and specialises in nineteenth-century periodicals, particularly the work of women. She has published in *Victorian Poetry*, *Victorian Periodicals Review*, and *Media History*. She is the author of *Women of the Press in Nineteenth Century Britain* (2000). Her forthcoming articles include 'Women in Publishing and Printing', in *From Ice Age Symbols to the Internet, an Encyclopedia of Graphic Communication*, ed. A. Rodriguez-Buckingham (2005), and a chapter on journalism and crime, ' "The Inside Story" – Crime, Convicts and Careers for Women', in *Crime, Madness and Sensation*, ed. Andrew Maunder and Grace Moore

(2004). She is currently working on the New Woman and journalism, including columnists writing for the illustrated weekly newspapers.

John Plunkett is Lecturer in Victorian Literature and culture at the University of Exeter. His publications include *Queen Victoria – First Media Monarch* (2003) and a three-volume collection, co-edited with Andrew King, *Popular Print Media 1820–1900* (2004). He is currently working on a reader on Victorian print media, and a long-term project, provisionally entitled 'Optical Recreations: A History of Screen Practice 1780–1900'.

Sheila Rosenberg was a contributor to, and then later an advisory editor and assistant editor for, the first three volumes of the *Wellesley Index* and was a founder member of RSVP. Publications include the section on serials (with Henry Rosenberg) in vol. 3 of the 2nd edition of *The New Cambridge Bibliography of English Literature* (NCBEL), 1969, and a chapter on the *Westminster Review*, 'The financing of radical opinion', in *Samples and Soundings*, ed J. Shattock and M. Wolff (1982). Her most recent articles include 'The "wicked *Westminster*": John Chapman, his contributors and promises fulfilled', *VPR*, 33 (2000). She is currently working on the contribution of John Chapman and his 'wife' to the French feminist movement in Paris in the 1870s and 1880s.

Johanna M. Smith is an associate professor of English at the University of Texas-Arlington, specializing in eighteenth- and nineteenth-century British literature and culture. She has published a book on Mary Shelley and several articles on subjects ranging from *Millenium Hall* to Raymond Chandler. Her most recent books are the second edition of *Mary Shelley: Frankenstein* (2000) and the co-edited anthology *Life-Writings by British Women 1660–1815* (2000). Her essay is part of a book she is currently completing on British women's interventions in the public sphere from 1752 to 1858.

Mark W. Turner is Lecturer in English at King's College, University of London. He is the author of *Backward Glances: Cruising the Queer Streets of New York and London* (2003), *Trollope and the Magazines: Gendered Issues in Mid-Victorian Britain* (2000), co-editor of *From Author to Text: Rereading* Romola (1998), and author of several articles on nineteenth-century media and culture. He co-edits the journal *Media History* and has recently guest edited a special issue of the *Journal of Popular Culture* on 'Reading and Pleasure'.

Introduction: Encountering the Press

Laurel Brake and Julie Codell

This book focuses on the unique characteristic of the Victorian periodical press – its development of encounters between and among readers, editors, and authors. By encounters in the press, we mean any set of articles or letters to the editor in which the writer, whether journalist or reader, responds to a published article in a periodical, often as a reply to special topics or issues of the day, or to other articles with which the respondent agrees or disagrees. These encounters may be in the form of debates or dialogues, and they function in several ways, notably as mediations of the topic under discussion in the press or as the content itself.

Essays in this volume explore writing by authors and journalists on a variety of topics, and by readers whose responses to articles and debates transformed them into active participants in Victorian debates. In their rich variety of voices and contexts, encounters addressed the most important subjects of the period: marriage and divorce, empire, local politics, science, religion, gender and class politics, and new claims of authority in social, political, and cultural matters. Encounters determined the contents and structure of many journals. Most nineteenth-century periodicals, whether review, magazine, miscellany, or newspaper, consist of individuals' contributions patched together and fitted, very practically, to the space, readership, and politics of the structure of a single periodical issue.

The concept of encounters is important not only because it mediates periodicals' social functions, but also because it offsets another tendency: a journal title promises a false unity, appearing to present, despite its many articles, topics, and illustrations, a unified policy, or set of beliefs, as if the journal itself were a single author. Although anonymity was intended in part to promote objectivity, the pressure of proper names broke through. Names of celebrity authors/contributors/editors such as George Eliot, William Thackeray, Walter Pater, and James McNeill Whistler are gradually published or implied following the growth of signature (the published attribution of articles to contributors) from 1865 onwards. By 1877 named celebrities dominate competition among upmarket periodicals to increase sales and popularity. Encounters in nineteenth-century journals also invoke other publications, parties and individuals by name, producing at times a racy topicality that signature would subsequently enhance. The monthly *Nineteenth Century's* 'symposium', for example, organised topical debates among named celebrity contributors, whereas in the case of periodicals adhering to anonymity, their titles gave the illusion of unity and appropriated the social and cultural functions of the author that Michel Foucault, historian of culture, has described: the author's name has now come to assume an heroic authority, unity, autonomy and control over all the written material attributed to that name, erasing in our minds the rich social and cultural influences that authors inevitably assimilate but may not always acknowledge.[1] By focusing on encounters in the periodical press, we can supplement the illusion of unity in periodicals and explore not the contribution of the individual celebrity writer, but the multi-vocal discourse of periodical texts by editors, writers, and readers.

Dialogue among diverse emerging publics from differing classes, genders, and new professional and political interest groups resulted. The spread of education and literacy meant that specialized discourses about art, politics, or economics became available to more readers for their consideration and commentary, a kind of secular Protestantism. Through this widening discursivity, individuals of emerging classes (Jürgen Habermas's notion of the bourgeoisie as a 'reading public')[2] could debate topics once reserved for aristocratic consideration in a new space, the 'emerging *public sphere of civil society*' (Habermas, 23; italics in original). In the nineteenth century, the public also became a source of opinions and judgments (Habermas, 2) and this set of emerging, diverse opinions constituted the encounters in the periodical press. Differences among groups were mediated by these encounters, as members of the public wrote in response to one another.

As the site of debates and encounters, the press emerged as a major public space for discourses about society, politics, culture, public order, and larger worlds of foreign and imperial affairs. Collective production and breadth of representation were among the defining strengths of journals. Any research on Victorian culture must consider how different newspapers and periodicals mediated key debates within the period. Every kind of writing appeared in the press, including much nineteenth-century fiction and poetry. Serialized in periodicals, literature was often fragmented, interspersed, and intertextual. These conditions of printing and reading raise historical questions such as why certain magazines supported some authors and not others, what editorial policies existed in each periodical, how much periodicals paid authors and editors, and their circulation and readerships, questions this volume addresses through the study of encounters.

Approaches to periodicals have changed in recent years and a study of these changes provides an account of the state of media history. Scholars often trace the history of a single topic or event, but such transjournal approaches may ignore the composite identities of individual titles. Other accounts are empirical and archival, employing statistical evidence of costs, circulation, and authors, or focus on aspects of the material culture of print. Still others are largely theory-based. Imagining the historical reader of periodicals is difficult, and can be based on subscription rates, the topics discussed, the language used, the politics expressed, personal communication between editors and authors, and letters on the correspondence page. This volume intends to intervene in a field that has been evolving for more than half a century, and its chapters show the fresh and varied strategies with which critics treat complex publications that are neither single-authored nor one-off. Essays in this volume, alive to the timely interactions and intertextuality of Victorian periodicals, do not exclusively focus on famous authors writing in the press, or media histories of well-known journals. Instead, they treat a wide range of journals, including weeklies such as *Eliza Cook's Journal* (1849–1854), *Punch* (1841–2002) and the *Dart* (1876–1911), an illustrated paper from Birmingham; popular monthlies such as the innovative *Cornhill Magazine* (1860–1975), and the Benthamite and then progressive, quarterly and then monthly *Westminster Review* (1824–1914); as well as short-lived periodicals, and 'class' journals that are addressed to a single topic or mode, such as illustration, gossip or satire. The methodology of this volume applies what D. F. McKenzie called the sociology of texts,[3] in which meanings stem both from texts treated as artefacts of material culture and from their functions in society.

The implications for media history of McKenzie's rescue of the study of text from the exclusions and hierarchies of bibliography and history were profound. Instead of devaluing ephemera and isolating individual texts as bibliographers tended to do at the time, McKenzie deprecated the narrowness of focus on one format, the book; instead, he cited the inclusiveness of a developing genre of bibliographical work, the short title index, to welcome *all* forms of print *and* the new media as objects of study. At the same time his active embrace of the *comprehensive* history of individual titles included ways that production, materials, and design produce meanings, as well as the conventional reliance on typography, and contributed to his contemporary French colleagues' re-formulation of the theory of the *history* of the book.[4] McKenzie's prac-tice challenged the convention in history, which was to raid the press for isolated quotations, without taking account of the politics and sociology of the serials from which they were lifted.

McKenzie's work was matched by other enabling approaches to the field, which now comprise the foundations of current research. From Michael Wolff's fertile imagination emanated not only a journal and a research society[5] dedicated to Victorian periodicals, but also two crucial reference projects edited by other scholars, which appeared over decades. The first, *The Wellesley Index to Victorian Periodicals* (1966–89)[6], recorded the contents of largely complete Victorian runs of each issue of 43 upmarket quarterlies and monthlies, and undertook basic research on each title, the index of which was prefaced by a scholarly headnote. Its pursuit of the identity of authors and attribution of individual arti-cles reflect its origins in English literature and its foregrounding of authorship, while promulgating links between periodicals and literature in its widest sense. Thus, by the end of its five volumes, there was an author index of journalists, and the basis for a subject index, which was realized in *Wellesley*'s subsequent publication on CD-ROM. While *Wellesley* characterized its selected journals as 'major', they only were recognised as such in our time by the huge stimulus to research afforded to them by their inclusion in *Wellesley*. This 'Index' was the first major stimulus to the reinvigoration of research in this field in Britain and the US.

In 1969 the third volume of the *NCBEL*[7] included a substantial list of newspapers and periodicals, and in 1976 the first volume of Wolff's other suggestion, the *Waterloo Directory* (Phase 1)[8], extended the horizon of *NCBEL* by publishing nearly 30,000 titles of Victorian serials. Since that debut, the *Waterloo Directory of English Newspapers and Periodicals* under John North has gone from strength to strength, appearing on CD-ROM in 1994, in a 10-volume edition (series 2) in 1998, and a 20-volume edition (series 3) in 2004, as well as online in 2001 and 2004. Both in its model for a bibliographical template for serials and its expanding profiles of numerous titles, informed by shelf-checks and accompanied in many cases by illustrations of title pages, it is a remarkable resource which continues to open up knowledge of titles which, if familiar at all, were each known to tiny numbers of specialists. The formidable variety and richness of the Victorian press are becoming discernible in these volumes.

Meanwhile, electronic availability of the contents of periodical titles themselves has been pioneered, by for example *ILEJ* (*Internet Library of Early Journals*), *PCI* (*Periodicals Contents Index*), *Palmer's Index to The Times*, *The Times* itself, the British Library's pilot, *Historical Newspapers Online*, and Brown University's Modernist Journals project that includes a portion of *The New Age* (1894–1938). The capacity to search journals electronically, to access them at home *and* irrespective of geographical proximity to library resources, and to download text easily has transformed the nature of intellectual work possible on journals as well as widening access. Soon, use of such material can be an expected part of *all* research in the period, from secondary school students to scholars. One of the most recently available electronic indexes that is particularly useful is an anthology of several Victorian indices. Called *Nineteenth-Century Masterfile* (in the UK) or *Poole's Plus* (in the US), it includes *Poole's* [subject] *Index to Victorian Periodicals*, W. T. Stead's indexes of the 1890s, and other indices of legal, religious, and psychology journals.

Our burgeoning access to periodical texts and the potential for research access releases have been paralleled by the fast-developing field of book history which, in its various national accounts, often extends to print culture and the press. The conventional separation of the study of books, periodicals and newspapers is beginning to give way, as it does in our volume, and journals such as *Media History* (1998 onwards)[9], which not only tuck print journalism into a media bed, beside film and video, broadcasting, photography and digital forms, but also look beyond national to global formations and discourses. This kaleidoscope of frameworks is the context of our studies of encounters in the Victorian press, encounters that themselves suggest restive formal and cultural dynamics.

Nineteenth-century periodicals were not normally univocal. Even within the earlier periodical convention of anonymity, a range of contributors and views were discernible. Serials can be described in the way that the Russian formalist Mickail Bakhtin describes literature: dialogic, multi-vocal, and intertextual.[10] Readers' letters to editors and responses to plots and characters in serialized novels effected changes in editorial views and in fiction writing. There are contending voices and arguments within journals (visible clearly in early *Punch*), between rival titles competing for similar niches (the *Saturday Review* [1855–1931] and its contemporaries), and between titles that represent competing political parties or positions (the Whig and Tory quarterlies in the first half of the century, such as the *Edinburgh* (1802–1929) and the *Quarterly* (1809–1967), respectively). Where politics was a key term, one indirect model was the adversarial rhetoric of Parliament. Radicals believed that newspapers were the parliament of the people, a connection reinforced by the imposition of newspaper taxes that restricted circulation of political information to those who could afford to purchase it. Late in the century, at the height of the power of nineteenth-century journalism, government *by journalism* was proposed by W. T. Stead (1849–1912), editor of the *Pall Mall Gazette* (1865–1923) and the *Review of Reviews* (1890–1936). This power was actually practised by the press, as the infrastructure of newspaper news-gathering and distribution became a system of political communication between reader-consumers and editor-owners who were also power brokers in politics and government.

While the encounters limned here are represented within the nineteenth century, the place of the Victorian press in modern media history is foreshadowed. It would be hard to find another field that is as faceted in its approach and range of reference as media history. Current feminist theory, for example, is likely to find significant areas of familiarity and difference in pieces here on women and work, class, gender, marriage and divorce. Anticipating modern, post-Victorian media history, these essays contribute an historical framework to the writing and study of media, too often limited to study of the last decades of the twentieth century. For example, the inroads of fiction into the nineteenth-century newspaper anticipated the recent exponential growth of feature content in dailies, just as the interaction characteristic of the Victorian press anticipates other media formats today such as talk shows. Authors in this collection are from a wide range of disciplines: literature, history, art history, political theory, history of science, and new fields such as colonial/imperial studies and cultural studies, a range that matches the multi-disciplinarity of the Victorian periodical press. Essays in this volume were selected and expanded from papers delivered at an international conference in London on the nature of encounters in the Victorian periodical press. They are arranged chronologically from the beginnings of the Victorian period in the 1830s and 40s to the very end of the century, as well as within topics on gender, class, urban life, and politics that emerged during this period.

Notes

1. Michel Foucault, 'What is an Author?' (1969), in *The Foucault Reader*, ed. Paul Rabinow (Harmondsworth: Penguin, 1984), 101–20.
2. Jürgen Habermas, *The Structural Transformation of the Public Sphere*, trans. Thomas Burger (Cambridge: MIT Press, 2000), 23.
3. *Bibliography and the Sociology of Texts: The Panizzi Lectures*, 1985 (London: British Library, 1986). A second edition of these lectures was published in 1999 by Cambridge University Press.
4. See Peter D. McDonald and Michael F. Suarez, S. J., 'Introduction', in *Making Meaning*, by D. F. McKenzie (Amherst and Boston: University of Massachusetts Press, 2002), 7: 'McKenzie's arguments, as appropriated by Darnton and Chartier, were crucial in helping to effect the turn away from quantitative, macrohistorical methods of traditional French book history to a new-style *histoire du livre* of the 1980s and 1990s emphasizing readers, materiality, and meaning'.
5. Now *Victorian Periodicals Review* (1968ff) and the Research Society for Victorian Periodicals (RSVP).
6. *The Wellesley Index to Victorian Periodicals*, ed. W. Houghton (vols 1–4), E. Houghton (vols 2–4) and J. Slingerland (vols 4–5) (5 vols; Toronto: University of Toronto and London: Routledge, 1966–89).
7. H. M. R. and S. K. R [Henry and Sheila Rosenberg], 'Newspapers and Magazines', *New Cambridge Bibliography of English Literature*, vol. 3, ed. G. Watson (Cambridge: Cambridge University Press, 1969), 1755–1884.
8. The first phase/volume was jointly edited by John North and Michael Wolff, and all subsequent volumes by John North.
9. The origins of *Media History* lie in the *Journal of Newspaper and Periodical Studies* edited by Michael Harris, 1984ff.
10. Mikhail Bakhtin, *The Dialogic Imagination*, ed. Michael Holquist, trans. Caryl Emerson and Michael Holquist (Austin: University of Texas Press, 1981).

Part I
Early Victorian Press Encounters

1
Civic Publicness: The Creation of Queen Victoria's Royal Role 1837–61

John Plunkett

> Assuredly, the reign of Victoria will be known as the reign of royal visits; it seems to have established an era of royal and imperial sociability.
>
> *Illustrated London News,* June 1844.[1]

What does a British constitutional monarch do? Month on month, year on year, what provides worthy employment for a sovereign, particularly one supposedly above the machinations of party-politics? In the profession of royalty the public engagement reigns supreme. Whether patronising diverse charities, touring countries in the Commonwealth, or honouring the latest newly built hospital, civic visits loom large in the modern conception of royal duties. This essay argues that Queen Victoria and Prince Albert, through the impact of a burgeoning newspaper and periodical press, set a progressive model for the serious duties and pleasurable diversions that we have come to expect from a constitutional monarchy. During the 1840s and 1850s, Victoria and Albert undertook an unprecedented number of regional tours, foreign visits and civic engagements. They forged a successful role for themselves that would be followed by future British monarchs. Their work ranged from an earnest social concern, as in Albert assuming the Presidency of the Society for Improvement of the Labouring Classes in 1848, to the more enlivening nature of their marine jaunts to Louis-Philippe and Napoleon III in 1843 and 1855 respectively.

The thread that binds together the diverse activities of Victoria and Albert is the extensive press attention that they received. Royal occasions, whether an exclusive court levee at Windsor or one of the many parish dinners given to commemorate the monarch's birthday, had always occupied a privileged position in the calendar of national events.

Despite the vast changes wrought by industrialism and political reform, the cumulative regularity of Victoria and Albert's activities, coupled with the media attention they received, ensured that the monarchy continued to dominate the public sphere. Royal events were increasingly indivisible from the way in which they were experienced through their media coverage. There was a new style of royalty that was as much inaugurated around Victoria and Albert as by them. The roles they created were inseparable from the modernity of their lives existing as royal news, disseminated as never before by prints, periodicals and newspapers. Although representations of Victoria have been the subject of several recent books, most notably by Adrienne Munich and Margaret Homans, these studies have tended to focus on analysing individual images.[2] Not enough attention has been paid to the new genres of newspapers and periodicals that were instrumental in creating an immediate relationship between Victoria and her subjects.

The engagements carried out by Victoria and Albert only had such an impact because they were keyed into the simultaneous development of popular weekly newspapers like the *News of the World*, *Lloyd's Weekly Newspaper*, the *Weekly Times* and *Reynolds's Weekly Newspaper*. These publications commenced in October 1843, January 1843, January 1847, and May 1850 respectively. The new, relatively affordable Sunday newspapers were aimed at the large number of readers who were either unwilling to afford a metropolitan daily paper or who did not have the leisure time to read one. The success of these newspapers established a genre that would dominate the popular press for the rest of the nineteenth century and beyond; in 1886 a survey of the working-class press by Edward Salmon could declare: 'Few working-class homes in England fail to "take in" some kind of paper on the day of rest.'[3] Predominantly liberal in outlook, with the notable exception of *Reynolds's Weekly Newspaper*, the enthusiastic royal coverage of the new weekly press marked a departure from the anti-monarchism that characterised unstamped radical publications of the 1830s like the *Poor Man's Guardian*. Similarly the Chartist newspaper the *Northern Star* was at it most influential in the late 1830s and early 1840s, and was superseded by the new Sunday publications.

The growth of the newspaper and periodical press was aided by equally far-reaching changes in graphic reproduction. Prior to the 1820s, cheap illustration was still primarily restricted to the woodcuts accompanying street ballads, published most famously by the Catnach Press of Seven Dials. The beginning of a rapid expansion in graphic culture took place with the introduction of steel-plate engraving in the early 1820s, a mode of reproduction that was taken up with great success by the literary annuals and the Books of Beauty. Nevertheless, the most far-reaching development to influence the graphic representation of Victoria before the advent of photography was a revival in wood-engraving and the subsequent development of an illustrated press. The 1820s saw the introduction of 2d illustrated miscellanies like *The Portfolio* (1823–5) and the *Mirror of Literature, Amusement and Instruction* (1823–41).[4] These were the precursors to the remarkable success of two illustrated periodicals that commenced in 1832, the *Penny Magazine* (1832–45) and the *Saturday Magazine* (1832–44). Inexpensive and high-quality illustrations were an important part of the attraction of these periodicals. It remained the case, however, that few newspapers gave illustrations of contemporary events. Thus, when the *Illustrated London News* commenced publication in May 1842 it was both innovative and impressive. Published weekly, the *Illustrated London News* provided an extensive supply of visual news, ranging from panoramic pullouts to small vignettes. In its ambitious and successful production of visual news, the *Illustrated London News* gave a new industrial and aesthetic dimension to wood engraving. It was soon imitated by publications like the *Illustrated Times* (1855–62), the *Pictorial Times* (1843–48), and the *Illustrated News of the World* (1858–63).

The changes in print and graphic media that I have just outlined became bound up with a new style of monarchy. They did so because in contrast to Victoria's consultations with her ministers – which invariably took place behind closed doors – her tours and visits took place as a series of specifically 'public' duties. There was a crucial symbiotic relationship between the civic publicness of Victoria and the publicity that these events received. Large royal setpieces were ideal for pictorial reportage. The communicative encounter between the monarchy and the press, traced from Victoria's accession in 1837 to Albert's death in 1861, shaped the news-values of the illustrated and Sunday presses, and, in so doing, helped to reinvent the position of the monarchy in national life. The focus of the rest of this chapter is therefore twofold. It traces the way that both the extent and the discursive shape of Victoria's coverage helped to promote her as a popular monarch.

During the 1840s and 1850s, attacks upon the monarchy as an institution have to be continually set against the much larger number of column inches of royal news that were engendered by the Queen's engagements.[5] By its *ipso facto* success, Victoria and Albert's civic publicness set the agenda for a royalist popular politics. (I am here using publicness in the sense defined by John Thompson, as in not just making visible but of making the experience of an event available to an audience not immediately present.)[6] Coinciding with the aftermath of the Reform Bill turmoil and the changing balance of power between the Crown, Lords and House of Commons, royal civic activities were invested with the discourse of popular constitutionalism. They were integral to the coterminous creation of Victoria as both a populist and a constitutional monarch, defining her royal role as well as producing a label that inspired endless platitudes. Recently, there has been an upsurge of interest in nineteenth-century populism and the discourse of constitutionalism. Well-known studies by Patrick Joyce, James Vernon and James Epstein have all drawn attention to the multiple ways in which notions of 'the People' and the constitution were deployed.[7] James Vernon has gone so far as to argue that constitutionalism was the major narrative of English popular political culture up until 1867. Despite the liminality, even the potential vacuity, of a term like 'the People', it was a crucial mobilising idiom and the cause of much con-testation.

One of the most oft-repeated platitudes concerning Victoria was that she had overseen the transition to a constitutional monarchy. At Victoria's death in January 1901, even the republican *Reynolds's Weekly Newspaper* felt able to assert that she was 'the example of a constitu-tional ruler and the founder of the Modern British Monarchy . . . she reduced meddling to the lowest terms and never imposed her will in an arrogant manner on her Ministers'.[8] As a monarch who had elevated herself above party politics, Victoria basked in the long glow of the Magna Carta and the Glorious Revolution, the culmination of the rights of the freeborn Englishman versus the autocracy of the Crown. Later, the Reform Acts of 1832, 1867, and 1884 would become part of the same constitutional mythology. This was a narrative whose potent hold was political, imaginative, historic. It seeped into every aspect of Victoria's role. Victoria's first tours and visits were endlessly played out through the interlinked discourses of the People and the constitution.

The populist invention of the British monarchy is often dated from the latter years of Victoria's reign. In a well-known argument, David Cannadine has contrasted the lack of grandiose royal ritual in the first half of the reign with the imperial extravaganzas of Victoria's Golden and Diamond Jubilees (1887, 1897) and the coronation of Edward VII (1902).[9] The pomp and circumstance of these late set-pieces is taken to exemplify Victoria's apotheosis as an imperial and national figurehead. This argument invariably downplays the significance of the Queen's activities during the first twenty years of the reign. The years between 1837 and 1861 were crucial in creating a successful model for the month-to-month duties of a popular British monarch. Pervading the multitudinous reports of the royal engagements of this period is the discourse of popular constitutionalism. Tours and visits were cast as a recognition of Victoria's reliance on the approval of her subjects, a celebration of the inclusivity and participation of the People in the political nation. Time and time again, the freely given support of the People was placed over and against the role of the organised Court pageantry. At Victoria's coronation, royal ceremony was widely derided as irrational, aristocratic and antiquarian. It was attacked as a being no more than a series of opulent gewgaws, a form of mummery designed to impress John Bull and prevent him from seeing the true state of the monarchy. The *Sunday Times*, then a radically-orientated newspaper, was typical in forthrightly declaring that if the coronation ceremony could not 'be simplified, adapted to the manners, laws and habits of the present time, it were better be abolished altogether'.[10] Subsequent royal events, which were perceived as being more informal and transparent, thus had an imaginative potency precisely because they were not over-laden with militaristic or aristocratic ceremony.

In a recent book, Frank Prochaska has argued that scholarship on the monarchy has neglected its substantive role in civil society.[11] Prochaska's own work focuses on the creation of what he describes as the welfare monarchy – the vital role played by royal philanthropy through the patronage of numerous charities and individuals. Victoria was a patron of, and not just a contributor to, 150 institutions, three times as many as George IV. Between 1831 and 1871, donations to institutions and individuals were equivalent to 15 per cent of the Privy Purse. Charity-work nevertheless comprised only part of the revivified prominence that Victoria and Albert enjoyed. The initial excitement occasioned by the new reign, which had been fostered by Victoria's coronation in 1838 and her marriage in 1840, settled down only in the sense that there was little diminution in her high-profile role.

Between 1840 and 1861, it is crucial to the whole style of Victoria's monarchy that she undertook a wide range of public engagements, and that she was seen to be doing them. Crucially, most newspapers treated Victoria's visits as an enactment of the reciprocal interest between Victoria and her subjects. As the *Illustrated London News* fawningly put it on the Queen's first tour of Scotland:

Abstractedly, the desire of a sovereign to hold communion with all classes of her people without regard to local or national distinctions, is an indication of a love of justice, and of that beautiful maternal affection which, in domestic life, cherishes no favourite in a family, but sheds its holy love on all alike.[12]

The comment is exemplary of the populist discourse attached to the queen's activities. In 1843, *The Times* similarly commented that Victoria's visits 'cement the union between the Crown and the people by a reciprocity of confidence.'[13] Again and again and again they were made to signify a popular constitutionalism – the monarch willingly placing herself before her People. Moreover, it is significant that the *Illustrated London News* regards the visits in terms of Victoria's maternal beneficence; the feelings inscribed into the visits are intimate and personal rather than simply a form of state duty. Instead of any contradiction between Victoria's femininity and her public role, they are conflated by the *Illustrated London News* so that each becomes the rationale of the other. Making the monarchy available to the People gave royal events an inclusive rhetoric that mitigated much potential criticism.

The majority of the metropolitan and provincial press echoed the *Illustrated London News's* sentiments. The extensiveness of the discourse of royal populism cannot be underestimated. On Victoria's tour of the midlands in November 1843, the *News of the World* claimed that her visits were only nominally visits to Sir Robert Peel, the Duke of Devonshire and the Duke of Rutland; they were in fact 'intended as visits to the people – all the working people as well as the burgesses in the different localities'.[14] For the *News of the World*, the Queen's most agreeable pleasure was in seeing, and in being seen. The *News of the World's* comments upon Victoria's tour of the midlands were in its reporting of the first major royal event to take place following its commencement in October 1843. They exemplify much of the future coverage given to Victoria by papers like *Lloyd's Weekly Newspaper* and the *Weekly Times*. Upon Victoria's visit to Louis Napoleon in 1855, for example, *Lloyd's Weekly Newspaper*, which had a predominantly artisan readership, made the typical declaration that 'it is not Victoria who visits Louis Napoleon, but England who visits France. It is not potentate embracing potentate, but people grasping people.'[15] The coverage of these weekly newspapers is all the more significant because they were amongst the most widely circulated of the period. By 1855, the *Illustrated London News* was selling approximately 155,000 copies a week, the *News of the World* 110,000, *Lloyd's Weekly Newspaper* 92,000, and the *Weekly Times* 76,000.[16] These figures place them well in advance of the majority of daily newspapers. Only *The Times* and, after 1855, the *Daily Telegraph* remotely approached such circulation. In 1861, the daily circulation of *The Times* was 65,000 copies, and the *Daily Telegraph* 141,000 copies.

The almost wholly supportive coverage of the monarchy by the new Sunday newspapers, the new illustrated press, and the existing metropolitan daily newspapers was the material embodiment of royal populism. Victoria's visits shaped a civic role for the monarchy but they were equally important through being turned into pleasurable reading or viewing matter. Francis Mulhern has argued that communities are 'not places but practices of collective identification'.[17] Reading about the monarchy in a newspaper, or viewing a print or photograph, were increasingly important everyday practices of collective identification. The promotion of Victoria's relationship with the People; the assertion of an unprecedented bond of intimacy between her and her subjects; the placing of her at the centre of an imagined national community – all these were achieved, at least partially, through the extensive coverage that was given to Victoria. This is especially so given that the circulation of newspapers usually increased significantly at the time of major royal events. At the wedding of the Prince of Wales, for example, *The Times* sold 108,000 copies compared to an average circulation of between 60,000 and 65,000 copies. There was a mutually supportive reciprocity between the cultural work carried out by the growth of newspapers, prints and periodicals, and the political claims of royal populism. Newspapers and periodicals had an essentially self-fulfilling function; they constantly enacted what they claimed simply to describe.

The number of newspapers commencing in the 1840s accentuated the novelty of the engagements undertaken by Victoria and Albert. It is important to emphasise that these activities were a significant departure from those of the previous three monarchs. The madness of George III had ensured his long closeting away at Windsor. George IV had visited Dublin in 1821 and toured Scotland in 1822; however his last years were notable for a similar reclusiveness, caused by a combination of ill-health and unpopularity. Although George IV had been an enthusiastic supporter of art and architecture, his patronage was never couched within the same framework of moral and civic progress as that of Victoria and Albert. Exhibiting more of a dilettante indulgence than a concern with industrialism and the manufacturing poor, projects like the Brighton Pavilion only seemed to guarantee more courtly extravagance and debt. The Queen Caroline affair and the debacle of his coronation hardly encouraged the type of civic visits undertaken by Victoria. William IV did not plumb the same depths of unpopularity as George IV, but he did not ascend the throne until the age of sixty-five in 1830. His age and his involvement in the Reform Bill prevented the type of popular constitutionalism that became so significant in Victoria's reign.

Commentators in the 1840s frequently used Victoria's visits to substantiate the break between her sovereignty and that of her Hanoverian predecessors. Comparing the movements of Victoria with their seclusion, the *Illustrated London News* was typical in noting with approval that 'the people of England had for many years been accustomed to look to their Sovereign as a fixture, which it would have been something astounding to have found out of its place, or moving out of its orbit, which was the rather circumscribed one, including Windsor, Buckingham Palace, St James, or now and then, Ascot'.[18] Rather than confining the Court to a single location, Victoria was lauded for bringing its economic benefits, and sharing its attractiveness, with her subjects. In conjunction with the development of an illustrated and a popular press, Victoria and Albert enthusiastically inaugurated a new style of royalty. A young couple touring different areas of the nation without the trappings of pageantry, frequently accompanied by their infant family, the visits could be invested with a heady mixture of romantic sentiment, family propriety, royal patronage, and local civic pride.

The making and the receiving of state visits, along with a plethora of minor civic engagements, dominated the public activities of Victoria and Albert throughout the 1840s and 1850s. Given that their nine children were also born during this period, they combined private domesticity with public diligence in a wholesome mixture that the newspaper and periodical press gave fulsome attention to. The couple established a precedent of royal duties, consisting of civic visits, military reviews, meetings and benevolent charity work. Visits and engagements followed on from one another in quick succession. A wryly-amused *Punch* noted Victoria's propensity for visitations by publishing, in two separate articles, a list of the prospective marine excursions over the next ten years and distinguished visitors over the next five years.[19] Marine journeys were to include calling on St Petersburg, New York, and the South Pole, while projected visitors ranged from Mehmet Ali in 1847 to the Emperor of Lapland in 1852. A full-page engraving captures the packed schedule of Victoria and Albert and *Punch*'s breathless attempts to keep up with their movements (Figure 1). Produced upon Victoria and Albert's return from Saxe-Coburg in 1845, the engraving neatly combines their travels with their tender regard for the royal hearth.

Victoria and Albert's visit to the midlands in 1843 is indicative of what was seen to be the Queen's willingness to patronise every part of the nation with her presence, honouring the industrial areas of Britain as

Figure 1 'There's no place like home', *Punch*, 9 (1845), 109. Courtesy of University of Exeter Library.

well as the inhabitants of London and Windsor. Each tour of a manufacturing area was given a weighty political symbolism on top of the more pragmatic pleasures of a general holiday for many of the local inhabitants. The tour of the midlands lasted for nine days and took in

Nottingham, Derby, Chesterfield, Belvoir Castle, Lichfield Cathedral, Coventry, and Leicester. There was also an excursion to Birmingham for Prince Albert, which managed to cram in guided tours of six factories before moving on to visit the town hall and the Free Grammar School. The opening of the Royal Exchange in 1844 by Victoria and Albert was seen in comparable terms as one of their many recognitions of the power of commerce, while events like their tour of Lancashire in late 1851 accorded the same respect to northern industrialism.

The impact of Victoria and Albert's civic publicness is particularly evident in the way their visits helped to forge a local consensus around the Crown. The provincial press's coverage of Victoria's visits to their own locality emphasises the iterative nature of royal populism. On Victoria and Albert's aforementioned visit to Birmingham in 1843, the *Birmingham Journal* declared that their presence would 'hardly fail to operate favourably on the somewhat conflicting materials that have, for a long time, constituted that capital's population'.[20] Radical, Tory and Whig worked together in order to organise the welcome to the Prince. Similarly, when Victoria and Albert visited Birmingham again in June 1858, this time to open Aston Park, the *Birmingham Daily Post* took great pride in declaring: 'The most democratic town in England must also be the most orderly in its loyalty'.[21] The very contrariness of the comment is telling. Birmingham's consciousness of its own radically-tinged civic pride meant that it went out of its way to prove its loyalty. Birmingham's feting of Victoria confirmed not its deference but the dignity of its democratic civic identity.

The various local prints and newspapers produced to commemorate a royal visit were never simply representations of the event: they were part of the communicative encounter between the monarchy and the press and shaped the nature of the occasion itself. In the days leading up to the Victoria's visit to Birmingham in 1858, the *Birmingham Daily Post* was full of advertisements for commemorative prints and sonnets. There was even a local satire, 'The Great Avatar', which promised caricatures of all the local dignitaries.[22] As well as giving fulsome coverage to the event itself, the *Birmingham Daily Post* produced an extra commemorative edition in order to meet the enormous demand for an account of the occasion. Although the print run of the commemorative edition was double the normal run of the newspaper, all copies were sold by four o'clock on the day of publication. The narrative consequently had to be inserted into its evening journal.[23] With a national press not yet in existence, the prominence of the provincial press was vital for propagating the narrative of royal populism.

The particular importance of municipal pride in this period meant that royal civic visits were far from being frivolously decorative. They were constitutive of Victoria and Albert's role. In terms that prefigure those of Bagehot in *The English Constitution*, *The Times* saw Albert's opening of the Royal Exchange in 1844 as an essential part of the post-Reform Bill political landscape:

> These great occasions are not far from being an integral part of our constitution. To the middle-classes, who may now almost be considered the ruling class of England, it has become nearly a right . . . that the great men of the country should pay them the compliment – we might say the homage – of appearing periodically.[24]

The Times is typical of the way in which these royal events were signified as a new position for the Crown, an *entente cordiale* between the monarchy and the middle-class. Moreover, as *The Times* unconsciously expresses, thanks to the newspapers and journals, the monarchy did indeed appear periodically. Albert's involvement with the Great Exhibition and Victoria's opening of the event was only the crowning glory of a constitutional role that encompassed a multitude of dinners, reviews and meetings. Ranging from enormous set-piece occasions to the briefest passing through of the royal train and the receiving of (yet another) platitudinous address from local dignitaries, the dutiful labour of Victoria and Albert was being never-endingly displayed for all to see.

The extent and the format of the engravings of royal events by the illustrated press reinforce the ideological stress upon royal populism. The standardised regularity of the *Illustrated London News* was at the core of a crucial difference between its constant supply of visual news and the various royal portraits that had traditionally been released as individual prints. As Chris Brooks has argued, whereas formal portraits are iconic, fixed in both convention and action, the illustrated press was concerned, above all, with the flow of contemporary events.[25] In an important epistemological shift, Victoria and Albert's relationship to their visual representation shifted from the iconic to the dynamic, from the portrait to the image. The succession of civic engagements and tours carried out by Victoria also accorded with the class-consensus that was promoted by the illustrated press. In its initial prospectus, the *Illustrated London News* decried the party-political alignment that characterised the metropolitan daily press. Ruled by the household gods of the English people, it declared that it would devote itself to depicting the 'beautiful chain, which should be fastened at one end to the cottage, at the other to the palace, and be electric with the happiness that is carried into both'.[26] During the 1840s and 1850s, the *Illustrated London News* did its best to emphasise this chain of connection through its regular coverage of Victoria's activities.

The distinctly modern experience of the monarchy provided by the illustrated press is demonstrated in an article by the novelist Catherine Gore, which was published in *Blackwood's Edinburgh Magazine* in 1844. Gore declared that the new art of illustration belonged to the quickness of the modern age. She predicted that the world of letters would soon be replaced by the world of emblems. Illustration would replace written matter because it allowed greater speed of comprehension. It was the ideal media to be 'available to those sons of the century always on the run'.[27] Gore predicted that MPs' portraits would soon be daguerreo- typed for the morning papers; the best artists would delineate Victoria's drawing-rooms for general consumption; and close-up engravings of boxing-matches would avoid the need for vivid description of the injuries received. Gore's prophecies reflect the excitement caused by the potential of the illustrated press. They demonstrate the way that pub- lishing developments created a novel yet immediate interaction with Victoria.

From its inception royal events loomed large in the news-values of the *Illustrated London News*. The very first number of the periodical was timed to coincide with a lavish historical costume ball hosted by Vic- toria. Five months after its initial publication came the Queen's first tour of Scotland, an episode that the *Illustrated London News* responded to with commercial relish and royalist gusto. After despatching two artists to shadow the royal party, the *Illustrated London News* devoted most of its resources during the following five weeks to portraying every aspect of Victoria's journey. Sixty-three engravings of the tour were eventually published, an exceptional number in comparison to the number of indi- vidual prints published in the late 1830s. Over the next twenty years, the illustrated press gave the activities of the royal family a consistently high degree of attention. Through recording the number of front-pages on which the *Illustrated London News* and its principal competitors included either an engraving or an article devoted to Victoria and Albert, it is possible to demonstrate the prolonged weight of attention devoted to the monarchy. Figure 2 shows the percentage of royal front pages of the *Illustrated London News*, the *Pictorial Times*, and the *Illus- trated Times*.[28] I have chosen the latter two papers to demonstrate the extent to which its principal competitors imitated the news-values of the *Illustrated London News*. Between 1842 and 1847, the percentage of

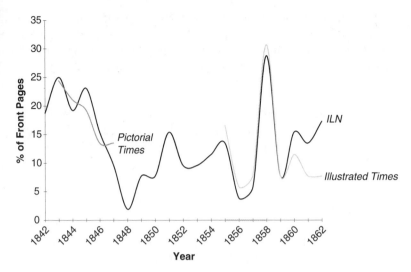

Figure 2 Front-page coverage of the British royal family 1842–62.

royal front pages of the *Illustrated London News* was 18.5. Similarly, for the *Pictorial Times* it was 18.3 between 1843 and 1847. While the *Illustrated London News*'s royal coverage was at its lowest in 1848, throughout the 1850s there continued to be substantial if rather formulaic coverage.

In addition to the extent of coverage by the illustrated press, its graphic reportage deployed the same ideological inclusiveness as the written journalism of most newspapers. In the *Illustrated London News* and the *Pictorial Times* there were innumerable depictions of Victoria and Albert either passing through triumphal arches in their carriage, arriving by the royal train, or stepping off the royal yacht, invariably surrounded by loyal and cheering crowds. This was popular constitutionalism at its strongest: the position of Victoria and Albert validated not by ceremony but by the approval of their subjects. When Victoria and Albert visited Louis-Napoleon in 1855, the *Illustrated London News* contrasted the informality with which they were greeted in Britain with the grand ceremonial reception that they would receive in Paris:

> The French love shows, are accustomed to and excel in them. . . . The whole aspect of the streets and public buildings offers itself to aid and impress the efforts of the Government when it desires to impress

the imagination of the spectators. In London the spectators are themselves the show. . . . Nothing but the presence of good-humoured, orderly, and rejoicing multitudes, can impart a ray of grandeur to them [the London streets]; and these, it must be said, are never wanting at the call of Loyalty or Duty.[29]

The mob versus the loyal People, despotic state pageantry versus consensual civic pride, the foreignness of spectacle versus English constitutional liberty, this is the series of ideological binaries that was endlessly deployed in articles and illustrations.

An engraving from the *Illustrated London News* of the queen's visit to Birmingham in 1858 is typical of the standpoint adopted by the illustrated press. The engraving can be tellingly compared with the coverage of the same event by the *Birmingham Daily Post*. In Figure 3, the royal couple have been reduced to small figures, recognisable only by Victoria's bonnet and parasol and Albert's top hat being lifted to the crowd. This was a visual grammar repeated so often that it became iconographic. The magnificence of the arch is in marked contrast to the unostentatious appearance of Victoria and Albert themselves. Their spartan coach, accompanied by only a small contingent of riders, is similarly set against the backdrop of the packed grandstands. Victoria and Albert are not the spectacle here: the spectacle is of popular constitutionalism and a public political sphere in which royalty was legitimated. After 1848, the contrast between the fate of other European monarchies and the reception of Victoria could not have been more acute. Barricades, chaos and insurrection as opposed to banners, cheers and illuminations.

An engraving of Victoria's visit to Liverpool in 1851 (Figure 4) replicates the same visual rhetoric. Victoria and Albert are no more than minuscule figures on the balcony of Liverpool exchange. What the engraving actually displays is the popular support for the Crown: the thousands of people huddled together in the pouring rain emphasize both the appeal of Victoria and the ordered loyalty inspired by the Crown. And, perhaps disturbingly, it is possible to read this individual engraving as symbolizing the extent to which these occasions went far beyond being about Victoria and Albert. The royal couple have been very literally effaced. The more the engravings and written journalism sought to make Victoria a representative figurehead, to promote her as a national focal point, the more she herself tended to personally disappear under the weight of that very populism. This engraving dramatises the dialectic between the power and powerlessness of Victoria, a tension which is at the heart of the monarchy's media-making.

Figure 3 'Queen Victoria's Visit to Birmingham', *Illustrated London News*, 3 July 1858, 1. Courtesy of University of Exeter Library.

Figure 4 'Queen Victoria's Visit to Liverpool', *Illustrated London News*, 2 Oct 1851, 489. Courtesy of University of Exeter Library.

By the end of Victoria's reign, the civic publicness of the royal family had become the accepted model for the role of the monarch as a national figurehead. After the death of Albert in 1861, Victoria's own long seclusion only served to accentuate the importance of her previous industry. It is no coincidence that republicanism was at its strongest during the late 1860s and early 1870s, when Victoria was perceived as receiving large amounts of money from the Civil List without performing any duties in return. While Victoria's creation as the Empress of India in 1876 added an imperial hauteur to her position, the subsequent decline of the British Empire has meant the monarchy losing its imperial gloss. Nevertheless, what has remained is the round of public functions and philanthropic duties. What has also remained is the extensive, sometimes intrusive, character of royal reportage. Although the illustrated press, for example, was well-established by the 1850s, it continued to expand. A new genre of women's illustrated newspaper, established principally by the *Lady's Newspaper and Illustrated Times* (1847–63) and *Queen* (1861–), was notable for the way it involved its readers in the life of the royal family. The first illustrated daily newspaper, the *Daily Graphic*, also commenced publication in 1889. The growth of new media like photography and cinematography similarly followed the established pattern of supportive royal coverage. Queen Victoria's Diamond Jubilee in 1897 and her funeral in 1901 were among the first major national occasions to be filmed. The communicative encounter between the monarchy and the various nineteenth-century media continued to reinvent the traditional aristocratic prominence of the monarchy.

Notes

1. 'The Royal Guests', *Illustrated London News*, 8 June 1844, 361.
2. Margaret Homans, *Royal Representations: Queen Victoria and British Culture 1837–67* (Chicago: Chicago University Press, 1998); Adrienne Munich, *Queen Victoria's Secrets* (New York: Columbia University Press, 1996).
3. Edward G. Salmon, 'What the Working Classes Read', *Nineteenth Century*, 20 (1886), 110.
4. See Brian Maidment, *Into the 1830s: Some Origins of Victorian Illustrated Journalism* (Manchester: Manchester Polytechnic Library, 1992), 5–7.
5. For radical attacks on the royal reportage of the press, see John Plunkett, *Queen Victoria – First Media Monarch* (Oxford: Oxford University Press, 2003), 56–67.
6. John Thompson, *The Media and Modernity* (Cambridge: Polity, 1995), 120–25.
7. James Vernon, *Politics and the People: A Study in English Political Culture, c. 1815–1867* (Cambridge: Cambridge University Press, 1993), Patrick Joyce, *Visions of the People: Industrial England and the Question of Class, c. 1848–1914* (Cambridge: Cambridge University Press, 1991). James Vernon, ed., *Re-Reading the Constitution: New Narratives in the Political History of England's Long Nineteenth-Century* (Cambridge: Cambridge University Press, 1995).
8. 'Our Glorious Constitution', *Reynolds's Newspaper*, 27 Jan. 1901, 4.
9. David Cannadine, 'The Context, Performance and Meaning of Ritual: The British Monarchy and the "Invention of Tradition", c. 1820–1977', in *The Invention of Tradition*, ed. E. Hobsbawm and T. Ranger (Cambridge: Cambridge University Press, 1983), 101–164.
10. Editorial, *Sunday Times*, 1 July 1838, 4.
11. Frank Prochaska, *Royal Bounty: The Making of a Welfare Monarchy* (New Haven: Yale University Press, 1995).
12. 'The Royal Visit to Scotland', *Illustrated London News*, 3 Sept. 1842, 257.
13. Quoted in Richard Williams, *The Contentious Crown: Public Discussion of the British Monarchy in the Reign of Queen Victoria* (Aldershot: Ashgate, 1997), 198.
14. 'The Queen's Visit to Her People', *News of the World*, 3 Dec. 1843, 4.
15. 'England meets France', *Lloyd's Weekly Newspaper*, 19 Aug. 1855, 1.
16. Quoted in Peter Sinnema, *Dynamics of the Printed Page: Representing the Nation in the* Illustrated London News *(Aldershot: Ashgate, 1998), 16.
17. Quoted in Terry Eagleton, *The Idea of Culture* (Oxford: Blackwell, 2000), 80.
18. 'Royal Visits', *Illustrated London News*, 31 Aug. 1844, 128. See also, 'London, 8 December, 1843,' *The Times*, 8 Dec. 1843, 4.
19. 'Victoria's Voyages for the Next Ten Years', *Punch*, 5 (1843), 128. 'The Queen's Illustrious Visitors', *Punch*, 7 (1844), 182.

20. 'Saturday, December 2', *Birmingham Journal*, 2 Dec. 1843, 4.
21. 'The Queen's Visit', *Birmingham Daily Post*, 15 June 1858, 2.
22. 'The Great Avatar', *Birmingham Daily Post*, 10 June 1858, 2.
23. 'To Our Readers', *Birmingham Daily Post*, 14 June 1858, 2.
24. Quoted in Williams, *The Contentious Crown*, 196.
25. Chris Brooks, 'Representing Albert', in *The Albert Memorial*, ed. Chris Brooks (New Haven: Yale University Press, 2000), 42.
26. 'Our Principles', *Illustrated London News*, 21 May 1842, 17.
27. Catherine Gore, 'The New Art of Printing', *Blackwood's Edinburgh Magazine*, 55 (1844), 47.
28. Whilst newspapers continued to have advertisements on their front pages, the illustrated press often led with a combination of engraving and article. Space restrictions meant that the most sumptuous illustrations were rarely on the front page, nevertheless, the engraving and article were usually of the one or two most important news items of the week.
29. 'Her Majesty's Visit to Paris', *Illustrated London News*, 4 Aug. 1855, 130.

2
'Nothing but a Newspaper': The Contested Space of Serial Fiction in the 1840s Press

Graham Law

> An attempt has just been made to give a new feature to Sunday papers. We allude to the project of filling a number of columns with tales of the imagination. Could we conceive the scheme to be other than decidedly prejudicial to the Sunday Press, and injurious to the public, we would adopt it, . . . but in our opinion a newspaper ought to be nothing but a newspaper, and it is as preposterous to introduce magazine stories into a journal, as it would be to make a magazine solely the vehicle for current news. . . .[1]

This essay focuses on the serialization of novels in British newspapers around the 1840s, describing the journals and writings concerned, and offering reasons for the rise and decline of the practice. Right from the start, as the epigraph taken from the *Weekly Dispatch* of 1841 suggests, the columns in newspapers given over to instalment fiction were contested space. Conflicts concerning the role of the newspaper novel include not only those between publisher and publisher, but also those between editor and author or reader, and are thus both external and internal. Internal disputes will be demonstrated by the tensions concerning the relative status of information and entertainment material across a wide range of journals. The most sustained instances will be found in two successful Liberal weeklies, the *Sunday Times* and *Illustrated London News* (*ILN*). As shown in detail in Table 1, both of these carried serials virtually throughout the decade, though with a degree of irregularity. External contests will be shown firstly in the exploitation of serial fiction in the ideological and circulation battles between the Radical *Dispatch* and its Conservative rival the *Era*, and secondly through the strategies employed by unstamped popular papers like *Lloyd's Penny Sunday*

Table 1   Serial fiction* in the Sunday Times and Illustrated London News around the 1840s

Signature	Title	Serialization
	Sunday Times (1822–)	
'From the Pen of a Popular Author' [W. Leman Rede]	The Royal Rake, and the Adventures of Alfred Chesterton	5 Jan 1840–14 Oct 1841, irregular
W. Harrison Ainsworth	Old Saint Paul's	3 Jan–26 Dec 1841
Richard Brinsley Peake	Cartouche	12 Nov 1843–10 Mar 1844
[Marguerite] Countess of Blessington	Strathern	12 Nov 1843–15 Dec 1844
Eugene Sue, 'Expressly Translated' for ST	The Wandering Jew	30 Jun–14 Jul 1844, incomplete
G. P. R. James	The Step-Mother	5 Jan 1845–4 Jan 1846
James Sheridan Knowles	Fortescue	4 Jan 1846–3 Jan 1847
Unsigned [W. Leman Rede]	The Man in Possession	24 Jan–11 Apr 1847, incomplete
Unsigned	The Ranger and His Guest: A Forest Tale	5 Dec 1847–9 Jan 1848
W. Harrison Ainsworth	The Lancashire Witches	2 Jan 1848–7 Jan 1849
'ABR' [Angus B. Reach]	The Great Scotch Mull	26 Aug–4 Nov 1849, irregular
	[In 'The Man at the Corner' Column]	
Unsigned	The Pauper's Daughter	11 Nov–30 Dec 1849
	[In 'The Man at the Corner' Column]	

Illustrated London News (1842–)

Author	Title	Dates
Henry Cockton	England and France; or, The Sisters	18 Mar–23 Dec 1843, irregular
Thomas Miller	Mabel Marchmont	6–20 Jan 1844
Miss Camilla Toulmin	The Adopted; or, Impulse not Principle	20 Jan–3 Feb 1844
Miss Louisa Stuart Costello	The Young Flagolet Player	10 Feb–24 Feb 1844
Miss [Julia] Pardoe	The Merchant's Daughter	9 Mar–23 Mar 1844
Baroness [E. C.] de Calabrella	Retribution	30 Mar–13 Apr 1844
'The Old Sailor' [M. H. Barker]	Fitz-Stephen	13 Jul–17 Aug 1844, irregular
Frederica Bremer, trans. Lewis Filmore	Hopes	8 Mar–15 Mar 1845
Unsigned	Otello: A Tale of the Opera	9 Aug–27 Sep 1845, irregular
Mrs [Catherine] Crowe	Gerald Gage; or, The Secret	10 Jan–14 Mar 1846, irregular
Camilla Toulmin	Gold; or, The Half-Brother	4 Jul–14 Nov 1846, irregular
Berthold Auerbach, trans. Mary Howitt	The Professor's Lady	13 Nov 1847–1 Jan 1848
W. Blanchard Jerrold	The Progress of a Bill	9 Sep–28 Oct 1848
Monsieur [Louis] Reybaud, trans. Juliette Bauer	Jerome Paturot: In Search of the Best Republic	11 Nov 1848–6 Jan 1849, incomplete[†]
The Brothers [Henry & Augustus] Mayhew	The Fear of the World; or, Living for Appearances	22 Dec 1849–23 Feb 1850, irregular
Thomas Miller	Fred Holdersworth; or, Love and Pride	19 Oct–28 Dec 1850, irregular
Augustus Mayhew	A Story of the Present Day	1 Feb–19 Jul 1851, irregular
William Carleton	The Squanders of Squander Castle	17–31 Jan 1852, irregular, incomplete[‡]

* Fiction published in 2 instalments or more.
† Abridged; 2nd vol. in resumé only.
‡ Novel in vol. reviewed 1 May 1852.

Times in mimicking 'legitimate' bourgeois publications like the *Sunday Times* itself. The skirmishing over the space of serial fiction should thus be understood, as the comments in the *Dispatch* suggest, as part of a larger battle over the redefinition of the newspaper as a news miscellany. This battle occurs in the context of the broadening social readership of the press after the 1832 Reform Bill and at the time of the Chartist demands for a proletarian franchise. As such the serial fiction battles of the 1840s can be seen as a rehearsal of the debate over the New Journalism later in the century.

However, before getting down to detail, it is necessary to outline the material conditions favouring the insertion of fiction into newspapers at the start of the Victorian era. Three main factors, all coming into play in the later 1830s, contribute to the emergence of the practice: changes in the British tax regime; new publishing activity in Paris; and developments in serial publication on the part of the London book publishers. Since this is by no means unfamiliar territory, here a brief summary can suffice. With the Reform Bill, the movement to repeal the taxes on knowledge gained strength. However, the result was a series of unsatisfactory Parliamentary compromises, unwanted by the established daily papers, and offering little encouragement to proprietors wishing to commence cheap journals aimed at a mass audience. Following significant reductions in the advertisement tax and paper duty, the cost of the newspaper stamp itself fell from fourpence to a penny. At the same time, however, the 1836 Newspaper Stamp Act increased the severity of the requirements concerning the security bonds to be posted against the issuing of criminal libel. It thus did little to reduce the fiscal burdens on small-scale publishers, so that the main stimulus was to the middle-class weekly papers.

The French *roman-feuilleton* also made its first appearance in 1836 in *La Presse*, a Parisian daily that had reduced its price by half and needed urgently to double its circulation to remain in profit.[2] The success of this venture, which represented the first use of a fully capitalist mode of production in the French fiction industry, made it a model for all progressive dailies, so that, throughout the following decades, the Parisian press played host to Romantic chroniclers of the stature of Balzac, Sue, and Dumas. English writers with an eye on the Parisian scene were quick to recognize the significance of this development. In 1843 Thackeray noted that:

> since the invention of the Feuilleton in France, every journal has its six columns of particular and especial report. M. Eugène Sue is still guillotining and murdering and intriguing in the *Débats* . . . ;

M. Dumas has his tale in the *Siècle*; Madame Gay is pouring out her eloquence daily in the *Presse*; M. Reybaud is endeavouring, with the adventures of Jean Mouton in the *National*, to equal the popularity which he obtained with 'Jérome Paturot:' in a word, every newspaper has its different tale. . . .[3]

Of course, the French *feuilleton* was a feature of the metropolitan daily newspaper, whereas the London equivalent would be found overwhelmingly in the weekly press. Yet there was at least one unsuccessful attempt to duplicate the Parisian model. This was in the *London Telegraph*, a threepenny daily starting up in February 1848 which lasted for only five months. In its opening issue it carried the first installment of Albert Smith's *The Pottleton Legacy* in a 'portfolio' at the foot of the front page. More generally, the appearance of works by, for example, Sue and Reybaud in translation in the London weeklies bears clear witness to this continental influence.

The later 1830s in Britain also witnessed a number of experiments in serial publication, these by the London book publishers, driven by the need to counterbalance the rigidity of the market for new work in volume form. This was increasingly dominated by lavish multi-volume editions, still sold at the inflationary prices scaled after the Napoleonic Wars, and aimed mainly at the circulating libraries. Though there were sporadic experiments with weekly serialization – including Ainsworth's *Jack Sheppard* in threepenny numbers from 1840, and Dickens's *Master Humphrey's Clock* (1840–1), the illustrated threepenny paper which carried *The Old Curiosity Shop* – the most successful formats for serial fiction quickly emerged as the independent monthly installment at a shilling and the half-crown monthly literary miscellany. As Robert Patten has shown,[4] the phenomenal popularity of the young Dickens, with *Pickwick* in numbers in 1836–7 and *Oliver Twist* in *Bentley's Miscellany* in 1837–9, was of crucial importance in establishing both modes of publication.

These developments in the serial market are now well understood. More generally, over the last thirty years or so, thanks to the activities of bodies like the Research Society for Victorian Periodicals and indexing projects like the *Wellesley*, the literary periodical highways of the nineteenth century – the metropolitan quarterly reviews and monthly miscellanies – are now clearly marked on the map. However, the task of charting the byways of the Victorian weekly, popular and provincial presses is still in its early stages. The phenomenon of publishing novels in newspapers in the decade before the campaign against the taxes on knowledge finally achieved success has therefore received remarkably

little scholarly attention. Thus this inquiry has been based on an extensive, though by no means exhaustive, survey of the contents of the metropolitan weekly journals around the 1840s (the official circulations of
the main papers concerned are indicated in Table 2),[5] supplemented by
a more casual glance at the daily and provincial press during the same
period.[6]

Tensions

As Table 2 again shows, throughout the 1840s the main Tory weeklies
had to measure their generally declining circulations in the thousands
rather than the tens of thousands increasingly claimed by their radical
opponents. Virtually all of these Tory journals were to turn to fiction as
an attraction at some point during that decade. Complete tales of fashionable life by the likes of the Baroness de Calabrella appeared regularly
outside 'the season' in the *Court Journal*, while the *Britannia* ran occasional sketches by Thackeray or Anna Maria Hall;[7] and, as we shall see,
both the *Britannia* and the *Era* offered serial stories on at least one occasion.[8] However, the most consistent newspaper venue for serial fiction
in the 1840s was undoubtedly the weekly with reformist tendencies.
First and most typical was the *Sunday Times*, a well-established sixpenny
whose stately front page echoed that of *The Times* itself, though it
concealed a lively combination of radical politics, crime coverage, and
sports intelligence.[9] Composed of eight broadsheet pages, the *Sunday
Times* carried serials from the beginning of 1840 through to the end of
1849, though with several gaps, notably one covering most of 1842
and 1843. The sequence began majestically in January 1840 with the
opening of Leman Rede's episodic *The Royal Rake*. The reason given for
the new venture was that '[i]n these stirring times men will scarcely find
leisure for the perusal of volumes', and there was a promise that the
'remaining chapters will appear on each succeeding Sunday throughout
the year, and be accompanied with an illustration'.[10] The novel did
indeed at first appear with weekly regularity and a small woodcut,
though it rambled on intermittently and unadorned into the autumn
of the following year. At the end of the decade, the sequence of serial
stories in the *Sunday Times* came to a humble and unannounced end
with the anonymous *Pauper's Daughter* in eight short installments.

Yet in between there was a series of popular serials by successful
authors running regularly throughout the year. On 20 December 1840
(page 4), the *Sunday Times* had prominently announced the 'Exclusive
Publication' of Harrison Ainsworth's *Old Saint Paul's*, 'To be completed

Table 2   Circulations of major stamped weekly newspapers, 1839–52

(Average per issue, thousands)*	1839	1840	1841	1842	1843	1844	1845	1846	1847	1848	1849	1850	1851	1852
Bell's Life in London (1822–86)	22.7	20.6	19.8	19.5	19.1	18.2	20.2	24.0	25.2	23.8	22.6	24.7	27.0	25.7
Bell's New Weekly Messenger (1832–55)	2.6	2.7	2.4	2.3	1.9	1.5	1.3	1.0	0.9	0.6	0.5	0.4	0.3	0.4
Bell's Weekly Messenger (1796–1896)	17.8	17.4	17.0	16.3	15.1	15.0	14.1	14.1	14.6	14.3	13.6	13.5	12.5	12.2
The Britannia (1839–56)	1.8	3.1	3.8	5.6	5.0	5.0	4.9	4.9	4.2	3.9	3.5	3.2	2.6	2.4
The Court Journal (1829–1925)	1.9	1.4	1.5	1.1	0.8	0.8	0.8	0.8	0.7	0.5	0.4	0.3	0.4	0.5
The Era (1838–1939)	3.6	3.4	4.7	4.6	4.0	4.3	3.9	3.3	4.4	4.4	3.7	4.3	5.6	5.6
Illustrated London News (1842–)	–	–	–	27.4	40.6	48.7	50.4	45.5	43.6	57.0	57.8	66.7	145.7	108.6
John Bull (1820–92)	4.4	4.2	3.9	3.6	3.2	2.8	2.5	2.5	2.3	2.3	2.3	2.1	2.1	2.1
Lloyd's Weekly Newspaper (1842–1931)	–	–	–	16.0	33.1	45.6	53.4	51.2	32.5	34.2	46.8	49.2	67.0	74.6

Table 2 Continued

(Average per issue, thousands)*	1839	1840	1841	1842	1843	1844	1845	1846	1847	1848	1849	1850	1851	1852
News of the World (1843–)	–	–	–	–	7.2	13.2	24.1	36.1	38.1	47.7	54.0	56.3	58.5	59.9
Northern Star (1837–52)	35.6	18.7	13.6	12.5	8.7	7.4	6.5	6.2	8.8	12.0	7.0	4.7	2.9	1.3
The Observer (1791–)	2.3	4.2	3.5	4.0	2.7	3.0	2.9	3.4	4.1	5.4	6.9	6.2	7.6	6.7
The Sunday Times (1822–)	13.3	20.2	21.2	21.0	17.6	16.9	18.2	17.9	15.1	14.6	14.1	13.0	12.3	10.3
Weekly Chronicle (1836–67)	25.8	21.7	19.4	17.8	13.3	7.2	6.1	5.0	3.3	2.9	2.2	1.6	2.4	2.1
Weekly Dispatch (1801–1961)	52.9	63.0	57.2	63.0	55.1	50.0	47.3	46.6	42.4	40.6	43.3	37.5	37.5	38.5
The Weekly Times (1847–1912)	–	–	–	–	–	–	–	–	15.5	20.7	34.8	39.2	58.6	57.0

* Calculated by dividing the annual Newspaper Stamp Returns by the number of issues (i.e. 52 for a complete year), rounded to the first decimal place.

Source: *A Return of the Number of Newspaper Stamps, 1837–50* and *1851–3*.

in Fifty-two Weekly Numbers, the First of which will appear in the Columns of that Journal on SUNDAY, 3rd of JANUARY, 1841', a schedule that was adhered to scrupulously. Later offerings included G. P. R. James's *The Step-Mother*, James Sheridan Knowles's *Fortescue*, and *The Lancashire Witches*, once again by Ainsworth. Though there was one Newgate adventure, Richard Brinsley Peake's tale of a French highwayman, *Cartouche*, and a silver-fork novel in the form of Lady Blessington's *Strathern*, the staple fare was the historical romance exposing fashionable aristocratic vice, in keeping with the political line of the journal.[11] As Table 2 shows, the weekly circulation of the *Sunday Times* jumped from around 13,000 in the late 1830s to over 21,000 in the early 1840s, with the two peaks during that decade coinciding with the appearances of Ainsworth's *Old Saint Paul's* and James's *The Step-Mother*. However, there then followed a gradual retreat to as low as 10,000 by the early 1850s, which the serialization of *The Lancashire Witches* during 1848 seems to have failed entirely to counter.

Less radical and more miscellaneous than the *Sunday Times* was the *Illustrated London News*, under the canny proprietorship of Herbert Ingram. Although consistently calling for reforms to alleviate the wretchedness of the lower orders, it was always happy to celebrate the latest royal and civic occasion in grand style. As Peter Sinnema notes,[12] it cultivated a 'respectable' family audience, directing some of its features specifically towards women and children, and rejecting the broader humour of the smoking-room. But its most distinctive feature, of course, was that it was the first British newspaper to give priority to engravings, which were lavish in both quantity and quality. Again priced at sixpence, and composed in its early years of sixteen folio pages with frequent supplements free of charge, it offered value for money for those who did not need to worry about money.[13] It was surely the novelty of the engravings which ensured that, even in its first year of publication, the *ILN* achieved a circulation well in advance of the *Sunday Times* at its peak, and sales had topped 100,000 copies before the newspaper stamp was abolished. Moreover, surges in sales correspond this time not so much to exciting new serial stories but rather to extraordinary public events visualized extensively in the paper: the revolutions in Europe of 1848, the Great Exhibition of 1851, and (though this is beyond the range of Table 2) the Crimean campaign of 1854.

The serials carried during the paper's first decade were in general rather shorter and less melodramatic than those in the *Sunday Times*, though the first was in many ways untypical. The paper started up only in May 1842, but by September there was already an announcement that the proprietors had made arrangements 'with one of the most eminent authors of the day, to produce in their journal a Work of Fiction, upon an entirely new plan, to be entitled, The Novel of the Moment'.[14] When the first serial novel eventually began its nine-month run in March 1843, it proved to be *England and France; or, The Sisters, A Romance of Real Life*, by Henry Cockton. Despite the promise of the sub-title, it turned out be a sentimental tale set during the Regency with scenes of the Napoleonic Wars. Presumably the proprietors had been anticipating something more along the lines of Cockton's recent serial successes, *Valentine Fox* in monthly parts (1840) and *Stanley Thorne* in *Bentley's Miscellany* (1840–42), both comedies of modern urban life.[15] More typical were the subsequent romances of contemporary English middle-class life by worthy authors like Thomas Miller and Camilla Toulmin, both of whom provided two serial novellas during the period in question. The proprietors seem generally to have encouraged titles like Augustus Mayhew's *Story of the Present Day*, or sub-titles like 'A Story of Life in the Middle Station' (for Toulmin's *Gold*). As Sinnema has suggested (170), 'the hegemony of a "house style" emerges in papers like the *ILN*, regardless of the individual writer's class position, sex or political commitments', and thus reassuring English domestic fiction was the norm in the early days of the *ILN*.[16] After a steady run of such works in the first half of 1844, the journal noted that

> The literary feature of introducing a series of *nouvellettes* from the pens of the first writers of our time, has met with a very general and gratifying approval. It seems to have harmonized with the *family* character of this newspaper, and to have fertilized the dry realities of the actual world with a pleasant stream of fiction to please the palate, and prompt the imagination of the young.
>
> (*ILN*, Preface to vol. IV, issued with Index, 6 July 1844)

The metaphors are mixed, but the underlying intention is clearly to suggest that fiction should complement rather than compete with the news, with the former figured as feminine and the latter as masculine material.[17] As we shall see, this gendering of space in the newspaper meant that serial fiction tended to suffer from an inferiority of status equivalent to the social and legal disabilites of women in early Victorian Britain.

The clearest evidence of the contested status of newspaper fiction – and this is apparent in other papers carrying serial novels as well as in the *ILN* – lies in its intermittency and irregularity. By these terms I intend not only unpredictable gaps within and between serial runs or narratives left incomplete, but also inconsistency of formatting, including position in the journal, size of type-face, and level of illustration. These phenomena admit of two rather different explanations. The first is that the novelists often wrote close to the weekly serial deadlines, and sometimes failed to maintain a steady supply. (We should note that significant delay just as much as total failure would have caused problems for the illustrators.) The second is that works of the imagination were classified, along with other entertainment matter, as of lower standing than the news stories: not that they were merely 'filler', but rather that they served a secondary, supplementary role (often gendered feminine, as we have seen), and were thus liable to curtailment and postponement when space was at a premium. In general terms, the first explanation often seems to apply in the case of the *Sunday Times* and the second in the case of the *Illustrated London News*.

Some bohemian romancers recruited by the *Sunday Times* were clearly less reliable suppliers of copy than the journeymen journalists who contributed the paper's political, criminal and sporting intelligence. Though there seems to have been no explanation or even acknowledgment in the paper itself of the fact that the translation of Sue's *Wandering Jew* vanished after only three parts, we do know what happened to Leman Rede's *The Man in Possession*. The author's sudden death from apoplexy on Saturday, 3 April 1847 forced the editor to make an announcement as early as Sunday, 11 April:

> The concluding lines of the foregoing chapter were the last ever penned by the hand of Mr W. L. Rede, the author of 'The Man in Possession,' and we are now reluctantly compelled to inform our readers that, in consequence of his death, the publication of this romance terminates with the chapter given this week.
>
> (*Sunday Times*, 11 April 1847, 3)

If Rede was sailing as close to the wind as this, it is unsurprising that *The Royal Rake* failed to keep to the regime set by the editor. A similar instance of bohemian unreliability seems to have contributed to the early demise of the *London Telegraph*, also owned by Herbert Ingram. In its specimen first issue, the daily *Telegraph* declared priorities similar to those of the *ILN*:

> Amusements will claim our care after business and politics . . . We shall contribute to cheerfulness by productions of our own, and a

prominent feature of the TELEGRAPH will be a tale by a celebrated writer.

A distinctive feature of our journal will be the place assigned to this tale. It will be at the bottom of the first page, which will always be separated from the rest of the paper and devoted to some entertaining matter.[18]

But it was only a few days before this 'portfolio' disappeared. A product of the celebrated pen of Albert Smith (then drama critic of the *ILN* as well as editor of the monthly *Man in the Moon*), the tale of *The Pottleton Legacy* was quickly down to two, and then even a single episode per week. Soon relegated to the back page and appearing at increasingly lengthy and irregular intervals, Smith's serial staggered to a conclusion in the final issue of the paper on July 8th. The story itself was popular enough when reissued the following year with illustrations by Phiz, so one must presume that daily deadlines were even more of a challenge than weekly ones for the bohemians of Grub Street.

The less volatile novelists taken on by the *ILN* (it is noticeable that many more women were recruited) seemed unlikely to fail in this way: the novellas at least were probably submitted complete before serialization commenced. Henry Cockton was perhaps the author most likely to cause anxiety, but in fact the editors seemed to have been embarrassed by a surplus rather than a shortage in the supply of *England and France*. The first few weeks of the run appeared regularly, in a similar position, generously spaced over three or four columns, and with the same number of engravings. But by the summer the instalments began to appear in odd corners, squashed in minuscule type into little more than a single column, with one or two engravings at best. At the same time a number of gaps appeared, often announced as due to 'the imperative pressure of news intelligence' (*ILN*, 24 Jun. 1843, 432), whether the funeral of the Duke of Sussex (6 May), the unsettled situation in Ireland (17 Jun., 24 Jun.), or the royal visit to France (16 Sep.). On more than one occasion the Chess and Fashion columns were 'unavoidably deferred' along with the 'Romance' (16 Sep., 182). Even the final episode, promised for 9 December, was delayed due to extensive illustration of the Queen's visit to the Midlands. In a similar way, gaps occurred in Catherine Crowe's *Gerald Gage* (7 Mar. 1846) and Toulmin's *Gold* (1 Aug. 1847), principally on account of visits by Prince Albert to, respectively, the Isle of Wight and Liverpool, while the momentous public events of the late 40s and early 50s explain the massive gaps punctuating the appearance of Augustus Mayhew's *Story of the Present Day*, or the abrupt curtailment of the stories by Reybaud and Carleton.

Thus one general reason for the gradual withdrawal of newspapers from the fiction market in the late 1840s is that these were increasingly 'stirring times'. The second revolution in Paris, as well as the second presentation of the Charter petition, generated far more than the average quantity of news copy, and encouraged the dropping of secondary material. That the revolutionary events on the continent in 1848 proved considerably more inflammatory than the increasingly conservative Ainsworth's medieval melodrama *The Lancashire Witches* was presumably a major reason why this was the last full-length serial novel to appear in the *Sunday Times*. This pressure on space affected not only journals with reformist and radical tendencies but also the Tory press itself, which was filled with reactionary fervour. In late summer 1848, after a lengthy break in 'Fortune: Some Scenes from Life', the anonymous serial that had begun in the *Britannia* on 27 May, the instalment was prefaced with a mild complaint. Under the signature 'Umbra', the author wrote:

> I had not intended to resume this tale, until, by more space being at the editor's disposal, I could have had a better assurance of its continuance without those interruptions which I must think destroy whatever interest it might otherwise possess. . . .
>
> Yet I am very far from accusing the editor's discretion in giving preference to the news of the day. Burke . . . said that if an audience, however intellectual, were collected in Covent-garden Theatre, and were fascinated by the acting of a Garrick or a Siddons, they would rise as one person and leave the place if told that a king were about to be really beheaded in the market-place. Can we wonder, then, that a journalist, whose province it is to chronicle the real and the actual, should lay by fiction to present his readers with those grand dramatic scenes which are continually occurring in a period of revolutionary excitement like this?
>
> But I hope now that my tale may be continued regularly.[19]

The author's hopes were to be disappointed, however, as the tale was relegated permanently to the shadows after September 9, when 'Fortune' ended abruptly *in medias res*.

Let us now turn from these various signs of internal tensions concerning the space of the serial novel, to overt external conflicts between journals opposing each other on ideological as well as economic grounds, whether Radical versus Tory, or Stamped versus Unstamped, in which imaginative fiction sometimes figures as a bone of contention or a weapon of war.

Battles

In 1840 the most powerful metropolitan weekly journal in terms of sales was the *Weekly Dispatch*, with a circulation around three times the size of that of its closest competitor (Table 2). The *Dispatch* was one of the survivors of the first generation of Sunday papers, dating from a period when to publish on the Sabbath was seen as a declaration of secularism and radicalism.[20] But unlike *Bell's Weekly Messenger*, which had opposed the Reform Bill and was now 'The Country Gentleman and Farmer's Journal', or even the *Observer* which was now rather more circumspect, the *Dispatch* maintained its rebellious spirit into the Victorian era. This was undoubtedly the main reason for its continuing popularity – salty political commentaries by 'Publicola' and 'Gracchus' were then a particular attraction. Yet on the reduction of the stamp tax, there were also clear signs that the weekly newspaper market was in for a shakeup. The creation of the *Weekly Chronicle*, which in 1837, due to its extensively illustrated coverage of the Greenacre murder case, briefly overtook the sales of the *Weekly Dispatch*, proved to be merely a foretaste of what would happen in the mid-1840s. Then John Browne Bell, instead of attempting to revamp his old *New Weekly Messenger*, by now in steady decline, decided to create an entirely new threepenny radical Sunday journal on modern lines, the *News of the World*. At around the same time, as we shall see in more detail shortly, a number of penny fiction publishers were to enter the cheap stamped Sunday newspaper market, notably Edward Lloyd with *Lloyd's Weekly* and George Stiff with the *Weekly Times*. And this, of course, was in addition to the dramatic success of Herbert Ingram's Saturday journal, the *Illustrated London News*. Already by 1850, as noted by Richard Altick[21] and as confirmed by Table 2, all four of these papers had comfortably overtaken the sales of the *Dispatch*.

Yet back in the late 1830s, after seeing off the challenge from the *Weekly Chronicle*, the *Dispatch* was clearly more preoccupied with the outrageous intrusion into its territory of a new Tory Sunday paper. Owned by the Licensed Victuallers' Association, the *Era* started up at the end of September 1838 as a general Conservative news weekly, though it later came to specialize in theatrical matters. The war seems to have started in the autumn of 1839, on the publication of the official Newspaper Stamp Returns for the preceding year, when the *Dispatch* mocked the average weekly sales of the *Era* during 1837–8, reckoning them at a paltry 1221 compared to its own prodigious 51,413. The *Era* reacted immediately to this 'wilful falsehood' on the part of the *Dispatch*, arguing quite reasonably that its figure should have been a substantial 9071, since only fourteen issues of the paper had appeared during the period in question.[22] One must suspect, however, that the Tory organ had been massaging its statistics by stamping sheets in advance, since, as Table 2 shows, it failed to achieve a circulation of even half that level over the next dozen years.

Another incident occurred a year later when the *Era* attempted to boost its sales figures by introducing serial fiction, beginning with Captain Marryat's 'The Poacher' (13 Dec 1840–23 May 1841).[23] Marryat's tale, reissued in volume form as *Joseph Rushbrook* in 1841, in fact betrays signs of his subsequent shift into the juvenile market, signs its radical opponent was quick to spot. The *Weekly Dispatch* was of the opinion that 'Captain Marryat has produced one or two works of moderate interest; but . . . he has spun his best yarn and now writes mere twaddle. The Captain is fast sinking into senility' ('To Correspondents', in reply to 'J. B.', 27 Dec 1840, 618). Further, and despite the fact that Marryat had stood unsuccessfully as a Liberal for the reformed parliament back in 1833, the *Dispatch* went on to charge that the *Era*'s new feature was evidence of a Tory conspiracy. The comments forming an epigraph to the present essay were thus not, as might at first sight appear, directed explicitly towards the long-standing radical rival the *Sunday Times*, but rather at its upstart rival the *Era*. That article went on to insist that it was a dereliction of the duty of an editor to deny space to the issues of the day – the need to repeal the Corn Laws and reform the Poor Laws – and concluded:

It may be very useful for Government and for Tory partisans insidiously, and by very slow degrees, to destroy the political press by gradually changing Newspapers into Magazines, but we will never suffer the public mind to be seduced from an interest in public affairs, and we would rather see Newspapers suppressed by the legal violence of the Attorney-General with corrupt and ignorant Juries, than have the inestimable blessing filched from us by the trick of diverting their character from foreign and domestic news to tales of the imagination.

('To the Readers of the Weekly Dispatch', 3 Jan 1841, 6)

To this the *Era* responded that, unlike its enemy, it had ample space to spare for literary matter, and proceeded to give the reasons:

> As to the diversion of the Sunday Press from its legitimate purpose, by weaving an effort of fancy with the parliamentary and general news, foreign and domestic, we hold it to be all pure, unadulterated 'blarney'; our space suffices for the whole; .... Should our contemporary wish to diffuse useful information alone, why fill some three or four columns weekly with Correspondence which, if it cost one penny to indite, is assuredly not worth a decimated fraction to peruse?
> ('Dispatch Versus Era', *Era*, 10 Jan 1841, 4)

The following week, the *Dispatch* could do little more than repeat both its allegations of a Tory plot and its mockery of the childishness of Marryat's story, concluding sourly that 'the butter-shops will be infinitely benefitted by Captain Marryat's tale, if we may infer from the vast number of papers on hand last week, and which we understand were on "sale or return" ' ('To Correspondents', the *Weekly Dispatch*, 17 Jan 1841, 30). It seems unlikely that the *Dispatch* was unaware that, at precisely this time, Ainsworth's *Old Saint Paul's* was beginning its run in the *Sunday Times* with a fanfare of publicity. The vehemence of the *Dispatch's* response to the *Era's* venture can thus perhaps be diagnosed as a displaced expression of its (justified) fears of the loss of its pre-eminence among the radical Sunday papers at a time of growing instability in the contemporary newspaper market. Such an interpretation is encouraged by a telling phrase from 'To the Readers of the Weekly Dispatch', asserting that 'We write not in a spirit of rivalry, for our circulation places us beyond any competition of the papers that have begun the new system', with its acknowledgment that papers other than the *Era* were involved.

Unlike these open hostilities between the *Weekly Dispatch* and the *Era*, my final instance concerns the use of fiction as a weapon in the guerrilla war conducted from the early 1840s by the unstamped Sunday press. These papers, aimed at a proletarian readership, were generally four-page folios with a garish woodcut beneath the heading banner (Morison, 255–62). Typically short-lived examples were [W. M.] *Clark's Weekly Dispatch* (1841) and *Bell's Penny Dispatch* (1842). The most persistent, however, was [Edward] *Lloyd's Penny Sunday Times and Peoples' Police Gazette*, which started in April 1840 and survived until towards the end of the decade. (The details are tentative as no complete runs seem to have survived.) The claim of these journals to avoid the stamp duty was that they were not technically newspapers, since their main appeal lay in lurid crime reporting that was at least semi-fictional. They also quickly followed the middle-class weeklies in offering melodramatic serial stories. *Clark's Weekly Dispatch*, for example, ran the American R. H. Dana's 'Two Years Before the Mast' in 1841, while *Bell's Penny Dispatch* ran a number of translations from the French the following year, including Paul de Kock's 'Man with Three Pairs of Trousers'. *Lloyd's Penny Sunday Times* normally carried a complete tale on its front page, but from September 1841 there was also a four-page Companion devoted almost entirely to serial stories, including quite a number by Malcolm Rymer, such as 'Blanche; or, The Fearful Mystery of the Doomed House' in 1841.

The nature of these developments helps to suggest the most fundamental reason why attempts to carry novels in respectable weekly newspapers were relatively short-lived in the period before the repeal of the stamp duty. If, by the early 1840s, the monthly serial had already clearly emerged as the dominant mode of periodical publication in the bourgeois world, by the middle of the same decade the weekly serial was becoming increasingly associated with the lower depths of the proletarian market. The urban 'penny blood', which by the later 1830s was already rapidly superseding the traditional rural popular forms of the ballad, broadside, and chapbook, is best understood as a miniaturized, plagiarized, parodic version of the bourgeois monthly serial.[24] Indeed, the prefix 'penny' itself in this period not only denotes the price but also connotes this process of diminution. Serial novels in penny weekly parts had begun to appear from as early as 1835. These were typically written by 'hack' writers like Malcolm Rymer and G. W. M. Reynolds, issued by Salisbury Square publishers such as W. M. Clark and Edward Lloyd, and distributed through channels anathema to the established booksellers, whether street hawkers or tobacconists' shops. The fashionable sub-genres of the bourgeois novel all soon had their reduced counterparts in the proletarian market. Blatant imitations of bourgeois best-sellers by Dickens and G. P. R. James, for example, became common – beginning with *The Penny Pickwick* from 1838 – as did tales of criminal heroes like Jack Sheppard, already celebrated by Ainsworth.

The unstamped penny papers, their titles filched from the legitimate Sunday newspapers, are thus to be understood as a further act of radical plagiarism (Morison, 257). This can be demonstrated most directly by aligning the heading banners of *Clark's Weekly Dispatch* and *Lloyd's Penny Sunday Times* with their bourgeois equivalents. Or again by noting such guerrilla tactics as the publication in the *Penny Sunday Times* on 3 September 1843 of a sketch entitled 'The Waltz of Death', as by 'C. G.

Ainsworth', in imitation of the 'Dance of Death' scene in *Old Saint Paul's*, which had not long finished its run in *The Sunday Times*. Clearly the bourgeois journals were anxious to distance themselves from such proletarian insubordination, just as they wanted to draw a line between their own activities as radical reformists and those of the red republicans. The initial precaution was thus to refrain from ostentatious illustration of the serials, as in the case of the *Sunday Times*, which used few engravings after the experiment with Rede's *Royal Rake*, and the final one to give up on fiction altogether, leaving the field to the penny imitators – the *Illustrated London News* being perhaps the last to withdraw.

We should note, however, that the proletarian Sunday papers did not themselves continue the battle beyond the end of the decade. The nature of the stamp legislation made them a hazardous venue for cheap fiction publication, and by the mid-1840s it was apparent that the safer course for the popular proprietors was to divide news and novels into separate periodicals. Alongside new penny-fiction-magazines like George Stiff's *London Journal* (1845–1912) and *Reynold's Miscellany* (1846–69), smaller in format but similar in content to the Companion to *Lloyd's Penny Sunday Times*, the Salisbury Square publishers began also to issue their own legitimate Sunday papers. These were still strong on crime and radical in opinion, but with no fiction and duly and legally stamped. The first and most successful was, of course, *Lloyd's Weekly*, which began life as *Lloyd's Illustrated London Newspaper*, a miniature twopenny imitation of Ingram's journal.

*

By the early 1850s, then, serial novels had all but disappeared from British newspapers. Yet it was not long before they were to return in quantity. As I have argued elsewhere,[25] as soon as the taxes upon knowledge were removed, serial fiction began to appear with increasing regularity in the weekly press. But this time the key developments were not in London but in the provinces, initially in Scotland where melodramatic novelists like David Pae quickly began to sell their serial stories piecemeal to papers like the *People's Journal* in Dundee, and then in the north of England when agencies such as Tillotsons of Bolton were set up to syndicate sensational novels by, say, Mary Braddon or Florence Marryat in journals like the *Newcastle Weekly Chronicle* or the *Sheffield Telegraph*. It was only well into the 1870s, however, when the weekly installment had largely lost its association with a proletarian readership, that metropolitan weekly newspapers returned to the fiction market in

any numbers. Society journals like Edmund Yates's *World* or new illustrated papers like the *Graphic* were among the first to get involved. After
the end of its first sequence of serials in the early 1850s, the *Illustrated
London News* had continued to feature complete tales with a seasonal
flavour regularly in its special Summer and Christmas numbers, and in
the early 1880s, due in large part to competition from the *Graphic*, it
reverted to a full programme of serial fiction.[26] But this time, far from
being given secondary status, the serials were among the leading attractions, and the accompanying engravings were often extravagant in
scale and style. Around the same time, serials by writers as well known
as Wilkie Collins began to appear in new popular Tory weekly papers
like *England* and the *People*, and under this provocation even the old
radical Sundays began to follow suit. In 1885 the *Weekly Dispatch* itself
began a series of socialist serials with works by John T. Day and Edith
Nesbit (as Fabian Bland), though these soon gave way to tales of adventure by, for example, W. Clark Russell. This widespread incursion of
fiction material into newspapers in the later nineteenth century has
rightly been treated as part of that more general development in the
later Victorian press that we know as the New Journalism.[27] The tensions and battles over serial fiction in the 1840s should thus be seen a
precursor of the cultural debates waged later in the century. W. E.
Adams, the republican editor of the *Newcastle Weekly Chronicle*, and a
member of Tillotson's first syndicate in 1873, recalled: 'I revelled as a
boy in the politics of the Dispatch'.[28] On the other hand, Edmund Yates,
a pioneer among the New Journalists, also looking back on the Sunday
papers of his boyhood in the 1840s, remembered them not for their
political comment but for their serials:

> [M]y newspaper-reading was confined to Sundays, when I devoted
> myself to the *Sunday Times* and the *Weekly Dispatch*. I suppose the
> latter was at the height of its fame just then; but the political letters
> of 'Publicola' and 'Gracchus' had naturally no attraction for me, and
> I was far more taken up with the glimpses of life revealed in the fash-
> ionable novels of Lady Blessington, instalments of which were
> published in the *Sunday Times*.[29]

Notes

1. 'To the Readers of the Weekly Dispatch', *Weekly Dispatch*, 3 Jan. 1841, 6.
2. See Lise Queffélec, *Le roman-feuilleton français au XIXe siècle* (Paris: Presses
   Universitaires de France, 1989), ch. 1.

3. Unsigned article by William Makepeace Thackeray, 'French Romancers on England', *Foreign Quarterly Review*, 32 (Oct 1843), 226–46; 226.

4. See Robert L. Patten, *Charles Dickens and his Publishers* (Oxford: Clarendon Press, 1978).

5. Table 2 incorporates data from both *A Return of the Number of Newspaper Stamps, 1837–50* (House of Commons Papers, 28: 42, 1852) and *A Return of the Number of Newspaper Stamps, 1851–3* (House of Commons Papers, 39: 117, 1854).

6. Serial novels seem to have appeared occasionally in the Scottish weekly press even in the decade before the abolition of the 'taxes on knowledge', a notable example being that of the early work of Robert Scott Fittis, whose tale 'The Mysterious Monk' began its run in the *Perth and Dundee Saturday Journal* as early as 16 July 1842. The closest I have come to a hit in the English provinces is the appearance of 'Sunshine and Shadow' by Thomas Martin Wheeler, former Secretary to the National Charter Association, in Feargus O'Connor's Chartist weekly *Northern Star* from 31 March 1849 to 5 January 1850. However, though the *Star* was initially published in Leeds, its production had shifted to London in 1843.

7. For details, see Alexander Andrews, *The History of British Journalism* (2 vols; London: Bentley, 1859), II: 255–6.

8. *John Bull* seems to have been an exception in this respect, as no serial fiction has been traced there throughout the 1840s.

9. *The Sunday Times* thus represented much more of a general news organ than the Sunday paper founded in the same year, *Bell's Life in London*, which, as its sub-title suggests, was principally a 'Sporting Chronicle'. However, *Bell's Life in London* was occasionally to carry fiction of a sporting cast, notably the 'Sporting Sketches' of R. S. Surtees (famous for the Jorrocks series), 25 Oct. 1846–27 Jun. 1847, reissued in volume form as *Hawbuck Grange* in 1847.

10. Unsigned notice in the *Sunday Times*, 5 Jan. 1840, 2.

11. As this list suggests, melodrama was the preferred mode, and indeed several of the authors concerned had made their names in the theatre, including Leman Rede, whose *Rake's Progress* had run so successfully at the Olympic back in 1833.

12. Peter W. Sinnema, *Dynamics of the Pictured Page: Representing the Nation in the 'Illustrated London News'* (Aldershot: Ashgate, 1998), 12–14.

13. In the early years a standard issue contained thirty engravings of varying sizes, as attested by many announcements of special supplements with extra illustration (e.g. 11 Mar. 1843, 176).

14. Unsigned notice in the *ILN*, 24 Sep. 1842, 310.

15. The title was changed when the novel appeared in volume form, with the *ILN*'s engravings by Kenny Meadows and 'Alfred Crowquill' (Alfred Henry Forrester) still intact. The first edition from Nodes (1844) had *The Sisters; or, England and France*, while the second from W. M. Clark (1851) had *The Sisters; or, the Fatal Marriages*. Perhaps the editors of the *ILN* had encouraged the author to emphasize the scenes of public and political life.

16. Though if the decade is reviewed as a whole, both the serials and their illustrations seem to inhabit rather less of an ideological strait-jacket than is allowed by Sinnema. If reassuring English domestic fiction was the rule in the early days of the *ILN*, it was a rule by no means rigidly enforced. There

are quite a number of exceptional stories that are manifestly outward-looking or reveal a satirical edge. Although the *ILN* was no friend of republicanism, it maintained close journalistic links with Paris and began a French edition in the summer of 1851. The serial fiction included translations not only from the French but also from Swedish and German, while more than one author worked Irish themes. An uncomfortable radical edge is much more apparent in the later serials by Blanchard Jerrold and William Carleton, than in the earlier work by Miller which Sinnema points to as a rare and partial breaching of the narrative hegemony in force in the paper (169–76).

17. Despite this encomium to the new 'literary feature', only one short serial story appeared in the *ILN* during the following eight months, and that a very uncharacteristic one, a short historical romance by M. H. Barker. During much of this period, the space previously occupied by the *'nouvellettes'* was given over to instalments of a lengthy history of wood-engraving by William Andrew Chatto.
18. Unsigned 'Address', *London Telegraph*, 1 Feb. 1848, 1.
19. Notice signed by 'Umbra', *Britannia*, 26 Aug. 1848, 554.
20. See Stanley Morison, *The English Newspaper: Some Account of the Physical Development of Journals Printed in London between 1622 and the Present Day* (Cambridge: Cambridge University Press, 1932), ch. 2.
21. Richard D. Altick, *The English Common Reader: A Social History of the Mass Reading Public, 1800–1900* (Chicago: University of Chicago Press, 1957), 342–3.
22. Unsigned notice, *Era*, 17 Nov. 1839, 90.
23. This was followed immediately by 'Bizarre Fables', unsigned, but in fact from the pen of 'Arthur Wallbridge' [W. A. B. Lunn] (30 May–26 Dec. 1841).
24. See Louis James, *Fiction for the Working Man 1830–1850* (London: Oxford University Press, 1963), ch. 3.
25. Graham Law, *Serializing Fiction in the Victorian Press* (Basingstoke: Palgrave, 2000), 23–35.
26. See *Indexes to Fiction in 'The Illustrated London News' (1842–1901) and 'The Graphic' (1869–1901)*, ed. Graham Law (Sta Lucia, Queensland: Victorian Fiction Research Unit, University of Queensland, 2001).
27. See Alan J. Lee, *The Origins of the Popular Press in England 1855–1914* (London: Croom Helm, 1976), 128–9.
28. W. E. Adams, *Memoirs of a Social Atom* (1903, 2 vols; reprinted in one volume with an introduction by John Saville, New York: A. M. Kelley, 1968), 39.
29. Edmund Yates, *Edmund Yates: His Recollections and Experiences* (2 vols; London: Bentley, 1884), ch. 2.

3
Textual Encounters in *Eliza Cook's Journal*: Class, Gender and Sexuality

Johanna M. Smith

The first article of the first issue of *Eliza Cook's Journal* (1849–54) was entitled 'A Word to my Readers', a title that seems to indicate a straightforward encounter between author/editor/publisher Eliza Cook and her readers. But of course no such encounter is without ambiguity. As Margaret Beetham reminds us, not only is it difficult to identify the actual readers of many journals, but any periodical 'works by positioning its readers in a particular way'.[1] Furthermore, the implied audience of *Eliza Cook's Journal* has been a matter of debate. In this article, then, I first consider ideological encounters in periodicals in general and specifically in what Brian Maidment calls journals of popular progress.[2] I next consider *Eliza Cook's Journal* as a popular-progress journal by examining its implied readership(s), looking briefly at the *Journal*'s positioning of 'the people' and its discourses of the arts, and then in some detail at its discourses of the sciences. From there I consider *Eliza Cook's Journal* as a women's periodical, examining both the possible relations of reader to editor and the ways that women are represented in the *Journal*'s fiction. I conclude by exploring the possibility of lesbian encounters in the *Journal* and its fiction. My aim is not to settle the question of the genre or the audience of *Eliza Cook's Journal* but to demonstrate the intractability as well as the richness of these questions.

I will begin with some general questions of ideological encounters in periodicals. The market for reading material, Scott Bennett points out, was 'one of the earliest consumer mass markets'.[3] Questions of ideological production for this market are complicated, for if we approach periodicals as 'forms of social discourse rather than as direct statements of social opinion',[4] then any periodical genre becomes 'a formal construction impinging on, but not necessarily identical with, ideological statement'. Hence, to deduce a periodical's implied consumer or reader we must find 'some equation between [its] expressed opinion or "content" and [its] social discourse or "address"'[5]. Finding that equation can be tricky for journals of popular progress, or journals dedicated to the education and advancement of 'the people.' The difficulty is that while the expressed opinion of such journals is fairly self-evident, their address tends to be less so. In other words, says Maidment, these magazines are not 'simple statements of an emergent social philosophy of secular self-help';[6] rather they show 'the self-doubts and anxieties of a developing middle-class self-awareness', and so they display 'contradictions in purpose'. Such contradictions become particularly apparent in cases of double address, i.e., where an implied audience is made up of both middle-class and artisan-class readers. Ideally, through double address the journals of popular progress might construct opportunities for 'rational discourse'[7] between classes, 'spaces outside of class conflict where the artisan and the genteel could begin to understand each other'. But the difficulties of finding a common language for such a textual encounter were immense.

These problematics of address are evident throughout *Eliza Cook's Journal*. On the assumption that this periodical is not widely known, I begin with some basic information. Published from May 1849 to December 1854, the *Journal* was a weekly whose circulation ranged from 50,000 to 60,000 – slightly greater, according to the *Waterloo Directory of Periodicals*, than that of its contemporary *Household Words*. The lioness's share of the *Journal* was written by Cook herself (generally one editorial, article, and poem per week); several serials and the occasional article were contributed by Eliza Meteyard (a.k.a. Silverpen); other regular contributors included Samuel Smiles, William Dalton, Anna Maria Sargeant, and Percy B. St. John. For three-half-pence the reader got sixteen pages of 'utility and amusement':[8] articles, editorials, 'Short Notes' on current events, snippets from other periodicals, poems, aphorisms, short biographies, book reviews, and Peter Parley's 'Lessons for Little Ones', as well as stories and serials for adults. Keeping this variety in mind, we can see the *Journal*'s first article, 'A Word to my Readers', as symptomatic of problematics of address. Cook denies 'appointing myself any *particular* right to lead or teach "the people"' ('Word' 1), and she repudiates 'the fashion so violently adopted of talking to 'the people,' as though they needed . . . self-sacrificing champions'. Although she is 'anxious' to aid '"the mass"' in their 'gigantic struggle for intellectual elevation', she adds that this 'development of progressive mind' requires only 'communion with truth' to succeed. Is Cook addressing here 'the people' themselves, to show her solidarity with them? Or the self-appointed 'champions', to show them how to aid rather than lead the people? Or both groups of implied readers?

To further muddy the waters, 'the people' is a particularly complex term of address. Certainly Cook's idea of a 'development of progressive mind' encapsulates 'the narrative of progress . . . formed around the advancement of knowledge' which Patrick Joyce considers 'one of the narrative principles active in a construction of "the people"'.[9] Furthermore, James Vernon argues that at periods when the language and politics of class were perceived as divisive, a discursive shift toward 'the people' might offer the possibility of 'transcending the factional forces of class'.[10] A year after 1848, when the class-based politics of Chartism had seemed to threaten revolution, Cook's use of 'the people' is perhaps registering such a shift. The fact that the Literary and Mechanics Institute sponsored by Samuel Courtauld for his millworkers subscribed to *Eliza Cook's Journal*,[11] for example, indicates an implied audience of both working-class autodidacts and their bourgeois employers. Despite such invocations of 'the people', however, the language of class seems pervasive in the *Journal*. Even articles that deplore 'Antagonism of Classes' or advocate 'Sympathy between Classes'[12] accept the fact of classes, and some articles verge on browbeating 'the people'. Several hammer away at 'the moral wreckage – the brutish degradation – the frightful social suffering' caused by drink;[13] many articles recommend savings banks, assurance societies, and other means of helping 'the people' towards 'sobriety, temperance, and worldly virtue'.[14] Just as middle-class intellectuals and professionals represented 'the people' as 'subject to reform and modification',[15] so too might a popular-progress journal. Thus the occasional hectoring tone in *Eliza Cook's Journal* signals the 'general formulas of domination' intended to produce 'the people' as 'subjected' or 'docile bodies'.[16]

That tone, however, is not ubiquitous. Another, less disciplinary model offered by the *Journal* is that of cross-class encounters through art. As one story puts it, a 'common love of art . . . makes the whole world kin'.[17] This ideal, of a space created by art outside class conflict, is most strikingly evoked by Eliza Meteyard's fiction. In her first story for the *Journal*, various classes – represented by a duke's haughty daughter, a virtuous shoebinder, a demagogic cobbler, a skinflint florist, and a reformed young thief – are brought together around the sickbed of a designer's daughter, in a tableau of community created both by 'human sympathy' and by an appreciation of beauty.[18] 'I shall recognize no class whilst developing Truth, and Beauty, and Good', Meteyard says in concluding this story ('Three', 10), and its subsidiary moral, that 'what beauty is to the eye, sympathy is to human souls', further indicates the importance she attaches to aesthetics. 'The New Crockery-Shop', Meteyard's second *Journal* story, presents beauty as 'essential' to 'the philosophy of progressive social life';[19] indeed, 'the primary principle of art' ('New', 38) is 'to awaken in the mass a craving for, and a capacity to appreciate, the great intellectual labors of their kind'. Later in her career Meteyard wrote several books about the work of Josiah Wedgwood, and in her *Journal* fiction too the applied arts are of particular importance. In 'The New Crockery-Shop', for instance, when the kind-hearted staymaker Ann Gussett buys a teapot of flowered china from poverty-stricken Madeline Barlow, 'the wondrous influence of [its] beauty' (23) has multiple effects: a diminution of the 'rudeness, disorder, and . . . uncomeliness of unrefined life' among Mrs Gussett and her apprentices; a consequent improvement in Mrs Gussett's business, such that she enables Madeline to marry Edward, a pottery designer, by stocking a crockery shop for them; and via their shop, 'artistic effects upon the surrounding population' (38) which range from an increase in household *objets* to a Mutual Improvement Association, a Temperance Society, and a Lending Library.

In 'The New Crockery-Shop', aesthetic labour is strictly gendered: men create, women appreciate.[20] In another of Meteyard's stories for the *Journal*, her serial 'The Bronze Inkstand', women tend to function as mediators in aesthetic encounters. The story begins with an object lesson for ladies in the proper valuation of 'people who have to labor'.[21] When Lady Aurore displays 'contempt' for working-class 'vulgarity' and lack of taste, this attitude is countered first by her father Lord Clare's belief in a relation of 'mutual good-faith, appreciation, and service' between the classes, and then by her companion Bertha's 'bold advocacy of art and artisans' (59). Overhearing Bertha's remarks, the 'respectable mechanic' (11) Oliver Thornway is inspired to design a bronze inkstand, modelling it on the nebula he observed through a telescope. He thus embodies Bertha's hope that the artisan classes will become 'more open-eyed to beauty' (42) and to the 'suggestive hints' for artistic production offered by the 'exact sciences'. Bertha in turn comes to embody two ways for a 'gentlewoman' (12) to further such a hope: she writes articles on the sciences in a popular style designed to be 'understood by many'; and she offers to help Oliver, not as 'patronage' (58) but 'in the spirit of one who loves art for its own pure, exalted sake'. If Bertha thus stands for women writer-reformers like Cook and Meteyard herself, as a gentlewoman she might also serve bourgeois women readers as a model for cross-class encounter. A model for working-class women is provided by Dolly Newport, not only in such 'ministries' (62) as arranging 'with loving hands' (59) Oliver's 'artistic little workshop', but also because her 'innocence and truth' (62) have 'strengthened and beautified' his art. The serial concludes with the prospect that Oliver will marry Dolly once she completes the schooling arranged by Bertha – another act that the *Journal*'s bourgeois women readers might emulate. And by this point Lady Aurore has learned a lesson in feminine appreciative encounter: recognizing 'how weak and prejudiced I have been' (70), she apologizes to Oliver, 'taking his hand – yes, his hand' (71), in earnest of her 'humility' before his 'genius'. Where the story began with Lord Clare's moral superiority to his daughter, it ends with their positions reversed: he misses his chance to marry Bertha because, unlike his daughter, he allows 'conventional pride of mere position and birth' to blind him to the merits of a class beneath his own.

A second illustration of double address in *Eliza Cook's Journal* and the encounters it might enable can be seen in the *Journal*'s discourses of science. One of the *Journal*'s objects was 'to shew the higher holiness and poetry of true Science', thereby 'attracting men onward through the love of Knowledge' towards 'their own happiness' and 'the prosperity of society'.[22] To speak more soberly, the *Journal* intends to popularize science in order to further both individual and social improvement. The implied reader here would seem to be simply a person with little or no technical expertise in, or specialized knowledge of, science, and so one would expect a single and straightforward address. But early-Victorian science was 'contested territory', for the questions of 'who should participate in the making of science' and 'what kind of stories should be told about nature' were 'still unresolved'.[23] Indeed, as Greg Myers argues, popularizers who explained scientific discoveries and their significance may well have been 'more important than the professionals in shaping the public image of science'.[24] Moreover, 'popularizers do not simply transmit or water down the writing of professionals, they transform scientific knowledge as they put it in new textual forms and relate it to other elements of non-scientific culture'.[25] This point is particularly relevant for mass-market periodicals, where science articles would be cheek by jowl with pieces on non-scientific subjects, and for popular-progress journals, where articles on scientific progress would be linked by placement with pieces on other areas of social improvement. And, as Meteyard's recommendation of popularized science in 'The Bronze Inkstand' will have suggested, the implied readers of such science would have been various. From the

Enlightenment on, ladies were 'cultivated as consumers of scientific knowledge',[26] and science popularizations ostensibly written for them and/or children were often read by un- or under-educated men as well – Michael Faraday's introduction to science, for example, came from Jane Marcet's popularizing *Conversations on Chemistry*.[27] Clearly, then, the address of popular science articles could have been (at least) double, and the implied reader of such articles in *Eliza Cook's Journal* included the working-class woman. An article on the Sanitary Movement addresses 'the people themselves' as it recommends 'habitual cleanliness, temperance, and domestic economy', but it also assures working-class women that they have the 'physical and moral well-being' of their class 'much in their power'.[28] The *Journal* often advocates 'domestic industrial training' for working-class women, 'with a view to their future sphere as wives, mothers, and housewives'.[29] Similarly, 'Education for Housekeeping' claims that most such women require 'industrial training of the most practical kind' in housekeeping,[30] and another article makes that case with the common moral/disciplinary argument that 'the comfortable home is the best antidote to the alehouse'.[31]

The science popularizations most obviously addressed to women readers are the articles and fiction about cookery. The articles demonstrate a movement away from the older idea of housewifery as a set of practical skills acquired by apprenticeship or training, to the newer idea of domestic science, a more theoretical body of knowledge and expertise. In a sense, that newer idea had begun in the 1790s with Count Rumford's 'Philosophical Cookery',[32] such as his experiments to prove that boiling was an 'unscientific' way to cook meat (Lewis, 18). By the 1840s, it was the science of chemistry which seemed 'the source of knowledge about the essential nature of matter',[33] including edible matter. Justus von Liebig was a 'prodigious' popularizer of the new chemistry,[34] and his books are often mentioned approvingly in the *Journal*. Best known for his work in organic chemistry and its applications in agriculture, pathology, and physiology,[35] Liebig was also interested in the reform of dietetics: his *Researches in the Chemistry of Food* (1847) advocated 'a scientific basis . . . for the culinary art'.[36] This book was favorably reviewed in the *Journal*, the reviewer agreeing with Liebig that cooking is 'a scientific process' and that '[t]he cook may learn much from the chemist'.[37]

The fiction about cookery in *Eliza Cook's Journal* takes this scientific discourse in a different direction. To illustrate, I turn to 'Mrs. Dumple's Cooking School', a serial written by Eliza Meteyard and published in the June 1850 issues of the *Journal*. The story characterizes cooking as a 'civilizing art',[38] and the epigraph, which recommends teaching cookery to 'the humbler classes' (86) so as to increase their 'comfort, temperance, health, and economy', confirms that the civilizing is to be class-specific and moral/disciplinary. Yet the story's address is double in speaking 'at once to different sections of [its] readership',[39] to middle-class reformers as well as the working classes.

The story begins with a lingering evocation of pre-industrial England. This rustic Eden is embodied in Margery Dumple, 'nurtured in the sweet virtues of chastity, charity, thrift, and admirable housewifery' (87) on her father's grange in the weald of Kent. It is also figured by the Dolphin Inn, a coaching inn managed by the widowed Margery; its glory days are past, coach travel and haulage having been superseded in the early 1840s by railways. The story's opening thus seems to address an audience nostalgic for an older, rural and agricultural England. Very soon, however, such backward-looking dislike of industrial progress is displaced onto 'quaint, old-fashioned' Tummus, the comic hostler. In contrast, Margery's housewifery, although old-fashioned, is linked to the progressive vision of Alderman Rudbery, a 'great city silk merchant' (88). He proposes to turn the Dolphin into a cooking school, where Mrs Dumple will teach charity girls 'the most needed lessons of our daily life' (89) and thereby do 'more for the social life of England than half the laws trumpeted in Parliament'. This proposal speaks to an implied readership of forward-looking advocates for self-help and popular progress, and we might take the story's textual encounters – of working man, wealthy merchant, successful tradeswoman, and charity girls – as modelling for that readership the social progress achieved in the story.

Yet these encounters are less egalitarian and more hierarchical than they are made to seem. Mrs Dumple's pupils are not so much agents of their own progress as signifiers that charity girls who are 'attentive, steady, cleanly, honest, frugal, and industrious' (104) will be rewarded with 'good places of all-work' (and/or husbands, as the mass wedding at the end of the serial attests). Any prospect of further upward mobility is explicitly foreclosed: Alderman Rudbery dismisses the idea of 'rais[ing] up cooks for hotels, or mansions, or palaces' (89), and Mrs Dumple aims only to produce cooks 'for hospitals, taverns, or schools, but also for humble fire-sides and narrow house-holds' (124). The story's Ragged School and Industrial School children are told that they will receive meals prepared at the Cooking School, on one condition: '*That condition is work*', intones Rudbery, for '[i]t is God's law' (125) that those who do not work do not eat.

As the working classes are instructed in the duties and virtues of their station, so women of all classes are given gendered lessons. One such comes to women readers via the subplot of Emma Field and her daughter. Seduced by a wealthy employer who had 'talked of marriage' (132), Emma fled from him, gave birth to a daughter, and 'sunk to her early grave'; her daughter fetches up at the Cooking School and, through Mrs Dumple's 'right teaching, and a noble sense of duty' (135), is enabled to tread 'the path her own unhappy mother had been lured from'. The implied audience of this subplot would be working girls but also, I believe, middle-class women, who would learn from it their responsibilities to girls of the lower orders. And they would also learn the rewards of such care. It is pertinent here that Mrs Dumple tops the story's classed and gendered moral hierarchies. Alderman Rudbery, although superior to her in financial and social (and, arguably, gender) position, achieved his success because Mrs Dumple 'was a mother to me, and led me to be what I am' (89). And Emma's 'cold, haughty, super-cilious' (134) seducer is allowed to take his daughter from Mrs Dumple only after 'long entreaty' (135) and only on condition that she continue to 'watch over the rearing of his child'.

Mrs Dumple's moral eminence leads to a consideration of the com-plicated ways in which textual encounters might interpellate women subjects. In *Eliza Cook's Journal*, articles and fiction which make large moral claims for housewifery and which characterize working-class women as 'shockingly ignorant' of it ('Education', 248) open spaces of intervention for the middle-class woman with the requisite household skills and moral/disciplinary qualities of 'cleanliness, thrift, regularity, industry' and order ('Education', 247). The educative role modelled in the *Journal* exemplifies one of the new functions of women under modern capitalism. As feminist historians have documented, the domes-tic woman was becoming less important in production but correspond-ingly more important in 'reproduction of conditions for labour power', not only 'material reproduction of the labor force' but also 'ideological reproduction of the relations of production'.[40] Overseeing a middle-class household and its servants was thus 'an exercise in class management',[41] and this 'active management of class power' included instructing working-class women in their duties. The articles in *Eliza Cook's Journal* on domestic industrial training might perform this ideological repro-duction. But they might perform another as well, by means of double address. As Elizabeth Langland puts it, 'middle-class women were pro-duced by domestic discourses even as they reproduced them to consol-idate middle-class control'.[42] If the *Journal's* articles and fiction work to discipline working-class women in 'submission to the ruling ideology'[43] of domesticity, they also work toward ideological reproduction of the dominant classes by inculcating middle-class women with 'the ability to manipulate the ruling ideology correctly'.

*

Double address indeed, in this range from instructing to improving, from scientific data to moral discipline, from women of the middle and lower classes to men of those classes. This multiplicity informs my exploration of the extent to which *Eliza Cook's Journal* may be categorized as a woman's magazine. Certainly its 'general aim' of improvement encompassed 'women's improvement',[44] and certainly the *Journal* published a number of articles on women's issues. Frequently aired were the plights of needlewomen[45] and of single women,[46] the shortcomings of women's education,[47] the dearth of occupations for women,[48] and their need for greater legal protection.[49] While Kathryn Gleadle is right to say that the *Journal* provided a 'platform for discussions of the woman question',[50] then, in fact it gave more than equal time to the conservative view of that question: consider the articles satirizing women's emancipation,[51] praising good wives and mothers,[52] and espousing such tenets of domestic ideology as women's domestic influence[53] and moral superiority.[54] In these ways the *Journal* 'tended to perpetuate the Victorian ideal of domestic femininity'[55]: again we see that Victorian women like Eliza Cook might be 'as much agents of hegemony as objects seized and defined by it'.[56]

But of course this does not necessarily mean that Cook's readers became a community of the right-minded. And we may further complicate the issue of textual encounter in *Eliza Cook's Journal* by approaching its women readers as what Georges Van Den Abbeele calls a 'community at loose ends'.[57] This idea of an unstable or uncompleted community develops from Lyotard's concept of the differend, which he defines as 'the unstable state and instant of language' that occurs when 'phrases of heterogeneous regimen' must be linked.[58] A differend is structured in such a way that its resolution in the terms of one regimen necessarily wrongs the other; hence, any linkage between them should 'bear witness to differends' by finding idioms for both regimens.[59] The most equitable linkage, then, enables a 'play of *differences* or "loose ends"',[60] a play that 'gives the differend "its due"' as what '*cannot* be reduced to a consensus'. It seems to me that the 'heterogeneity and blurred boundaries' of a periodical[61] – its refusal of a single authorial voice, its mix of genres and discourses – makes possible textual encounters that enable readerly communities at loose ends. And I would now propose that one of the loose ends in the community of *Eliza Cook's Journal* and its readers is lesbian women.

What follows is necessarily speculative; as Leila Rupp points out, 'there is no easy way to find the lesbians in lesbian history'.[62] But Martha Vicinus argues that 'a lesbianism can be everywhere without being mentioned', and that this non-naming can be 'the very mechanism that reinforces its existence as a defined sexual practice'.[63] So I am pursuing 'the possibilities of the "not said" and the "not seen"'[64] as conceptual tools for understanding a lesbian history 'dependent upon fragmentary evidence, gossip, and suspicion'. My first point of speculation is Eliza Cook herself. Her contemporaries repeatedly noted her 'mannish' appearance: Tennyson considered her an example of 'physical masculinity' feminism;[65] Gansevoort Melville described her hair, short and parted on the side, as 'most boyishly dressed';[66] and Mary Howitt recalled that Cook's clothes, such as lapelled jackets showing shirt front and ruffles, followed 'a very masculine style, which was considered strange at that time'.[67] From the 1830s on Eliza Cook was well known as a poet, and perhaps her 'masculine' appearance was perceived as artistic eccentricity, but there seem to have been rumours about her sexuality as well. One commentator notes that the 20-year-old Cook's intimacy with the granddaughter of a Kent landed proprietor caused 'insinuations of a most absurd kind' in the 'scurrilous' publications.[68] In the 1840s Cook seems to have had a romantic friendship with the American actress Charlotte Cushman;[69] indeed, one of Cushman's biographers states quite baldly that Cook 'fell in love with her'.[70] Cook and Cushman sometimes wore matching dresses, a practice that signified both their friendship and their 'differen[ce] from heterosexual women'[71] – to Elizabeth Barrett Browning, for example, Cushman's later relationship with Mathilda Hays was marked as 'a female marriage' in part by their matching clothes.[72] Finally, Cook wrote several poems to and about Cushman, two of which were published in the *Journal*. For all these reasons, some women readers may have come to *Eliza Cook's Journal* expecting that it would give the sexual differend its due.

My second speculation concerns such a differend in several *Journal* stories by Eliza Meteyard. She seems to have been far less flamboyant than Cook, and although she was unmarried she did not, to my knowledge, attract the kind of sexual speculation that Cook did. Indeed, most commentators stressed her domestic virtues; she supported an aunt and two younger brothers by her writing, and she was widely praised for 'behav[ing] so nobly to her relatives'.[73] But several facts – her stated enthusiasm for 'social and industrial communities' based on 'human equality',[74] her contributions to such radical publications as *Douglas Jerrold's Weekly* and *Tait's Edinburgh Journal*, and a repeated concern that her ideas were too advanced even for this audience[75] – all suggest that she was at least unconventional in some ways. One area of unconventionality, I am postulating, is the presence in several of her stories of what Marilyn Farwell terms 'lesbian narrative space'.[76] Female desire is 'inconceivable' in most Western narratives, says Farwell, because they are 'structured by gender difference' into an active/male space and a passive/female space; hence they follow a 'necessarily heterosexual' trajectory.[77] When a woman becomes primary to another woman or concentrates on a woman rather than a man, however, the usual narrative dualisms and dichotomies are disturbed. A 'disruptive space of sameness' emerges,[78] and this is the lesbian narrative space. When such a space appears in Meteyard's stories, it is sometimes subsidiary to a tale's other aims. In 'The New Crockery-Shop', for instance, Mrs Gusset's relation to Madeline, although far more prominent in the narrative than Madeline's relation to her husband, is finally subordinate to the story's main focus on aesthetic community. And although another story concludes on a tableau of the heroine not with her new husband but with her housekeeper, this space of gender sameness is also one of class difference, in which the two women remain 'the truest mistress and servant'.[79]

Two of Meteyard's stories, 'The Hidden Ring' and 'Lucy Dean, the Noble Needlewoman', do foreground a lesbian narrative space. Initially 'The Hidden Ring' seems structured by heterosexual desire, as both Anne and Dora achieve the marriages they desire. But Dora's husband then exposes her to scandal and calumny by insisting that their marriage remain secret; it is Anne who establishes Dora's innocence, and this moment occurs in what Farwell calls a 'space of sameness'. Anne finds Dora asleep and sees the girl's wedding ring (usually concealed on a chain around her neck) reposing on her 'matchless bosom';[80] kissing the ring, Anne tells Dora that their 'faith and trust in the virtue of our sex' (58) shall be 'the sign of our sisterly friendship and affection'. This physical contact and the pledge of 'human sympathy' (56) between women stand in sharp contrast to the 'jealous' (29) and 'secret' love of Dora's husband.

Meteyard's serial 'Lucy Dean, the Noble Needlewoman' suggests quite strikingly a sexual 'play of differences'. The tale appeared in March and April of 1850, when emigration to Australia was being proposed as a remedy for the desperate situation of London needlewomen. Among the story's opening epigraphs is Edward Wakefield's claim in *A View of the*

Art of Colonization that successfully colonization 'all depends' on women,[81] and in that respect the story is conventional enough. Lucy is inspired and aided by Mary Austen to emigrate to South Australia; there the miners' 'rude nature visibly softened under the pure and blessed influence' (378) of her 'moral worth' (363), and she introduces order, regularity, and clean linen into the new settlement. Her efforts are rewarded with the mass nuptials of thirty miners; eventually she marries her erstwhile employer, and Mary Austen too emigrates and marries. Unlike the great majority of propagandists for women's emigration at this time, however, Meteyard tends to soft-pedal the matrimonial opportunities women might find in Australia. Her emphasis is rather on Mary Austen's reaching out 'so nobly from the depths of her woman's heart to her suffering sister women' (315), on women helping themselves and each other. Furthermore, as Catherine Gallagher points out, the one relationship in the story with a significant 'emotional dimension' is that between Mary and Lucy.[82] Toward her fallen sister Nelly, Lucy displays only 'sternness' (331); it is Mary Austen who prevents Nelly from drowning herself, and when the sisters finally meet in Mary's presence, Lucy refuses to acknowledge or speak to Nelly until Mary joins their hands and says '*Be one, for you are Sisters*' (394). It is true that Lucy sometimes worships Mary from afar, and Joseph Kestner is certainly right to see Mary as 'a myth of the triumphant priestly woman'.[83] Yet one such priestly moment is the prelude to close physical contact between the women: Lucy kneels before Mary 'as a disciple might before the holiest teacher' (330), but then 'buried her face' in Mary's lap. Similarly, when Lucy is later 'deeply moved' (343) by Mary's 'angel' kindness (342), she again 'buried her face upon the lady's lap' (343).

Throughout, Meteyard's serial follows a narrative pattern of such 'fleeting' but crucial 'moments of intensity and love between women'.[84] In the trajectory of such narratives, heterosexual couplings are preceded by 'emotional reconciliations between female protagonists',[85] reconciliations which serve as 'a displaced covert climax' before 'the final release of narrative tension' in marriage. Although Mary and Lucy both marry men, they are first quasi-married to each other: their benefactor joins their hands, saying that it is 'wiser' (395) to thus 'unite woman and woman together' than to 'unite man and woman in one'. And later when each woman takes a husband, there seems a deliberate ambiguity in the statement that 'Mary Austen and Lucy Dean were married in Sydney by the colonial bishop'. Also telling in this respect is the story's final tableau: Mary and Lucy, 'sitting hand in hand on the broad sands' (395) of the new world, together embody 'the spiritual faith' of 'the SOUL of WOMAN!' Gallagher reads this scene as a union of mothers, but it seems to me rather to crown the two women's many moments of romantic, even passionate, friendship.

I began by saying that scholars have debated the implied audience of *Eliza Cook's Journal* and the genre to which it belongs. I hope that, rather than foreclosing such debates, I have added to them by factoring in the possibility of a lesbian readership and a lesbian narrative space in the *Journal*'s fiction. In other words, I hope I have demonstrated that it is the 'play of differences or loose ends' that characterizes the textual encounters of *Eliza Cook's Journal*.

Notes

1. Margaret Beetham, *A Magazine of her Own? Domesticity and Desire in the Woman's Magazine, 1800–1914* (London: Routledge, 1996), 12.
2. Brian E. Maidment, 'Magazines of Popular Progress and the Artisans', *Victorian Periodicals Review*, 17 (1984), 83–93.
3. Scott Bennett, 'Revolutions in Thought: Serial Publication and the Mass Market for Reading', in *The Victorian Periodical Press: Samplings and Soundings*, ed. Joanne Shattock and Michael Wolff (Leicester: Leicester University Press, 1982), 226.
4. Maidment, 'Magazines', 85.
5. Ibid., 86.
6. Ibid., 86.
7. Ibid., 87.
8. 'A Word to my Readers', *Eliza Cook's Journal*, 1 (5 May 1849), 1.
9. Patrick Joyce, *Democratic Subjects: The Self and the Social in Nineteenth-Century England* (Cambridge: Cambridge University Press, 1994), 149, 175.
10. James Vernon, *Politics and the People: A Study in English Political Culture c.1815–1867* (Cambridge: Cambridge University Press, 1993), 300.
11. Judy Lown, *Women and Industrialization: Gender at Work in Nineteenth-Century England* (Cambridge: Polity, 1990), 152.
12. 'Antagonism of Classes', *Eliza Cook's Journal*, 7 (16 June 1849), 110–11; 'Sympathy between Classes', *Eliza Cook's Journal*, 4 (26 May 1849), 59.
13. 'Drinking!', *Eliza Cook's Journal*, 39 (26 Jan. 1850), 194.
14. 'Arts Wanted!', *Eliza Cook's Journal*, 237 (12 Nov. 1853), 42.
15. Anita Levy, *Other Women: The Writing of Class, Race, and Gender, 1832–1898* (Princeton: Princeton University Press, 1991), 47.
16. Michel Foucault, *Discipline and Punish: The Birth of the Clinic*, trans. Alan Sheridan (Harmondsworth: Penguin, 1977), 137–8.
17. 'Buy Images!', *Eliza Cook's Journal*, 173 (21 Aug. 1852), 266.
18. Eliza Meteyard, 'The Three Hyacinths before Heaven', *Eliza Cook's Journal*, 1 (5 May 1849), 8.
19. Eliza Meteyard, 'The New Crockery-Shop', *Eliza Cook's Journal*, 2–3 (12–19 May 1849), 3: 37.
20. Three stories in *Eliza Cook's Journal* do focus on women creators, but only one of them presents a woman becoming a successful artist as well as 'an

ornament to her sex' ('The Singing Girl', *Eliza Cook's Journal*, 45 [9 Mar. 1850], 291); the other stories, 'The People's Artist' and 'The Poetess', instead suggest that it is all but impossible for a woman to achieve both artistic success and domestic bliss.

21. Eliza Meteyard, 'The Bronze Inkstand', *Eliza Cook's Journal*, 79–83 (2–30 Nov. 1850), 79: 12.
22. I quote the advertisement written by Cook and bound at the end of the British Library's volume of *Eliza Cook's Journal* 1–35 (shelfmark PP6004/d).
23. Bernard Lightman, ' "The Voices of Nature": Popularizing Victorian Science', in *Victorian Science in Context*, ed. B. Lightman (Chicago: University of Chicago Press, 1997), 204–5.
24. Greg Myers, 'Science for Women and Children: The Dialogue of Popular Science in the Nineteenth Century', in *Nature Transfigured: Science and Literature, 1700–1900*, ed. John Christie and Sally Shuttleworth (Manchester: Manchester University Press, 1989), 191.
25. Ibid., 171.
26. Ann B. Shteir, *Cultivating Women, Cultivating Science: Flora's Daughters and Botany in England 1760–1860* (Baltimore: Johns Hopkins University Press, 1996), 2.
27. Myers, 173.
28. 'Health – The Homes of the People', *Eliza Cook's Journal*, 8 (23 June 1849), 114.
29. 'Homes and Housewives', *Eliza Cook's Journal*, 260 (22 Apr. 1854), 405.
30. 'Education for Housekeeping', *Eliza Cook's Journal*, 250 (11 Feb. 1854), 248.
31. 'Comfort at Home', *Eliza Cook's Journal*, 166 (3 July 1852), 159.
32. W. G. Lewis, *The Cook: Plain and Practical Directions for Cooking and Housekeeping; with Upwards of 700 Recipes*, rev. ed. (London: Houslton and Stoneman, 1849), 15.
33. Robert Bud and Gerrylynn K. Roberts, *Science vs. Practice: Chemistry in Victorian Britain* (Manchester: Manchester University Press, 1984), 38–9.
34. Margaret Pelling, *Cholera, Fever and English Medicine 1825–1865* (Oxford: Oxford University Press, 1978), 125.
35. Christopher Hamlin, 'Providence and Putrefaction: Victorian Sanitarians and the Natural Theology of Health and Disease', in *Energy & Entropy: Science and Culture in Victorian Britain*, ed. Patrick Brantlinger (Bloomington: Indiana University Press, 1989), 96–8.
36. Justus Liebig, *Researches on the Chemistry of Food*, ed. William Gregory (London: Taylor and Walton, 1847), 124.
37. 'Liebig on Nutrition, Diet, and Cookery', *Eliza Cook's Journal*, 130 (25 Oct. 1851), 413.
38. Eliza Meteyard, 'Mrs. Dumple's Cooking School', *Eliza Cook's Journal*, 58–61 (8–29 June 1850), 59: 103.
39. Helen Rogers, 'From "Monster Meetings" to "Fire-side Virtues"? Radical women and "the People" in the 1840s', *Journal of Victorian Culture*, 4 (1999), 59.
40. Catherine Hall, *White, Male and Middle-Class: Explorations in Feminism and History* (Cambridge: Polity, 1992), 51, 52.
41. Elizabeth Langland, *Nobody's Angels: Middle-Class Women and Domestic Ideology in Victorian Culture* (Ithaca: Cornell University Press, 1995), 8.

42. Ibid., 11.
43. Hall, 53.
44. Pauline A. Nestor, 'A New Departure in Women's Publishing: *The English Woman's Journal* and the *Victoria Magazine'*, *Victorian Periodicals Review*, 15 (1982), 94.
45. 'On the Best Means of Relieving the Needlewomen', *Eliza Cook's Journal*, 116 (19 July 1851), 189–91, and 'Work for Stafford House', *Eliza Cook's Journal*, 209 (30 Apr. 1853), 1–3.
46. 'A Brief Chapter on Old Maids', *Eliza Cook's Journal*, 21 (22 Sep. 1849), 333, and 'Old Maids', *Eliza Cook's Journal*, 78 (26 Oct. 1850), 403–5.
47. 'Men and Women – Education of the Sexes', *Eliza Cook's Journal*, 85 (14 Dec. 1850), 97–99, and 'The "Young Idea" – Female Education', *Eliza Cook's Journal*, 147 (21 Feb. 1852), 270–1.
48. 'The Ladies' Guild', *Eliza Cook's Journal*, 122 (30 Aug. 1851), 277, and 'Employment of Young Women', *Eliza Cook's Journal*, 36 (5 Jan. 1850), 145–7.
49. 'The Legal Wrongs of Woman', *Eliza Cook's Journal*, 197 (5 Feb. 1853), 225–7, and 'Treatment of Women', *Eliza Cook's Journal*, 119 (9 Aug. 1851), 225–7.
50. Kathryn Gleadle, *The Early Feminists: Radical Unitarians and the Emergence of the Women's Rights Movement, 1831–51* (New York: St Martin's, 1995), 44.
51. 'Emancipated Women', *Eliza Cook's Journal*, 252 (25 Feb. 1854), 273–4, and 'Women's Rights Convention', *Eliza Cook's Journal*, 238 (19 Nov. 1853), 62–4.
52. 'Seven Requisites of Female Character', *Eliza Cook's Journal*, 19 (8 Sep. 1849), 295–6, and 'Mothers of Distinguished Men', *Eliza Cook's Journal*, 226 (27 Aug. 1853), 283–6.
53. 'Home Power', *Eliza Cook's Journal*, 35 (29 Dec. 1849), 129–31.
54. 'Woman', *Eliza Cook's Journal*, 7 (16 June 1849), 107–8, and 'Women: Their Social Position and Culture', *Eliza Cook's Journal*, 179 (25 Sep. 1852), 337–9.
55. Nicola Thompson, *Reviewing Sex: Gender and the Reception of Victorian Novels* (London: Macmillan, 1996), 123.
56. Levy, 35.
57. Georges Van Den Abbeele, 'Introduction', in *Community at Loose Ends*, ed. Miami Theory Collective (Minneapolis: University of Minnesota Press, 1991), ix–xxxvi.
58. Jean-Francois Lyotard, *The Differend: Phrases in Dispute*, trans. Georges Van Den Abbeele (Manchester: Manchester University Press, 1988), 13, 29.
59. Ibid., 13.
60. Van Den Abbeele, xviii.
61. Margaret Beetham, 'Towards a Theory of the Periodical as a Publishing Genre', in *Investigating Victorian Journalism*, ed. Laurel Brake, Aled Jones, and Lionel Madden (Houndmills: Macmillan, 1990), 25.
62. Leila Rupp, 'Finding the Lesbians in Lesbian History: Reflections on Female Same Sex Sexuality in the Western World', in *The New Lesbian Studies: Into the Twentieth Century*, ed. Bonnie Zimmerman and Tony McNaron (New York: Feminist, 1996), 158.
63. Martha Vicinus, 'Lesbian History: All Theory and No Facts or All Facts and No Theory?', *Radical History Review*, 60 (1994), 58–9.
64. Ibid., 64.
65. Qtd. in Carl Woodring, *Victorian Samplers: William and Mary Howitt* (Lawrence: University of Kansas Press, 1952), 104.

66. Qtd. in Joseph Leach, *Bright Particular Star: The Life and Times of Charlotte Cushman* (New Haven: Yale University Press, 1970), 180.
67. Mary Howitt, *An Autobiography*, ed. Margaret Howitt, 2 vols (London: William Isbister, 1889), II: 37.
68. *Notable Women of our Own Times* (London: Ward Lock, 1883), 141.
69. Lisa Merrill, *When Romeo was a Woman: Charlotte Cushman and her Circle of Female Spectators* (Ann Arbor: University of Michigan Press, 1999), 141–50.
70. W. T. Price, *A Life of Charlotte Cushman* (New York: Brentano's, 1894), 61.
71. Vicinus, 60.
72. Qtd. in Vicinus, 64.
73. Howitt 2, 149.
74. Eliza Meteyard, 'Introduction', *The Nine Hours' Movement: Industrial and Household Tales*, by E. Meteyard (London: Longmans, 1872), xi.
75. Gleadle, 45, 96.
76. Marilyn Farwell, 'Heterosexual Plots and Lesbian Subtexts: Toward a Theory of Lesbian Narrative Space', in *Lesbian Texts and Contexts: Radical Revisions*, ed. Karla Jay and Joanne Glasgow (London: Onlywomen, 1992), 93.
77. Ibid., 94, 95, 97.
78. Ibid., 93.
79. Eliza Meteyard, 'The Immortality of Kindness', *Eliza Cook's Journal*, 25 (20 Oct. 1849), 389.
80. Eliza Meteyard, 'The Hidden Ring', *Eliza Cook's Journal*, 27–30 (3–24 Nov. 1849), 30: 57.
81. Eliza Meteyard, 'Lucy Dean, the Noble Needlewoman', *Eliza Cook's Journal*, 46–51 (16 Mar.–20 Apr. 1850), 46: 312.
82. Catherine Gallagher, *The Industrial Reformation of English Fiction: Social Discourse and Narrative Form 1832–1867* (Chicago: University of Chicago Press, 1985), 141.
83. Joseph Kestner, *Protest and Reform: The British Social Narrative by Women 1827–1867* (London: Methuen, 1985), 146.
84. Bonnie Zimmerman, ' "The Dark Eye Beaming": Female Friendship in George Eliot's Fiction', in *Lesbian Texts and Contexts: Radical Revisions*, ed. Karla Jay and Joanne Glasgow (London: Onlywomen, 1992), 140.
85. Ibid., 139.

Part II
Encountering Gender and Class

4
Encountering Time: Memory and Tradition in the Radical Victorian Press

Ian Haywood

> Let us, therefore, unite to obtain an immediate Literary Reform, and the only sure method of acquiring it is for the people to read only those good works which do them justice, and let works which wickedly trample on their rights, and unjustly elevate their oppressors, lie mouldering on the shelves, uncut, unread, unnoticed, and unknown. This is the easiest and most rational method of obtaining a speedy Radical Literary Reform. The remedy lies in the hands of the intelligent people, and these ought to employ it, for the sake of themselves and posterity.
>
> *(Chartist Circular, 1840)*

> The proletariat has formed upon this basis a literature, which consists chiefly of journals and pamphlets, and is far in advance of the whole bourgeois literature in intrinsic worth.
>
> (Frederick Engels, *The Condition of the Working Class In England*)[1]

> Rainborough knew what he was about.
> The Chartists knew what they were about.
>
> *(Sunday Citizen, 18 June 1967, leader)*

'Like every generation that preceded us, we have been endowed with a *weak* Messianic power'.[2] The words of the Marxist critic Walter Benjamin will form the basis of this essay, in which I want to investigate and illuminate some of the ways in which the radical press of the nineteenth century tried to overcome two forms of temporal provisionality. The first, which is peculiar to oppositional political culture, is the 'curse', to borrow Kevin Gilmartin's term, of exclusion, liminality, and imitation:

the consciousness of radical ideologies that they are ultimately para-
sitical forces owing their existence to the dominant culture which they
seek to join or conquer.[3] As Iowerth Prothero puts it:

> Radicals tended not to see politics as a permanent, on-going activity
> involving manoeuvring, clashing, compromising interests, but to see
> reform as once-for-all negative changes and the implementation of
> justice . . . radicals more often reacted to than created widespread
> political excitement, conflict, or crisis.[4]

The second, more generalized form of contingency, is the mechanical
succession of chronological time itself, 'empty homogeneous time' in
Benjamin's formulation, from which meaningful 'moments' must be
identified or produced. As a Marxist allied to the emerging Frankfurt
School, Benjamin refuted facile Hegelian notions of Enlightenment progressivism; an effective, materialist historicism must 'make the continuum of history explode' with 'the presence of the now' by grasping 'the
constellation which its own era has formed with a definite earlier one'.
Once this connection is made (presumably through a penetrating analysis of the determining influence of class forces), history will be 'shot
through with chips of Messianic time'. This mode of revelatory understanding and mobilization of history transcends narrow definitions of
empirical accuracy: 'To articulate the past historically does not mean to
recognize it "the way it really was". . . . It means to seize hold of a memory
as it flashes up at a moment of danger'.[5] Benjamin's startling and moving
proposition privileges the radical use and relevance of the past, its 'Messianic' potential, over 'empty' historicism; it also provides a way out of
that renowned classical Marxist conundrum, that 'The tradition of all the
dead generations weighs like a nightmare on the brain of the living'.[6] In
this essay I hope to show that for readers and producers of the radical
Victorian press, tradition and memory did not constitute a 'nightmare'
dialogue with the past, but could function as 'chips of Messianic time',
sources of identity, hope and continuity. The dynamic resource of mass-
produced print was both the medium and the message.

My examples are drawn from the two most outstanding popular
radical newspapers of the Victorian era: the Chartist national newspaper
the *Northern Star* (1837–52), and the prolific and long-lived *Reynolds's
News* (1850–1967). Some attention will also be given to *Reynolds's News*'s
neglected forerunner, *Lloyd's Weekly Newspaper* (1842–1918). The discussion of the *Northern Star* will demonstrate the ability of radical editors
to exploit the paratextual features of the printed page to generate a

symbolic or metaphorical reading of the 'news'; the analysis of *Reynolds's News* will look at the techniques of reader participation in the construction of tradition, notably during 'jubilees' and commemorative events.

The culture of remembering in the popular Victorian radical press has its roots in the foundational or 'dangerous' moments of its own history. The immediate success of the *Northern Star* is a tribute to the central agency of the radical periodical form in providing cohesion and inspiration for a mass reform movement. The paper informed, guided and motivated its readers.[7] But any review of the radical Victorian press must also focus on the achievements of those perplexing entrepreneurs, Edward Lloyd (1815–90) and George W. M. Reynolds (1814–79). So many contradictions emanate from the careers of these two pressmen that their talents fully deserve Fanon's brilliantly coined epithet, 'phobogenic'.[8] An aura of disrepute has hung over both men to the present day, though their success in forging a new kind of popular literature with radical credentials has also long been recognized. They exist on the borderline between respectability and scandal, popular enlightenment and 'trash', journalistic innovation and populist regression.[9]

In the early 1830s, Lloyd was active in the unstamped wars while Reynolds nurtured his renegade republican politics as a journalist in Paris. Both men then used plagiarism of Dickens as a stepping stone to popularity. In 1842, a year of political turbulence and widespread disturbances, Lloyd launched his innovative *Lloyd's Weekly Newspaper*.[10] The paper advocated Chartism and supported European nationalist struggles, but it also supplied its readers with the more facile and sensational pleasures of crime reporting and sport. Lloyd trumpeted proudly the paper's advanced technological means of production (the rotary press) as a beacon of modernity and industrial mass production. Lloyd also developed radical new methods of marketing, including paying his workers in coins stamped with his own visage. Concurrently, Lloyd monopolised the growing urban market for cheap serial fiction. His 'penny bloods' have secured his reputation for posterity as a downmarket publisher, but his followers at the time seemed unperplexed by the apparent discrepancies in his cultural standards. As Virginia Berridge has shown in her indispensable (and as yet unrivalled) study of the paper, *Lloyd's Weekly News's* business columns even attracted a loyal petit-bourgeois readership.[11] One of Lloyd's greatest commercial coups was appointing the well-known liberal critic Douglas Jerrold as the paper's editor in 1852. Later in life Lloyd subscribed to a narrow, 'Victorian' notion of respectability by disowning his 'Salisbury Square' fiction, but his readers remembered and celebrated his wider revolutionizing of popular literature in the 1840s.[12]

Reynolds lagged behind Lloyd in becoming a market leader in cheap serial fiction and newspaper proprietorship, but his extreme republicanism and his meteoric rise as a Chartist activist in 1848 meant that Reynolds's politicization of popular literature was more overt and more enduring. After successes with the highly popular *London Journal* (1845–1906) and his own *Reynolds's Miscellany* (1846–69), Reynolds moved into the radical newspaper field with the short-lived *Reynolds's Political Instructor* (1849–50), out of which grew his greatest legacy, *Reynolds's Weekly Newspaper*, launched in May 1850. By the early 1860s, with all taxes on newspapers abolished, Reynolds's and Lloyd's Sunday weeklies commanded over half a million readers.[13] The scale and significance of this achievement cannot be overestimated.

The importance of the nineteenth-century radical press for our understanding of Victorian popular politics and popular culture is now established.[14] Beginning with several pioneering articles by Raymond Williams in the early 1970s, critics have focused on the special contribution of the popular Sunday weekly in the formation of a new species of commercialized radical newspaper. Lloyd and Reynolds inherited two 'popular' print traditions which they managed to fuse together: the didactic and activist methods of the radical weeklies of the unstamped wars, and the more sensational pre-industrial pleasures of chapbooks, ballads, and dying speeches which by the 1830s had transmogrified into serialised fiction and crime reporting. The lowering of the stamp duty in 1836 only temporarily banished the popular radical press: a mere six years passed between the reduction and the appearance of *Lloyd's Weekly Newspaper* in 1842, and only one year before the emergence of the *Northern Star*, which rocketed to a circulation of around 50,000 by 1839.[15] Williams argues that Reynolds was a central figure in the emergence of this new popular press: 'the limits and pressures of the whole social development are well summed up in this contradictory but powerful figure and form', though the same might be said of Lloyd.[16] The attempt by the state to 'replace' the tradition of the radical weekly with 'the simulacrum of popular journalism that we still have in such large quantities today' had failed.[17]

Most critics attribute the success of *Reynolds's News*[18] to its populist politics: in common with Reynolds's fiction, the paper presented a melodramatic view of class politics.[19] As Patrick Joyce points out, melodrama was by no means a class-exclusive discourse. It undoubtedly 'made a particular appeal to the lowly, the excluded and the powerless' but it also 'spoke to a socially mixed audience', including genteel women.[20] This explanation of Reynolds's popularity, that in order to be commercially successful he indulged in an old-fashioned critique of political corruption, can be found in both Williams and Berridge. Their scepticism about Reynolds's motives has been influential. Tim Randall, for example, describes the politics of *Reynolds's News* unsympathetically as 'a diffuse radicalism'.[21] Randall argues that Reynolds exploited the 'irreversible decline' of Chartism by 'offering a rhetorical patina of radicalism'.[22] Compare this faint praise with Joyce's identification of *Reynolds's News* as the 'clearest expression' of the discourse of 'radical populism': the paper 'served as an essential bridge between the old radicalism and the new', keeping alive (in Patricia Hollis's words) the 'old analysis' of a 'predatory' landed ruling class, and feeding its readers' appetite for an untheorised, anti-monarchical, anti-statist republicanism.[23] Anthony Taylor has also underlined the paper's vital role in sustaining popular republicanism and anti-imperialism in the teeth of the late Victorian revival of the cult of the monarchy and empire, and Rohan McWilliam notes that historians have begun to reappraise the accuracy and relevance of the so-called 'old' analysis of political corruption in the light of the continuing power of the aristocracy in the nineteenth century.[24]

But these achievements must not be allowed to overshadow *Reynolds's News*'s persistent advocacy of the labour movement and organic working-class institutions. There is a sense of providence about the purchase of the paper by the Co-Operative movement in the 1920s, as the support for co-operative principles was a prominent feature of the paper's politics from its inception, and was fully consistent with Reynolds's republican advocacy of the 'democ-soc' reforms of the French revolution of 1848. The paper helped to naturalize such 'foreign' ideologies and blend them with nativist traditions of artisanal and agrarian radicalism. This 'diffuse' radicalism both reflected and imagined the multi-faceted radical cultures of its readers and provided a constant focus for their political desires, anxieties and fantasies. As we shall see, steadfastness became a central trope of the paper's appeal and efficacy, and adherence to the foundational moment and the foundational values of the paper was a crucial element in this mythology. As Aled Jones points out, the popular press of the late nineteenth century looked back nostalgically to the mid-century period when its power was at its height and as yet politically untamed by the forces of large-scale capital.[25] At the end of the century, the jubilee readers of *Reynolds's News* rallied around their undeviating loyalty to the paper's origins in the Chartist and revolutionary past, a period when, according to Margot

Finn, a 'radical internationalist culture' created and sustained an 'imagined community of labour'.[26] Commemoration was a ritualised remembering and enactment of a self-sustaining salvatory narrative, a triumph of messianic time. The cultural and political history of *Reynolds's News* was constructed on the page by its producers and readers who jointly owned its cultural capital.

The dominant method for the construction of 'messianic' time and the transmission of plebeian traditions in the nineteenth-century radical press was not the writing of 'homogeneous' historical narrative but the commemoration and remembering of 'moments of danger'. E. P. Thompson notes that the emerging working class developed their own 'martyrology' and a 'demonology', and this symbolic, quasi-religious system of beliefs and values played an important role in the formation of class-consciousness.[27] The symbolic, ritual and ceremonial aspects of radical culture are now recognized by historians as a vital source of collective expression and communal identity: this new phenomenology of radicalism incorporates social customs and leisure pursuits as well as more orthodox political activity and institutions: poems and marching songs, conviviality and toasting, the naming of children, funeral orations, and the inscriptions on flags and banners can now all be regarded as radical representations and discourses which display and perform 'thick descriptions' or shorthand versions of radical history and its causes.[28] All this semiotic activity was reproduced, synthesised and circulated in the pages of radical periodicals. Thus the radical press became an archive of collective memory. As we shall see, this was by no means a passive or straightforwardly reflectionist process. The symbolic lexicon of radicalism condensed and distilled the rational, ongoing critique of injustice and oppression into an easily recognized, accessible, and practical language of verbal and visual signifiers or monuments.

Radical symbolic activity was at its most intense during those 'moments of danger' when 'messianic' and 'empty' chronological time seemed most likely to merge. The starkest illustration of this process can be found in the repressive legislation enacted by the state in the wake of the Peterloo massacre of August 1819. An unprecedented clause in the infamous Six Acts outlawed the carrying of radical banners at rallies.[29] The Six Acts also, predictably, subjected the radical press to harsh new regulations, including the widening of the definition of a newspaper to include the radical weeklies, which then made them subject to the 4d stamp duty. The state hoped this would price the radical press out of the plebeian reader's orbit, but in the longer term this tactic only increased the cultural capital of the radical movement by creating a new force, the 'unstamped' press. Inadvertently, the state provided the radical Victorian press with a vital pre-history and a new monument, the heroic unstamped wars of the early 1830s.[30] When a radical Victorian periodical evoked Peterloo, therefore, it did more than remember its victims; Peterloo was a synecdoche of the first 'heroic' phase of nineteenth-century mass radicalism and its press, and a talismanic reminder that out of defeat could come renewal.[31] It seems appropriate, therefore, that my first example of a radical encounter with Victorian time should involve remembering Peterloo.

The front page

In the summer of 1842 England saw a spectacular assertion of working-class power. A lockout by factory owners in the industrial regions provoked a wave of mass strikes during which Manchester ground to a halt as the city fell to an occupation by organised labour (in order to close down factories, workers emptied the boilers, which gave the popular nickname 'Plug Riots' to the action). Even more alarmingly for the authorities, the Chartist movement saw an opportunity to forge an alliance with the industrial working class. In August 1842 this 'moment of danger' peaked during a series of meetings in Manchester between Chartists and labour leaders. Although support for the Charter was secured, the promised federation never materialised, and a truly revolutionary moment declined into a series of violent and often bloody skirmishes. The state retaliated with mass arrests and imprisoned hundreds of Chartists and labour activists.[32]

It may seem odd, therefore, that on the front page of the *Northern Star* for 20 August 1842, in the midst of this unfolding drama, we do not find a report on the conflict. Instead, there is a report on the erection of a monument in Manchester to commemorate Henry 'Orator' Hunt, with a large accompanying illustration (Figure 5). Henry Hunt was a firm favourite of northern radical martyrology, as it was his botched arrest which sparked the Peterloo massacre on 16 August 1819. The text situates Hunt's career within the mass radical agitation of the postwar years, with Peterloo as the narrative closure of this phase of radical history. Peterloo is visually revived in the lower half of the front page which reproduces a famous print of the massacre. These two images, which frame the front page and dominate the written text, seem to be counterpointed: the lower image is the violent, turbulent past, the upper image is the present which has emerged causally from those traumatic events; the past is the present's prehistory, full of sound and fury,

Figure 5 'Monument to the memory of Henry Hunt', front page of the *Northern Star*, 20 August 1842.

congested movement and massed human energy; the present is the calm monumentalism of more civilised times; this metonymic reading of the images emphasises distance, poignancy, emotion recollected in tranquillity: a mood, indeed, of remembrance.

But another, more radical reading of the relationship between the images is just as possible. If Michael Wolff is correct in his belief that 'the basic unit for the study of Victorian cultural history is the individual issue of a Victorian periodical,' we must be alert to the situatedness of paratexts within each periodical and how this might affect the reader's response.[33] As soon as the reader of this issue of the *Northern Star* turned over the front page and looked at page three, he or she found a graphic account of the disturbances. The effect of this displacement of dramatic 'news' from its more usual position on the front page is to profoundly alter the meaning of the front page's visual imagery. The function of the Peterloo print, which previously had a logically sub-servient position as the historical reality behind the Hunt monument, is powerfully inverted. The image is now proleptic, preparing the reader for the 'new' Peterloo described on the inside pages. The reversal of the hermeneutic logic of the front page symbolically expresses the radical desire that the closure of the new conflict will also be reversed, with the people victorious. Put more bluntly, the people will be revenged, but such an inflammatory idea need never be stated. Once the emphasis on 'messianic' commemoration has been established, the sense that 20 August (1842) is a reincarnation of 16 August (1819) becomes operative. The reader of the paper, who is always-already a potential activist, exists psychically between these two dates, with the Hunt monument a reminder of the promise of eventual peace.[34] The reports of the conflict inhabit simultaneously the immediate present and the symbolic past; the 'empty' chronology of 'news' is charged with the typological agency of radical intervention in history. Similarly, the reports are both a representation and form of radical action. The accounts are peppered with self-conscious references to Peterloo: the orderliness of the people, the violent intentions of the state.[35] The evocation of Peterloo means that any use of direct force by the authorities is immediately delegitimised, and any violent response by the people will be authorised as a purely defensive measure or the result of deliberate provocation:

> The authorities are at a loss what to do: for the works are all standing, and the people walking the streets in the most orderly manner. Every plan that has been devised has been tried to make the people break that peace, that there might be a pretext to re-enact the bloody work of 1819, but without avail.   (20 August 1842, 3)

At this point in the paper's coverage, the plot thickens further. The Hunt monument is reintroduced into the narrative to make the point that the rights (and rites) of radical commemoration are also under attack. One report informs the reader that the open-air festival which has been arranged to celebrate the founding of the Hunt monument, and at which the Chartist leader Feargus O'Connor was engaged to speak, has been prohibited. This registers the state's fear of messianic remembering, and uncannily echoes the original 'plot' of Peterloo in which the state silenced a radical event by seizing Hunt's body and the symbols (particularly flags) which surrounded it. Another report, however, tells us that the celebration has taken place a few days later in a more muted, genteel guise of a tea party, and without O'Connor (the passage of time between the two reports is of course a feature of a weekly paper, and while this meant that some of the dramatic immediacy of the daily newspaper was lost, it also meant that greater narrative pleasure could be derived from the successive reporting of the same 'story').

O'Connor's absence may seem a clear marker of defeat, diminution, and even feminization, but it is important to realise that genteel conviviality was an established part of the radical repertoire, and did not necessarily deplete class consciousness: fundraising, radical toasting, and informal organisation could all be combined with the respectable taking of tea.[36] The *Northern Star* presents the tea party as mocking or goading authority:

> under the very finger of oppression did the working people show that they are able not merely to uphold their principles, but even to do it pleasantly, and extract from it matter of amusement.
>
> (20 August 1842, 7)

Genteel conviviality is transformed into a form of successful non-violent direct action, repelling the state's offensive against free speech and the rights of assembly. The triumphalist wink of 'amusement' adds a mischievous, masterful carnivalesque closure to this micro-narrative of resistance.

Of course the *Northern Star* was not fantasizing that the repressive state apparatus could be defeated solely by taking tea, but the *bricolage* of its reports provided its men and women readers with different levels at which they could vicariously enter the struggle and identify with its participants.[37] The accounts of fierce pitched battles and skirmishes between workers and the military constituted a more conventional 'heroic' and masculine form of action. But the added charge and significance of these confrontations derives again from the symbolic resonances of historical reference. One of the most spectacular and orchestrated battles took place at the mill owned by Hugh Birley, who was targeted by workers precisely because he was known to have been a member of the Yeoman Guard who attacked the crowd at Peterloo.[38] Another iconic moment, the storming of the Stockport Union Workhouse, evoked an even more celebrated revolutionary event than Peterloo, the taking of the Bastille in July 1789. The fact that the victorious Lancashire 'mob' proceeded to distribute the workhouse's store of about 700 loaves of bread to the assembled poor was also reminiscent of scriptural miracle. Soon after this exalted triumph, troops shot down many strikers, but this parallel with the Peterloo massacre was always likely to be part of the script. The deeper victory of the people was the right to remember and construct their own history and traditions, a victory of actions but also of representation on the printed page.

Readers remember . . .

Reynolds's Weekly Newspaper: A Journal of Democratic Progress and General Intelligence was first published in May 1850. Announcements about the launch in *Reynolds's Miscellany* emblazoned its appeal to the 'enslaved masses' and declared that the paper would be a 'staunch, fearless, and uncompromising friend of popular principles' and would campaign for European republicanism and against 'monopolists of power, the privileged orders, and the favoured classes of society'.[39] There would also be 'light reading and amusement . . . as well as political disquisitions'. These announcements were placed above adverts for *Lloyd's Weekly Newspaper*, which is praised as a 'colossus of the press'; this shows just how closely Reynolds modelled his paper on Lloyd's.[40]

As a legally stamped paper, the initial cost of *Reynolds's News* was 4d, though this soon fell to a penny in the early 1860s. Most of the front page of the first issue reports on the continuing revolutionary struggles in Europe, which by this point were in crisis. In an editorial, Reynolds exhorts the working class to 'assemble of an evening to read or hear read the journals that are favourable to their cause' and to 'study foreign politics, which open so vast a field for enlightenment, and furnish so many glorious champions worthy of admiration'.[41] Reynolds had been an ardent admirer of French republicanism since his youth, and all his publications reflect this, but it is important to note that he assumes his readers are responsive to internationalism, an undervalued component of British radicalism. Anti-imperialism (including support for the Commune in 1871, and opposition to the Boer war) and a European socialist outlook were enduring features of the paper. Based on this evidence, it is not the case, as many twentieth-century left critiques of populism would have us believe, that British popular culture in the nineteenth century was uniformly the dupe of imperialist ideology, nor that the older, more organic radical public sphere declined into commercialism and conservatism.[42] The first issue of *Reynolds's News* also reported numerous Chartist meetings, and the paper retained a strong domestic political agenda, agitating for Co-Ops, Irish freedom, and the Social Democratic Federation. Although some of these were new causes, the basic political orientation of the paper remained consistent and inscribed in its founding moment: popular sovereignty, and resistance to monopolies of power in the land, the state, religion, and finance. The paper's relations with its readers seemed to validate this vision: although the readers were also consumers, the paper's democratic politics and its cheapness aimed at overcoming or dissolving the cash nexus, and fostering a collective identity, an 'imagined community of labour'.

Though it may be difficult for the anti-populist instincts of the political left to accept the fact, Reynolds and Lloyd turned bourgeois modes of cultural production to democratic ends. To accept this fact is salutary, as it cautions us against essentialist thinking about the relationship between radicalism and commercialism, and opens a window onto a flourishing nineteenth-century tradition of popular political print culture which combined useful knowledge with forms of sensational pleasure.[43] Reynolds and Lloyd were accorded genuine respect in their time as architects of a new kind of popular press. Charles Mitchell, the compiler of the first *Newspaper Press Directory* in the mid 1840s, categorised the political orientation of *Lloyd's Weekly Newspaper* as 'Democratic' politics, and added, ' it is peculiarly the poor man's paper'.[44] His praise for *Reynolds's News* in 1851 was more measured but indicated the paper's hybrid pleasures: 'but for its violent politics, it might be characterised as a good family paper'.[45]

In 1900 *Reynolds's News* celebrated its fifty-year 'jubilee'. A special supplement reviewing the paper's history was produced in May 1900. In his article '*Reynolds's*, 1850–1900', R. Wherry Anderson noted 'the founding of the journal as the outcome of the great popular agitation of the time'.[46] Although Reynolds's personal identity was indelibly stamped on the paper, its deeper value was its transmission of this originating 'moment of danger'. Anderson's words are not to be dismissed as mere self-regarding puff. The front page of the first issue of the paper was reproduced so that the original aims of the paper could speak for themselves. Moreover, this sense that the paper began as the product and expression of an intense phase of mass radical action was also proclaimed vividly in the testimony of readers. The paper validated its collective identity by handing over the construction of its past to its readers, who were invited to send in their recollections of the paper's earliest days. The letters which emerged from elderly readers who had been with the paper from its inception comprise a moving and fascinating oral history of mid-Victorian radicalism. One reader remembers Marx and Engels in the 1840s, another refused to attend at the great Chartist demonstration at Kennington Common in April 1848, and another was present at the arrest of Ernest Jones.[47] These snapshots of the 'great popular agitation of the time' have the emotional power of the unveiling of preciously preserved photographs, but their effect is not simply nostalgic. The relation between the memorializing present and the turbulent past (the Hunt monument to the Peterloo print) is dynamic and reciprocal: the invocation of the popular politics of the 1840s places the paper in a vital historical and radical tradition. This foregrounding of the situatedness of the reader in a 'messianic' temporal continuum cannot be achieved through the routine, 'homogeneous' reporting of 'news'; the latter is actually defined by the absence of a metadiscourse of the historical conditions of its own authority.

The most intriguing jubilee letter in *Reynolds's News* does not contain references to political luminaries but, like the Chartist tea party, recalls a genteel form of political pleasure. A reader writes in with a memory of a Chartist excursion to Gravesend (13 May 1900). The remarkable fact about this event is the acuteness and appropriateness of the reader's memory. In only the fourth number of the paper, 26 May 1850, there is an account of this very trip, which Reynolds himself took part in (26 May 1850, 7). The report makes clear that the aesthetic and moral dimensions of the excursion cannot be separated, in fact and import, from radical politics. The excursion, itself a new form of popular pleasure made possible by cheap railway fares, gave activists and their families an opportunity to escape from the city and enjoy pastoral beauty, but after a game of cricket and a stroll 'along green lanes', the community of Chartists gather to sing the Marseillaise. The reporter's interpretation of the excursion is combative: Chartists and republicans have refined sensibilities and are not dehumanized monsters. Chartists are capable of 'rational enjoyment of the pleasures within their reach'; far from being 'the reviled destructives of the English press' they 'know how to appreciate the beauties as well as the bounties of Nature'. The vignette illuminates in miniature that massive political and cultural battle between moral reformers and radicals which began in the Jacobin 1790s and directly influenced the formation of 'Victorianism'. The Evangelical offensive of the first half of the nineteenth century demonised radical politics as unrespectable and unEnglish, the 'Other' of civilised Christian values. This misrepresentation was an attempt to deny the high degree of convergence between the moral aspirations of radicals and 'improvers': respectability and intelligence was a common goal, but for radicals this higher state could only be guaranteed through democratic political reforms, while for conservatives and Evangelicals the essential reforms were spiritual and moral. So the micro-narrative of the singing of the Marseillaise in the Kent countryside by a community of Chartist daytrippers is intimately bound up with all those 'moments of danger' which comprise radical history. It has as much 'messianic' value as a 'condition of England' novel.

I want to conclude with a much later but very apposite illustration of the radical press recalling and foregrounding its formation in political 'encounters' of the mid-nineteenth century. The radical remembering of origins figured prominently in the self-representation of the final moments of *Reynolds's News*. In June 1967, under its new title the *Sunday Citizen*, the paper finally closed. The paper announced proudly, 'it is 117 years since George William MacArthur Reynolds founded this newspaper to support the People's Charter' (4 June 1967, front page). The final leader went on to place the paper in a longer tradition of popular dissent stretching back to the Peasants' Revolt and the Levellers. At the point of extinction, the paper produced one of its most memorable examples of popular political discourse and the mobilization of radical time:

> Rainborough knew what he was about.
> The Chartists knew what they were about.
>
> (18 June 1967, leader)

It is inconceivable that such sentiments would be phrased and aired in this way in today's popular press. The editorial assumes the reader's familiarity with a tradition of radical nationalism but retains the populist, even 'tabloid' register of informality.[48] With hindsight, the poignancy of the language is deepened further, as the demise of the *Sunday Citizen* symbolized the end of an era of cultural history in which the popular-radical press 'knew what it was about' (Curran and Seaton). With that perspective in mind, a new 'encounter' with the Victorian origins of the mass-circulation newspaper has much to teach the present day.

Notes

1. Frederick Engels, *The Condition of the Working Class in England* (London: Grafton, 1984), 166.
2. Walter Benjamin, 'Second Thesis on the Philosophy of History', *Illuminations* (London: Fontana, 1977), 256.
3. 'Radical discourse was haunted by its own inevitable extinction, which figured by turns as an imminent curse and a painfully deferred promise' (Kevin Gilmartin, *Print Politics: The Press and Radical Opposition in Early Nineteenth-Century England* (Cambridge: Cambridge University Press, 1996), 60). Though I have severe reservations about Gilmartin's readiness to adopt this post-structuralist position regarding the 'contradictory structure of radical representation' (127–8), I do subscribe to his characterisation of nineteenth-century radicalism as a movement which had an intense relationship with history and time.

4. Iowerth Prothero, *Radical Artisans in England and France, 1830–1870* (Cambridge: Cambridge University Press, 1997), 35.
5. Benjamin, 257.
6. Karl Marx, *The Eighteenth Brumaire of Louis Napoleon, Marx and Engels: Basic Writings on Politics and Philosophy*, ed. Lewis S. Feuer (London: Fontana, 1974), 360.
7. For a full discussion of the Chartist press, see Dorothy Thompson, *The Chartists: Popular Politics in the Industrial Revolution* (Aldershot: Wildwood House, 1984), chapter 2.
8. Frantz Fanon remarks that to dominant culture blacks are 'phobogenic', a 'stimulus to anxiety': *Black Skin, White Masks* (New York: Grove Press, 1982), 151.
9. The best summary of Reynolds' life and works can be found in three sources: E. F. Bleiler, Introduction and Bibliography to George W. M. Reynolds, *Wagner the Wehr-wolf* (New York: Dover, 1975); Louis James and John Saville, 'G. W. M. Reynolds', Volume 3 of *Dictionary of Labour Biography*, ed. Joyce Bellamy and John Saville (London: Macmillan, 1976), 46–51; Rohan McWilliam, 'The Mysteries of George W. M. Reynolds: Radicalism and Melodrama in Victorian Britain', in *Living and Learning: Essays in Honour of J. F. C. Harrison*, ed. Malcolm Chase and Ian Dyck (Aldershot: Ashgate, 1996). Also useful is Trefor Thomas's Introduction to his edition of George W. M. Reynolds, *The Mysteries of London* (Keele, Staffordshire: Keele University Press, 1996), particularly his discussion of Reynolds's working methods. Reynolds's reputation has also been recuperated by labour historians working on 'late' Chartism. See McWilliam; Patrick Joyce, 'The constitution and narrative structure of Victorian politics', in *Re-Reading the Constitution: New Narratives in the Political History of England's Long Nineteenth Century*, ed. James Vernon (Cambridge: Cambridge University Press, 1996), 65–74, and *Democratic Subjects: The Self and the Social in Nineteenth-Century England* (Cambridge: Cambridge University Press, 1994), 82; Margot Finn, *After Chartism: Class and Nation in English Radical Politics 1848–1874* (Cambridge: Cambridge University Press, 1993), 112. By comparison with the growing interest in Reynolds's career, very little critical work has been done on Lloyd, and his achievements are seriously in need of a revaluation. The best accounts of his work are to be found in two sources: for the fiction, see Louis James, *Fiction for the Working Man 1830–1850: A Study of the Literature Produced for the Working Classes in Early Victorian Urban England* (London: Penguin University Books, 1973); for the journalism, see Virginia Berridge, 'Popular Journalism and Working-Class Attitudes 1854–1886: A Study of *Reynolds's Newspaper, Lloyd's Weekly Newspaper* and the *Weekly Times*', Ph.D., 2 vols (University of London, 1976); Mike Shirley, 'On Wings of Everlasting Power: G. W. M. Reynolds and *Reynolds's Newspaper* 1848–1876', Ph.D. (University of Illinois, 1997).
10. The paper began life as *Lloyd's Illustrated London Newspaper* on 27 November 1842, priced 2d, but after a brush with the stamp duty authorities (who claimed it carried news) the paper was relaunched in January 1843 as *Lloyd's Weekly London Newspaper* and sold for 2½d, still well below the price of most of its rivals.
11. Berridge, chapter 2.
12. See *Lloyd's Weekly Newspaper*, 13 Apr. 1890. This issue reported Lloyd's death,

and heralded his achievements as the 'pioneer of the cheap press'. Joseph Hatton's chapter on Lloyd in *Journalistic London* (1882) is entitled 'The Father of the Cheap Press.'

13. Alvar Ellegard, 'The Readership of the Periodical Press in Mid-Victorian Britain', *Victorian Periodicals Newsletter*, 13 (1971), 3–22. By the end of the century *Lloyd's Weekly Newspaper* became the first weekly to pass the one million mark. See also Stephen Koss, *The Rise and Fall of the Political Press in Britain. Volume One: The Nineteenth Century* (London: Hamish Hamilton, 1981), chapter 1.

14. See Eugenio F. Biagini, *Liberty, Retrenchment and Reform: Popular Liberalism in the Age of Gladstone, 1860–1880* (Cambridge: Cambridge University Press, 1992), 20–8. Biagini uses *Reynolds's News, Lloyd's Weekly Newspaper*, the *Weekly Times*, and the *Newcastle Weekly Chronicle* as historical sources, and notes that for the nineteenth-century radical reader, 'the very act of buying was a political act' (21). The political importance of *Reynolds's Newspaper* had long been recognised. H. R. Fox Bourne, one of the early compilers of newspaper history, regarded the paper as 'a formidable spokesman for the most irreconcilable portions of the community' (H. R. Fox Bourne, *English Newspapers: Chapters in the History of Journalism*, 2 vols (London: Chatto and Windus, 1887), 2: 348). In the 1930s, Simon Maccoby claimed that *Reynolds's News* was the most influential radical newspaper of the late nineteenth century, calling it a 'flourishing Ultra' (Simon Maccoby, *English Radicalism 1853–1886*, 3 vols (London: George Allen and Unwin, 1938), 1: 410–11).

15. David Vincent, *Literacy and Popular Culture: England 1750–1914* (Cambridge: Cambridge University Press, 1989), 248.

16. Raymond Williams, 'The Press and Popular Culture: An Historical Perspective', in *Newspaper History from the Seventeenth Century to the Present Day*, ed. George Boyce, James Curran and Pauline Wingate (London: Constable, 1978), 49.

17. Raymond Williams, 'Radical and/or Respectable', in *The Press We Deserve*, ed. Richard Boston (London: Routledge and Kegan Paul, 1970), 16.

18. For convenience I use the shortened form of the paper's title, which changed several times in its history. For the first year the paper was called *Reynolds's Weekly Newspaper: A Journal of Democratic Progress and General Intelligence*; in 1851 it was modified to *Reynolds's Newspaper: A Weekly Journal of Politics, History, Literature and General Intelligence*, and by the end of the century it had become *Reynolds's Newspaper* with the masthead 'Government of the People, by the People, for the People.'

19. See three articles by Anne Humpherys: 'G. W. M. Reynolds: Popular Literature and Popular Politics', *Victorian Periodicals Review*, 16 (1983), 78–89, reprinted in *Innovators and Preachers: The Role of the Editor in Victorian England*, ed. Joel H. Wiener (London and Westport, Connecticut: Greenwood Press, 1985); 'Popular Narrative and Political Discourse in *Reynolds's Weekly Newspaper*', in *Investigating Victorian Journalism*, ed. Laurel Brake, Aled Jones and Lionel Madden (Basingstoke: Macmillan, 1990); 'Generic Strands and Urban Twists: The Victorian Mysteries Novel', *Victorian Studies*, 34 (1991), 463–72.

20. Joyce, 1996, 184. The possibility that a complex, suppressed proto-feminism exists in Reynolds's work has understandably intrigued contemporary critics, though the focus has been on the fictional narratives rather than the

journalism. For a sophisticated feminist analysis of Reynolds's textual strategies, see Ellen Bayuk Rosenman. 'Spectacular Women: *The Mysteries of London* and the Female Body', *Victorian Studies*, 40 (1996), 31–64; Trefor Thomas, 'Rereading George W. M. Reynolds's *The Mysteries of London*', *Rereading Victorian Fiction*, ed. Alice Jenkins and Juliet John (Basingstoke: Macmillan, 2000). For Thomas, Reynolds's work teems with 'forbidden textual pleasures of violent sensation, political subversion, and sexual titillation' (65). Reynolds's popularity with genteel women readers is underutilized in more general studies of Victorian women's periodical reading. See Sally Mitchell, *The Fallen Angel: Chastity, Class and Women's Reading, 1835–1880* (Bowling Green, Ohio: Bowling Green University Popular Press, 1981); Kate Flint, *The Woman Reader 1837–1914* (Oxford: Clarendon Press, 1993); Margaret Beetham, *A Magazine of her Own? Domesticity and Desire in the Woman's Magazine, 1800–1914* (London: Routledge, 1996).

21. Tim Randall, 'Towards a Cultural Democracy: Chartist Literature 1837–1860', M.Litt. (University of Birmingham, 1994), 207.

22. Ibid., 213.

23. Joyce, 1991, 65–74. In *Democratic Subjects*, Joyce praises Reynolds and Lloyd as 'innovative' in their ability to give the mass reader 'features with a radical edge, the chaste pleasures of improvement, and the titillations of sensation' (Joyce, 1994, 82). See also Patricia Hollis, *The Pauper Press: A Study in Working-Class Radicalism of the 1830s* (Oxford: Oxford University Press, 1970), viii.

24. Anthony Taylor, 'Commemoration, Memorialisation and Political Memory in Post-Chartist Radicalism: The 1885 Halifax Chartist Reunion in Context', in *The Chartist Legacy*, ed. Owen Ashton, Robert Fyson and Stephen Roberts (Woodbridge, Suffolk: Merlin, 1999); McWilliam, 192.

25. Aled Jones, *Power of the Press: Newspapers, Power and the Public in Nineteenth-Century England* (Aldershot: Ashgate, 1996), chapter 5.

26. Finn, 21–2; see also chapter 3, *passim*.

27. E. P. Thompson, *The Making of the English Working Class* (Harmondsworth: Penguin, 1977), 661.

28. See: Clifford Geertz, *The Interpretation of Cultures* (London: Hutchinson, 1975), chapter 1; Eileen Yeo, 'Culture and Constraint in Working-Class Movements, 1830–1855', in *Popular Culture and Class Conflict 1590–1914: Explorations in the History of Labour and Leisure*, ed. Eileen and Stephen Yeo (Brighton: Harvester Press, 1981); James Epstein, *Radical Expression: Political Language, Ritual and Symbol in England, 1790–1830* (Oxford: Oxford University Press, 1994), chapter 3; Paul Pickering, *Chartism and the Chartists in Manchester and Salford* (Basingstoke: Macmillan, 1995), Part Two; James Vernon, *Politics and the People: A Study in English Political Culture, c. 1815–1867* (Cambridge: Cambridge University Press, 1993), 119–26.

29. *Parliamentary Debates* [Hansard], vol. XL (3 May – 13 July 1819), 1665–6.

30. The classic accounts of the unstamped press are still unrivalled: Joel Wiener, *The War of the Unstamped: The Movement to Repeal the British Newspaper Tax, 1830–1836* (Ithaca and London: Cornell University Press, 1969); Hollis.

31. E. P. Thompson, 660.

32. See Mick Jenkins, *The General Strike of 1842* (London: Lawrence and Wishart, 1980). It is worth recalling that *Lloyd's Weekly Newspaper* was established in the immediate aftermath of the strike, and the paper expressed considerable

sympathy with the northern working class, victims of 'the ravages of distress and the wantoness of oppression' (*Lloyd's Weekly Newspaper*, 1 Jan. 1843, leader).

33. Michael Wolff, 'Charting the Golden Stream: Thoughts on a Directory of Victorian Periodicals', *Victorian Periodicals Newsletter*, 13 (1971), 27–8.

34. The idea that the radical press effected a 'psychological reorientation' of its readers is discussed in James Curran and Jean Seaton, *Power without Responsibility: The Press and Broadcasting in Britain* (London and New York: Routledge, 1997), 18–19.

35. For Peterloo, see Donald Read, *Peterloo: The 'Massacre' and Its Background* (Manchester: Manchester University Press, 1958). For Hunt, see John Belchem, *'Orator' Hunt: Henry Hunt and English Working-Class Radicalism* (Oxford: Clarendon Press, 1985).

36. Prothero, 283.

37. Laurel Brake makes the useful point that periodicals were a 'communication circuit' of intrinsically intertextual discourses (Laurel Brake, 'Writing, Cultural Production, and the Periodical Press in the Nineteenth Century', in *Writing and Victorianism*, ed. J. B. Bullen (London and New York: Longman, 1997), 54–72. See also Vincent, 252.

38. See the *Northern Star*, 13 Aug. 1842, 5.

39. *Reynolds's Miscellany*, vol. 4 (Jan.–July 1850), 272.

40. *Reynolds's Miscellany*, 4: 416. It is worth noting that Reynolds may only have been repaying a debt, as *Lloyd's Weekly Newspaper* had promoted Reynolds's works throughout the 1840s. See, for example, the issues for 9 April 1843 (6), and 8 November 1846; the latter announces a 'splendid' new illustrated periodical, *Reynolds's Miscellany* (11).

41. *Reynolds's Weekly Newspaper*, 5 May 1850, leader. On the back page of the first issue, Reynolds's intention of permeating all levels of the literary culture of the working class is made clear in a report of a decision by the Provisional Committee of the National Charter Association (on which Reynolds served) to establish a Tract fund and reach the 'cottage hearth' of the isolated and demoralised agricultural worker: 'at home, by his own hearth, he could digest the unanswerable arguments lucidly explained in the Tracts before him' (8). The spectre of the politically literate peasant had haunted the British state since the 1790s.

42. See John Mackenzie, *Propaganda and Empire: The Manipulation of British Public Opinion 1880–1960* (Manchester: Manchester University Press, 1985); Theodore Adorno and Max Horkheimer, 'The Culture Industry', *Dialectic of Enlightenment* (London: Verso, 1979); Jürgen Habermas, *The Structural Transformation of the Public Sphere: An Inquiry into a Category of Bourgeois Society* (London: Polity Press, 1989), 181–5.

43. On this topic, see Iain McCalman, *Radical Underworld: Prophets, Revolutionaries and Pornographers in London, 1795–1840* (Cambridge: Cambridge University Press, 1988); Jon Mee, ' "Examples of Safe Printing": Censorship and Popular Radical Literature in the 1790s', in *Literature and Censorship*, ed. Nigel Smith (London: The English Association, 1993); Marcus Wood, *Radical Satire and Print Culture 1790–1822* (Oxford: Clarendon Press, 1994).

44. Charles Mitchell, ed., *The Newspaper Press Directory* (London: Charles Mitchell, 1846), 70–1.

45. Charles Mitchell, ed., *The Newspaper Press Directory* (London: Charles Mitchell, 1851), 133.
46. *Reynolds's News*, Jubilee Supplement, 27 May 1900, front page. George Jacob Holyoake also contributed an article, 'The Great Triumphs of Democracy', in which he regrets that the masses are still too duped to demand a 'greater equalization of fortune' (2). The diamond jubilee of *Lloyd's Weekly Newspaper*, on 30 November 1902, passed with barely a mention in the paper.
47. *Reynolds's News*, 20 May 1900, 8. An 88-year-old reader named 'Rambler' recalls reading the very first issue of the paper on the banks of the Ganges river, and kept the issue until it rotted.
48. On nationalism in this context, see Hugh Cunningham, 'The Language of Patriotism', in *Patriotism: The Making and Unmaking of British National Identity. Volume 1: History and Politics*, ed. Raphael Samuel (London: Routledge, 1989), 57–89; Tony Benn, *Arguments for Socialism* (London: Verso, 1979), chapter 3.

5
Preaching to the Ladies: Florence Fenwick Miller and her Readers in the *Illustrated London News*

Barbara Onslow

Within the flourishing society and fashion columns, specifically aimed at women in the newspapers of the eighties and nineties, women writers continued the established practice of engagement with their readers. Such dialogue had long been a feature of Victorian women's magazines.[1] Florence Fenwick Miller's relationship with readers of her lively 'Ladies' Page',[2] in the *Illustrated London News (ILN)*, repays attention in the light of her expressed views on the journalist's power to influence. An ardent suffragist, she blended fashion with feminism to promote those women's causes she supported. In doing so she met her readers on rather different terms from those commonly governing encounters between the reading public and the lady journalists who wrote their fashion, shopping and social pages.

The varying strategies by which columnists at once constructed a 'readership community', to which actual readers might theoretically contribute, and controlled such real contributions to meet their own agenda, are well illustrated by the *Englishwoman's Domestic Magazine (EDM)*. This periodical, founded by Sam Beeton, played a pivotal role in developing the tradition of reader participation, and provides a useful background against which to assess Florence Fenwick Miller's engagement with her readers.

Matilda Browne's 'Spinnings' by 'Silkworm' in the 1870s created a persona with whom readers could share their diverse and fragmented concerns over shopping, fashion, and the practical issues of domestic life. 'Silkworm', for those who wrote to her, seems to have been a virtual companion; as one correspondent put it, 'I look for your spinnings with a sort of affectionate interest, and feel as if we were friends.'[3] The engagement was reciprocal, or at least presented as such.

During a painful period, when for three months 'sorrow, sickness and death' were 'constant visitors in my home circle and among my friends', 'Silkworm' shared her feelings of despondency over her work, confessing that the editor suggested dropping the column for a while 'but I know how many dear and kind ladies depend upon my report as to novelties &c at this season and I have therefore tried to be useful if not entertaining.'[4] Judging from her closing column some months later, 'Silkworm' welcomed her correspondents' support in both her professional and private lives. 'Spinning at the Seaside' alerted faithful readers to her future plans (for a book of crochet patterns), but also thanked them, in deeply emotional terms, for their letters of sympathy. 'It is worth while to be ill and suffering . . . to fold the useless hands, and to endure the bitter pains, to receive such love and sympathy, such universal kindness and goodness.'[5]

As a site for readers' engagement with the *EDM*, 'Spinnings' had been preceded by the 'Englishwoman's Conversazione', where the nature of the relationship was very different. Sam Beeton controlled the 'Conversazione' through his selection of, often lengthy, extracts from letters, and by his commentary on the correspondence, delivered, as Margaret Beetham puts it, by an editorial persona 'teasing, authoritative and implicitly masculine'. Beeton allowed, indeed encouraged, debate on an eclectic range of issues – romantic worries, rights for women, and the infamous 'tight-lacing' and 'correction of servants'. These latter two shocked certain readers, but seemingly titillated others, to the extent that some charged the magazine with publishing, wittingly or unwittingly, pornography masquerading as domestic controversy.[6]

The correspondents' voices in the 'Conversazione' are both more individual and explicit – (letters were often quoted verbatim) – and more vulnerable to critical editorial exposure, than are those who addressed 'Silkworm'. The robust and entertaining debates Beeton set up gave licence to his editorial persona to chastise and interrogate. In contrast, Matilda Browne, though restricting the individual voice to occasional surfacings in a quoted sentence or reference, seems, when speaking of her collective correspondents, always to be trying to address their needs. She gives information because 'I have been requested by many ladies to do so', or delights in the response to an item on Scottish textile producers. 'Not only does the Silkworm find her Spinnings liked and her labours useful, she has the further pleasure of introducing the finest specimens of Scottish art and manufacture to ladies who possess taste and judgement'.[7] Readers are simultaneously flattered and consoled by the sense of belonging to a discriminating, sympathetic female circle where domestic problems may be shared, and often solved.

Annie Swan's 'Over the Teacups' in *Woman at Home* in the 1890s, drew upon some of the 'Conversazione's' subject-matter and structures, but replaced its 'jovial masculine authority' with 'sympathy and moral seriousness' offered by a distinctly feminine persona who treated her correspondents as equals.[8] In this respect the tone of her column was derived from 'Silkworm' rather than Beeton.

Florence Fenwick Miller certainly endorsed the crucial importance of the 'right tone' in journalism, but it was not one associated with the feminine persona. For her, periodicals were

> the pulpits from which our modern preachers are most widely and effectively heard, and the right tone of which is, therefore, of the first consequence to society. For every hundred persons who listen to the priest, the journalist . . . speaks to a thousand . . . [and] may effectively influence the thoughts and consciences and actions of thousands in the near future.[9]

Her 'right tone' thus carries a moral implication. Her successful career, spanning some forty years, as columnist, leader writer and periodical editor, suggests that she also understood the phrase to mean the 'tone' that would attract readers, making them susceptible to the journalist's preaching.

Florence Fenwick Miller was equally well-known as a feminist activist as she was a columnist. She lectured in the suffragist cause, was a London School Board member, and the first treasurer of the International Woman's Suffrage Committee. A sister journalist, in summarizing her prolific writing career, said, '[F]ashions and domestic concerns have not fallen much under her notice'. Yet such concerns would clearly be expected in any regular woman's feature in a weekly paper. Her 'Ladies' Page', therefore, ingeniously combined frivolity with incisive commentary on serious feminist issues, designed to influence readers and draw attention to initiatives in which they could and, it is implied, *should* participate.[10]

Her skill in pleasing readers was attested by contemporary journalists. In 1888, when Oscar Wilde was planning the *Woman's World* with Cassell's, he fancied that a 'Notes' column on current topics would be of 'considerable' commercial value to the publishers if written, not by himself, but by a well-known woman like Mrs Fenwick Miller. There 'are many things in which women are interested about which a man really cannot write . . . I mention Mrs Fenwick Miller as her notes in the *London News* are so admirable'.[11]

Fanny Green bracketed her with Mrs Humphry, 'Madge' of *Truth*, and Miss Faithfull in the *Ladies' Pictorial*, as contributors of successful women's columns.[12] When she became proprietor and editor of the feminist *Woman's Signal* it enjoyed a new lease of life under her innovative and energetic management,[13] a revamping which, Mary Billington claimed, broadened its appeal: '[S]he is fast raising [it] from the hopeless faddism and 'anti-man' partisanship which formerly distinguished it'.[14]

Mary Billington's reference to Mrs Fenwick Miller's 'record of dress and feminine doings' in the *Illustrated London News* as 'one of the features of that stately weekly' suggests a New Journalism development of 'Spinnings'. The 'Ladies' Column' in its various guises does indeed physically foreground shopping and fashion, whether at Ascot, the gallery private views, the Queen's Drawingrooms, or the sales at Peter Jones. Yet the construction of its readership is far from the intimate, domestic circle defined by 'Spinnings' or 'Over the Teacups'. The titles, 'Ladies' Column' and later 'Ladies' Page', demarcate the territory for the female sex, but its tone is markedly different from the cosiness of the chit-chat connoted by spinning and afternoon tea.[15] It shares instead the astringency, the combativeness, and the authority of the masculine persona of the editor of 'Conversazione'. It also occludes the *individual* correspondent as effectively as did 'Silkworm' in her warm cocoon.

Florence Fenwick Miller, however, as conscious of her 'real' readers as she was of the requirements of her journal, was the consummate journalist, in the sense that Arnold Bennett understood it, as a good writer matching her material to the character of the paper. By the eighties the *Illustrated*, founded in 1842, but since 1869 facing competition from another prestigious metropolitan pictorial, the *Graphic*, enjoyed an impressive circulation. Holiday issues could reach over half a million. Though mildly liberal in its political tendency, the paper avoided the more avantgarde views of 'New Woman' writers.[16] Mrs Fenwick Miller's opening article tactfully spelt out her intention: to treat of 'matters specially interesting to ladies, as they arise in the great world week by week'. The traditional 'woman's sphere' may have been 'Society, Dress, Domesticity and Charity' . . . [but] 'To that is now added Culture, Thought and Public Welfare . . .'. Nevertheless, she assured her readers, she would touch on such topics 'with a light hand' (*ILN*, 6 March 1886, 233).

Though addressing women, she was probably always aware, and, since she so often included direct advice to politicians in the column, very likely hoped, that her readers would include men. The *Illustrated London News* was after all a paper, defined not by the sex of its target reader-ship but by being a pictorial paper, noted as much for its illustrated war coverage as for its images of royal occasions.[17] Mrs Fenwick Miller's main political thrust was directed at women's affairs, but she believed that it was necessary to influence the minds of *men* as well as those of women, just as she considered that a woman's achievement must be judged as that of a human being (rather than of a woman).[18] That her column ran for so long, from 1886 to 1918, by which time she was 64 years old, suggests that she pleased enough, and did not alienate too many, of the *Illustrated*'s readers.

If Annie Swan's 'Teacups' readers shared emotional problems, what does Florence Fenwick Miller's column construct as the shared interests of *her* readers? Fashion certainly: descriptions of the gowns of society ladies – the elegant, and the ludicrous, (which gave more scope for sar-donic touches), and practical advice. Sales bargains at Peter Jones seem more of interest than the finer points of a mantle.[19] The 'doings' of society, here defined as royalty, members of the aristocracy involved in philanthropic causes or reform, politicians – (the Gladstones were friends) – and the artistic and literary community. Domestic matters for the middle-class household – recipes, tips, advice on table-decorations, sales bargains in glassware, china and linen. But this was the icing on the cake. The *raison d'être* of the 'Ladies' Page' was more substantial fare.[20] It kept its women readers up-to-date on the achievements of other members of their sex, including those living outside the capital in provincial cities. 'Ladies' Page' readers shared a world of charitable and political initiatives to which they were encouraged to respond. They inhabited a commu-nity in which information on what *had* been done, and judicious drop-ping of associated titled names, gave moral support to those more timid readers who yet hoped to improve the lot of their sex.

The column's persona was Mrs Fenwick Miller's public 'platform' self. Her signature immediately identified her as the activist and lecturer, her name 'almost too well known to need any remarks about her news-paper work'.[21] When eventually she used a pseudonym it was 'Filomena', one already well-aired in her syndicated 'Letter' in provin-cial papers. Many readers would have known who 'Filomena' was, and might have enjoyed her transparent disguise, when, making a point about women's position after the First World War, she packed her column with substantial quotation from the vote of thanks to Mrs Fawcett by the President of the Women Writers' Franchise League, a lady no less than Mrs Fenwick Miller (*ILN*, 8 April 1916, 474).

Under various by-lines, she shared with readers her opinions, but not her feelings. To this extent she adopted the masculine tradition of Beeton, and Arnold Bennett's columns in *Woman*. Even her occasional personal revelations, apart from those that were a matter of taste (e.g. on selecting table-decoration or flowers), were usually linked to political and public issues. Readers did not learn of her little daughter Irene's gown at a children's charity fancy-dress ball because Mrs Fenwick Miller wished to construct a sense of the writer's family, but because, in her campaign for women's higher education, she seized the opportunity to garb Irene as a Doctor of Science 'in scarlet damask gown, with hood-lining and facings of black silk' (*ILN*, 29 January 1887, 117). Where 'Silk-worm' might admit to being 'passionately fond of babies' when writing up a lifelike baby doll in a toyshop,[22] Mrs Fenwick Miller reveals only personal foibles that are part of her feminist agenda. So she discusses the importance of names and styles. She disliked female forms of address, calling 'Mrs Chairman' a sort of mermaid or centaur-like designation. On several occasions she supported women who, having established a professional reputation, chose to maintain their maiden style after marriage.

There is, however, so little hint of private emotion that it comes as a surprise when she occasionally uses the first person plural instead of the third person. A striking example occurs during the First World War in an item dismissing the Women's Peace Congress in Holland. The columnist suddenly allies herself to her British readers: 'Women of neutral nations, if they have the heart, may pass pointless, abstract peace resolutions, but *we* are 'in it' with our men!' (*ILN*, 8 May 1915, 606).

The sense of personality in her column derives from a combination of style, the recurrence of her 'Hobby-horses', and her distinctive opinions on 'small matters'. Her witty, acerbic commentary is a version of 'gossip' which can be enjoyed by both sexes. She may not, like Annie Swan, encourage a sense of readers as her equals through intimate discussions of personal worries, but neither does she adopt the tone of patronage so characteristic of ladies' columns written by men. If she expressed her views forcefully, they were never intended to separate the sexes but rather to castigate the ignorance and folly of individuals of both sexes. Her irony is never sharper than when attacking foolishness, whether women's absurdities in dress or men's idiocies of opinion. The men were often named, but largely as a result of her practice of identifying those in public life and shielding lesser mortals.

Like any modern columnist writing for a weekly, which has to appear always up-to-date, she naturally made use of current talking-points, as well as recent events, in sourcing her copy. She thus engaged in the wider forum of the press, contesting or drawing moral support from the views of others. News items from other journals were reported to make them more widely known or to provide a peg for her own opinion. In this way she could return to her 'Hobby-horses' with a good excuse. Readers were constantly reminded by little instances that illogicality and wrong-headedness were not the prerogative of women.

The debate over women 'cross-riding' (as opposed to side-saddle) brought her out against medical correspondents to the *Field* who claimed it was 'dangerous and injurious to the female frame'. 'Doctors' she pointed out 'are but men like others, and are apt to support their half-conscious prejudices by hasty dicta'. Professional qualifications were no guarantee of reliability. 'We all know doctors who were found to say that women could not possibly, from their physical configuration, study as long and as deeply as men; and it was not till women had made many brilliant University successes that this theorising was silenced' (*ILN*, 15 March 1890, 348). An article in *Woman's World* charging doctors with exploiting nurses provided material for the column of 13 May 1890. A news item about an 84-year-old man's request to a lady guardian to find him a suitable 50 to 60 year old woman as his wife prompts the reflection on the self-deception of men 'about their perennial attractiveness to the other sex', and the 'preposterous' way in which English male novelists[23] depict women as 'passé' in their late twenties or early thirties, in contrast to the attitude of Balzac and de Maupassant (*ILN*, 20 March 1897, 400).

During the War, when women were bombarded with officious advice on coping with inflation, she remarked the absurdity of the gentleman urging middle-class housewives to trek out to the street-stalls in the poorer districts to buy cheap cuts of meat.[24] These stalls only got the wholesalers' leavings, which was a limited supply. What would happen if women followed his recommendation?

> The limited supply of cheap, left-over foods would be gone in no time, most of the invading bags would go home empty, and the prices would be raised next day. Perhaps our lecturer saw half-a-dozen ox-tails on his street-stall. But if he induced three thousand housewives to travel to buy at the cheap market, the miracle of the loaves and fishes would not be paralleled . . .

Identifying with her readers, she suggests instead using less meat and making, like the French, wider use of flavourings in pulses, vegetable dishes and stews – 'all this is our duty now' (*ILN*, 24 June 1916, 808).

Women were thus encouraged to take pride in their domestic skills and superior knowledge of practical economics. They were flattered, not by some 'Silkworm' identifying them as women of 'taste and judgement', but by the assurance that they belonged to a sex quite the equal of men, in some ways superior. They were the people who managed the practicalities of life, organizing, and coping with the pressures of wartime conditions. They were thus assured of their powers, without any suggestion of being 'anti-Man' or advocating the extremes of New Womanhood. Their domestic strengths were valued alongside their sex's professional ones as artists, writers, doctors, teachers, or reformers.

The 'Ladies' Page' was prepared to argue with male contributors to other journals yet did not seek a dialogue through the medium of readers' letters. Indeed on at least one occasion readers were actively discouraged from expecting it. On 14 June 1890, she remonstrated,

> My correspondents will easily understand that it is impossible for me to reply to them here, or to mention the subject of their letters except when they are of general interest. But it does not seem to be so well understood that it is unreasonable to expect me to answer letters privately.   (762)

Lady correspondents had that week apparently asked her for the name of the best registry office for governesses in Paris, a recommendation for a life insurance office, and her opinion on which of two operas one should go to. She had also been asked to advise on supplying pianos to Board Schools[25] and been invited to join an international society 'with the object of having somebody in every large town in the world to whom members . . . in travelling could go as friends!' The exclamation mark concluding her description of the invitation – which one presumes was ignored – suggests not only the impracticability of the scheme but her reluctance to admit 'as a friend' unknown members of the public. Equally, she refused to subscribe to the illusion of a coterie of unknown readers as her 'friends'.

Nor did she regard answering queries as part of the contract between columnist and reader. She dealt harshly with an impertinent male correspondent, rash enough to enquire from her where he might purchase 'stays for men' (*ILN*, 5 February 1887, 148). He was firmly told to contact a men's shop. Yet she published a summary of her response in her column, perhaps to warn off other such individuals, perhaps to pre-empt any suggestion that her column was a site for corset controversies, or perhaps to amuse her readers with a minor instance of the folly of some men.

Readers were encouraged to action, not dialogue. Usually when correspondence surfaced in the 'Ladies' Page' it involved a matter of public interest.[26] A case in point is the responses to an item on the nursing of the poor. In January 1888 she had criticized a scheme proposed by the Duke of Westminster for 'nurses with badges' (qualified nurses) to attend the sick poor in their own homes. She recalled a girlhood experience of medical assistance in poverty-stricken households where a solitary utensil might have to serve for washing the patient and preparing and serving the soup, and straw and 'evil-smelling clothing, too ragged to be worn' comprised the bedding: 'I will say no more, for fear of shocking my readers'. She thought trained nurses working in private homes would find even the domestic conditions of a clerk's or 'poor, solitary governess's ménage' too difficult to work in. They 'are not famous for 'making shift' and doing their best without fuss, with the appliances that are to hand.' The poor would, therefore, be better treated in hospital (*ILN*, 14 January 1888, 36).

On 18 February, acknowledging receipt of several letters on the subject of home nursing, she utilized two of them. She gave details from a report by 'Miss W' on the work of district nurses in the Paddington and Marylebone Association, and she discussed the letter sent by Mr Henry C. Hurry of the Metropolitan Nursing Association. His letter illustrated the dangers of the kind of forceful writing by which Florence Fenwick Miller attracted her readers. He had misunderstood her, thinking she disparaged the efforts of the nurses he represented. She responded: 'Far from it; I recognise fully that even half-an-hour's daily attention from a trained nurse may be most valuable, and I distinctly spoke of the good work done by the district nurses. Especially in chronic cases, which no hospital can keep . . .' (160). She made haste to make amends by publishing the addresses of both organizations so that interested readers might make contact.

Engaging in debate with other periodical contributors whose work was in the public domain might have its hazards, though in the *Illustrated* Florence Fenwick Miller rarely attempted to keep up a running argument with any individual. There were, however, other risks associated with bringing individual readers into the public arena of a column, as Sam Beeton had discovered when he was accused of inventing letters or being duped by his correspondents. The case of the Karl Pearson letters provided Florence Fenwick Miller with a salutary lesson, and probably contributed to her reluctance to make much use of readers' letters over subsequent years. It certainly determined her never again to print a correspondent's name.

On 31 May 1890 she launched a vigorous attack on 'a correspondent, signing himself "Karl Pearson"' who had forwarded to her

> a letter addressed to him by a third person, and evidently not intended for my perusal. This, on reflection, he will no doubt perceive to be an impropriety, and I consider myself barred from alluding to that letter. But Mr. Pearson's own communication is suggestive, and may be referred to, because it contains one of the most common blunders about the position of women.   (700)

He had complained that she, who sought to advance women's causes, had nevertheless criticized another woman's work. The precise nature of the criticism is not revealed. Any reader checking back over recent columns would find the only obvious candidate[27] to be Lady Burdett-Coutts. Florence had attacked the lionizing of 'Mr Stanley', whom she considered a buccaneer and cynical exploiter of Africans, at parties such as the 'Bohemian and thronged gathering' given by Lady Burdett-Coutts. But not only did she admire her works, praising her elsewhere, but this item had appeared only the previous week, which scarcely leaves time for the correspondence and article to be written and delivered. Pearson's letter led to a vigorous rebuttal. She would not refrain from criticizing another woman just because she supported women's causes, precisely because men so often reflected 'the blunders of one woman' upon the entire sex:

> It is a serious flaw in the reasoning apparatus of the mighty that men should so constantly do this with regard to women. If a woman with a fortune makes a foolish use of it, 'See', they cry. 'the mischief of trusting *women* with control over money!' But when the 'Jubilee Plunger' tosses a quarter of a million to the winds in a couple of years, nobody argues thence in a similar way about all men. . . . Somehow, one hardly every hears the reverse. One does not hear that 'women are great scholars' because Miss Ramsay was Senior Classic . . . that 'women are great organisers' because Miss Nightingale reduced chaos to order in the Crimea; or that 'women are great novelists' because there are no names higher in that branch of our letters than

those of Marian Evans (George Eliot), Charlotte Brontë and Jane Austen.[28]

The same illogicality is not, of course, applied to men. 'Fancy any man refraining from blaming Mr Karl Pearson for sending round a private letter because of 'the solidarity of the male sex'! (700–2).
The whole passage is a fine piece of rhetoric, and her overall argument persuasive, but its impact may have been diminished in the minds of readers when, a fortnight later, Mrs Fenwick Miller was obliged to print a retraction. This she embedded within the piece about unsolicited letters. It was clearly an embarrassment and her apology was offered without a trace of effusiveness:

> Mr. Karl Pearson informs me that he did not send me the letters written by himself and another person, and purporting to come from him, to which I referred a fortnight ago. Hence my impression that he had forwarded on to me a private letter from a third person is quite erroneous; he has not done anything of the kind, and my receiving the letters is a trick of some person unknown, by which I am sorry I was misled. (762)

Florence Fenwick Miller's own scruples over the passing on of private correspondence to a third party, however, prevented her from enlightening her public further. The general reader is left as bemused as ever as to the original cause of the dispute, and may well have the impression that the offending letter itself was bogus. This was presumably what Karl Pearson suggested, for the first of her three letters (Pearson Papers, University College London, 763/4 dated 2 June 1890) to him discredits the idea that an 'evil-disposed person has used your name & *copied your caligraphy [sic] so closely*'. Her response sheds light on the incident. She claims he *did* send her a letter, because this one is similar to the handwriting of that earlier one signed with his name, and its accompanying reply 'was undoubtedly in the writing of the proprietor of the *[?Women's] Penny Paper . . .*'.
She proposes a completely different solution to 'the mystery'. Perhaps the person who sent the letters was that selfsame editor. She asks him to check if she *was* the culprit, in which case she herself will make amends for her wrongful accusation. The editor in question was the outspoken Henrietta Müller who founded the *WPP* in 1888. She knew

Pearson through the Men and Women's Club, and had joined Florence on the London School Board in the 1879 election.

The corrections, crossings-out, ellipses, and insertions in Florence Fenwick Miller's letter suggest a writer in haste, somewhat agitated, and revising her thoughts as she wrote. She nevertheless, despite regrets over any unfairness, defends the thrust of her article. 'Of course the *point* of what I wrote about 'the solidarity of sex' remains unaltered. . . .' Her second note, on a half sheet dated 3 June, reiterates the emphasis on the incidental accusation of impropriety, rather than the argument of her articles, and reveals the cause of Karl Pearson's original complaint. Referring to an enclosure on which she had drafted a paragraph – presumably the one that eventually appeared – for his approval:

> I do not understand you to deny that you wrote to the Editor of the [?*Women's*] *Penny Paper* protesting against my taking exception to what I consider her absurd demand for a seat in the H. of C.? [House of Commons] What you wish me to know that you did not do is – send on to me that letter & her reply?

Back in early April, though without identifying the perpetrator, she had savaged the 'absurd demand'. 'The claim to enter the Reporters' Gallery of the House of Commons, which a lady has lately put forward, would be called preposterous if made by a man employed on an insignificant little penny weekly very recently started, and having a small circulation. [It] . . . is none the less or the more preposterous when made by a woman.' Space, she argued, was so limited that many papers, including nationals with substantial circulations, were unable to obtain a seat, so the lady's claim could quite reasonably be rejected on grounds other than sex and was effectively playing 'with the interests of women for the advertisement of individuals and their interests' (*ILN*, 5 April 1890). A lengthy, less business-like PS, emphasising her regrets, told Pearson the incident had determined her never again to print a correspondent's name, ending coyly, '*Please* tell me you forgive me!' (Pearson, 763/4, 3 June 1890).

Pearson's reply must have been kindly for the final letter thanks him for 'the generous spirit' in which he accepted her apology 'for an inadvertence wh [sic] my judgement shd [sic] have saved me from . . .' (Pearson, 763/4, 6 June 1890). He had evidently also contacted Henrietta Müller, who after asking him to call at her office as she preferred not to write about it, finally admitted she sent the letters privately to the *ILN*'s editor '[s]imply as an interesting comment' on matter in his journal, adding naively that it never occurred to her he would '*indirectly* make public use of it' (Pearson, 767/6, 2 & 19 June 1890).

Ironically, Mrs Fenwick Miller eventually assumed the proprietorship of *WPP*'s successor. Only a few months after the Pearson incident the *Penny Paper* became the *Woman's Herald*, and in 1892 was sold to Christina Bremner working with Lady Henry Somerset, from whom, under yet another title, the *Woman's Signal*, she acquired it in 1895. In retrospect the modern reader may speculate as to whether she had a slight suspicion about the source of the letters, but found the copy too good to miss, and, working at the speed she did, – she was astonishingly prolific – did not allow herself time for reflection. She must have known who Karl Pearson was, yet rather than capitalize on this she wrote of her correspondent 'signing himself "Karl Pearson"' as if she could not quite believe that it were him.[29]

As one traces the column's structure and concerns over time, the engagements with correspondents of both sexes suggest that its author maintained its declared function – as a space in which 'matters specially interesting to ladies, as they arise in the great world week by week' could be aired – primarily by the construction of a *general* readership, rather than involving individuals. Her column accorded her not only steady employment but 'by far the largest audience she had ever addressed'.[30] It was to that huge, inclusive readership of the *Illustrated London News*, men as well as women, that Mrs Fenwick Miller addressed her ideas.

Yet those actual correspondents, as much as the individuals in those audiences she addressed from public platforms, would have reminded her of the multiplicity of views and attitudes of that readership. Occasionally, as we have seen, they sharply recalled to her the risks one could encounter in that profession of journalism to which she attached such significance. In terms of the balance of power it is the authorial, authoritative persona, depending upon intellectual argument rather than shared sympathies, who dominates the arena of a column that markedly eschews any illusion of a female coterie.

Nevertheless, as her contemporaries attested, and the longevity of her 'Ladies Page' (from 1886 to 1918) bore out, she was essentially the consummate journalist. Conscious of the requirements of a journal which sought an extensive middle-class audience, she kept her initial promise to touch on her subjects 'with a light hand', promoting her causes effectively within the 'New Journalism' formula of information, gossip and entertainment.

Notes

1. Well-known ones include Mrs Humphry, 'Madge' in *Truth*, and Annie Swan in *Woman at Home*.
2. Originally 'Ladies' Column' (see footnote 10). I have employed one term throughout to avoid confusion; see Florence Fenwick Miller, *Harriet Martineau* (London: W. H. Allen. 1884), 164–5. Though she married Frederick Alford Ford in 1877, she retained her own surname.
3. See Margaret Beetham, *A Magazine of Her Own? Domesticity and Desire in the Woman's Magazine, 1800–1914* (London and New York: Routledge, 1996), 80–1.
4. (Matilda Browne), 'Spinnings in Town', *Englishwoman's Domestic Magazine*, 16 (Jan. 1874), 39.
5. (Browne, Matilda), 'Spinnings at the Seaside', *Englishwoman's Domestic Magazine*, 16 (1874), 319.
6. See Beetham, 82–4, and also her account of this column and the shorter-running 'Cupid's Letter Bag', 69–70.
7. (Matilda Browne), 'Spinnings in Town', *Englishwoman's Domestic Magazine*, 4 n s (1868), 46 and 160.
8. Beetham, 166.
9. Fenwick Miller, 164–5. It seems to me significant that this quotation comes from her biography of Harriet Martineau, a journalist she much admired, and who already had the reputation of possessing a 'masculine understanding'. Mrs Fenwick-Miller attacked individual men but, like Martineau, did not disdain the masculine traditions of journalism.
10. M. F. Billington, 'Leading Lady Journalists', *Pearson's Magazine* (July, 1896), 105. The format changed over time, becoming literally 'The Ladies' Page' in November 1895, with a leading illustrated fashion article by 'Paulina Pry', later 'Sybil'. Fenwick Miller's contribution was demoted to 'Notes' (for a period signed 'F. F. M.'). This change seems linked to her assumption of the editorship of the *Woman's Signal* early that October. I am unable to identify 'Paulina Pry'. Rosemary Van Arsdel refers to her as 'an assistant'. (Rosemary T. Van Arsdel, 'Mrs Florence Fenwick Miller and the *Woman's Signal*, 1895–1899', *Victorian Periodicals Review*, 15 [1982], 128ff. By mid-1898, though 'Ladies' Page' retained its additional space it was by-lined solely 'Filomena', Fenwick Miller's pseudonym. Dress was amalgamated with other topics but the line-drawings identified the page with Fashion.
11. Simon Nowell-Smith, *The House of Cassell 1848–1958* (London: Cassell and Company, 1958), 258. In the event Wilde himself, if sporadically, wrote the column, which included Literary Notes. Fenwick Miller produced one substantial article on the friendship between Mary Seton and Mary Stuart.
12. Green, Fanny L., 'Journalism as a Profession for Women', *The Monthly Packet of Evening Reading*, 2 n s (1891), 503.
13. See Van Arsdel 'Mrs Florence Fenwick Miller', 107–18, and chapter 13 in Rosemary T. Van Arsdel, *Florence Fenwick Miller: Victorian Feminist, Journalist, and Educator* (Aldershot: Ashgate, 2001).
14. Billington, 106. Billington was a successful correspondent and sketch-writer for a number of papers, notably the *Daily Telegraph*.

15. Both 'Spinnings' and 'Over the Teacups' are redolent of feminine activity, spinning having long been associated with woman's work, and afternoon tea, though gentlemen might well be present, being very much under the control of the lady of the house, who poured the tea. Additionally, both terms have connotations of talk – spinning tales; ladies' tea parties as an opportunity for gossip.

16. See Graham Law, *The Illustrated London News (1842–1901) The Graphic (1869–1901) Indexes to Fiction* (Queensland, University of Queensland, 2001), vi–vii and 6; and Graham Law, 'New Woman Novels in Newspapers', *Media History*, 7, 1 (2001), 22.

17. Joseph Hatton focuses upon this aspect of the paper in his sketches of London journalism. Joseph Hatton, *Journalistic London, Being a Series of Sketches of Famous Pens and Papers of the Day* (London: Sampson Low, Marston, Searle & Rivington, 1882), 225ff.

18. When editing the *Woman's Signal* she tried to get copies into the reading rooms of public libraries where men would see them (see Van Arsdel, 1982).

19. Typical of her sardonic manner is her description of the 'sallow, dark, short and plump' middle-aged lady at the Royal Academy Private View, unfortunate enough to catch her eye. Perhaps difficult to miss, attired in yellow printed silk 'commonly used for piano draping', patterned with large terracotta flowers, and cut low to expose 'a liberal allowance of dusky neck' (*ILN*, 10 May 1890, 602).

20. Her scale of priority frequently led the fashion element to be woven into accounts of some public meeting or charity event, or linked to issues like practical clothing for horse-riding or war work.

21. Billington, 105.

22. (Matilda Browne), 'Spinnings', *Englishwoman's Domestic Magazine*, 3 (1867), 371.

23. Thomas Hardy was one offender.

24. He claimed to be 'secretary of a medical society'. Inflation was severe. She quoted price rises of 'at least forty per cent'.

25. She was known for her work on the London School Board.

26. Similarly 'Silkworm' had publicized, at a reader's request, the 'poverty and destitution' of specialist needleworkers in Northern Ireland, adversely affected by 'tatting fever' (Browne, 'Spinnings in Town', 160).

27. Lady Colin Campbell's gown being thought more appropriate to blondes than to her 'pronounced, even bold, brunette style of beauty' seems too trivial to be in the frame.

28. The 'Jubilee Plunger', Ernest Benzon, became notorious for the fortune he lost gambling on horses.

29. Karl Pearson (1857–1936), described as the 'founder of the twentieth-century science of statistics', was then Professor of Applied Mathematics and Mechanics at University College London, but his interests were far wider than mathematics. He was later appointed the first Galton Professor of Eugenics. Between 1880 and 1884 he lectured widely in London on German culture, Luther, Marx and socialism. See *Dictionary of Scientific Biography* and *Dictionary of National Biography*.

30. Van Arsdel, 2001, 125.

6
Knowing Hodge: The Third Reform Bill and the Victorian Periodical Press

Patricia O'Hara

Although few Victorians in the 1880s could claim actual contact or social intercourse with the male agricultural labourer, known colloquially as 'Hodge', many would have had ample opportunity for discursive encounters with him in the pages of the periodical press. The closing decades of Queen Victoria's reign witnessed events and political legislation that made the rural working classes the object of intensified discussion in writings across a spectrum of discourses that included Parliamentary reports and debates, as well as folklore studies, novels, pamphlets, agricultural societies' reports, and the local and national periodical presses. The Third Reform Bill of 1884–85 'elevated [Hodge] to the dignity of a British citizen'[1] but even as Hodge the voter was acknowledged to be 'a mighty factor in the development of our social history',[2] he was anxiously identified as 'an unknown quantity',[3] 'an enigma',[4] a 'cipher'.[5] During the years surrounding the Parliamentary debates and the passage of the franchise bill that granted the male agricultural labourer the vote, the enterprise of knowing Hodge became an imperative, politically consequential undertaking. This project of knowing Hodge was an essentially discursive one, and it yielded lively, dissonant conversations in the Victorian periodical press in articles about the rights and social conditions of the male farmworker. Analysis of those conversations demonstrates the constitutive role of the press in the formation and sustaining of a political, national identity in late-Victorian England.

A substantial body of periodical literature was devoted to rural labourers in the last three decades of the century, and the Victorian press emerged as the site for the tendentious political and epistemological struggle over whose knowledge of the rural agricultural labourer was authoritative. Often preoccupied with the manifold social problems that arose from the agricultural depression and rural depopulation, these writings scrutinized agricultural labourers' housing, working conditions, education, and moral and social tempers. In the politically-charged years surrounding the passage of the Representation of the People Act of 1884, questions about the electoral fitness of agricultural labourers and their likely political allegiances lay at the centre of many of these social analyses. As the political body was being reconfigured, periodical readers encountered contending versions of the 'tillers of the soil' that each claimed authoritative knowledge of the hearts and minds of the peasant 'whose case is stated not by himself but for him'.[6] In this essay I juxtapose two sets of articles that stated the case for the labourer during the period that historian R. J. Olney has called the 'most strenuous period in English rural politics',[7] and I examine the ways that these encounters with Hodge were thematized and engaged in the re-formation of national identity in late-Victorian England. The first was an 1883 series on the English peasantry published in the studiously non-partisan *Longman's Magazine*, a series that included pieces by novelist Thomas Hardy and by journalist and country writer Richard Jefferies. The second set of articles, in the liberal, politically-invested *Fortnightly Review*, was penned by leaders of the Radical labour movement, including Joseph Chamberlain, Jesse Collings, Henry Broadhurst, and Alfred Simmons. Although the 'knowable Hodges' who materialized in these articles do little to make known the subjectivity of the 'folk of the furrow',[8] they disclose a great deal about the circulation of political values in the periodical press.

In its February 1883 number, *Longman's Magazine* announced a 'series ... in which the peasantry of different parts of the United Kingdom will be discussed by writers with *special local knowledge*'. Founded in the wake of the folding of *Fraser's Magazine*, the monthly *Longman's* was committed to uncontroversial, intelligent but popular reading fare – serialized fiction and commentaries on the arts, travel, and natural curiosities. It eschewed politics, quite manifestly so, for instance, in the publicity announcement of its inception: 'Longman's Magazine will not be devoted to the interests of any party, or any particular school of thought, whether political, religious, or social. Its space will seldom be devoted to politics, which mainly occupy the attention of the daily and weekly press'.[9] Given its editorial mandate and mass-market aspirations, it is perhaps surprising that *Longman's* launched its peasant series less than a year into its publication and precisely when the agricultural labourer was the subject of so much public political discourse and debate.[10] Less surprising, however, is its turning, for 'special local

knowledge' of rustic life, to Thomas Hardy and Richard Jefferies, authorities of a distinctly literary order, whose contributions to this peasantry
series followed Justin McCarthy's inaugural 'The Irish Peasantry'. By
1883 Hardy and Jefferies were the Victorian reading public's pre-
eminent chroniclers of rural life, Hardy in the Wessex novels that
included the early *Under the Greenwood Tree* (1872), the 'pastoral' *Far
from the Madding Crowd* (1874; and first serialized in *Cornhill Magazine*),
and *The Return of the Native* (1878); and Jefferies in novels and numerous periodical contributions, notably the series of essays that ran in the
conservative *Standard* and that had been recently collected into the
volume, *Hodge and His Masters* (1880).[11] In fact, in the same issue in
which the peasantry series was announced, *Longman's* readers could
have read both Hardy's 'The Three Strangers', a tale of 'agricultural
England' 'By the Author of "Far from Madding Crowd" ', and Jefferies's
'Bits of Oak Bark', a piece of descriptive country writing 'By the Author
of "The Gamekeeper at Home" '. Hardy's 'The Dorsetshire Labourer'
appeared in July 1883 with Jefferies' 'The Wiltshire Labourer' following
in November of that same year. Neither Hardy's 'Dorsetshire Labourer'
nor Jefferies' 'Wiltshire Labourer' approach anything like hard-line party
views, although their representations of labourers enmeshed in a
process of rural depopulation and social change are freighted with
political implications on the eve of the Parliamentary debates on the
enfranchisement of the 'agricultural labourer – the lowest scale in the
country population'.[12]

By way of preparing the readers of *Longman's* to encounter the hereto-
fore obscure Dorsetshire labourer, Hardy's essay opens by claiming
privileged knowledge of the 'class that lies somewhat outside the ken
of ordinary society'[13] – a rhetorical manoeuvre characteristic of periodical writings about labourers during these years. The essay moves to
impart that special knowledge to the 'ordinary' *Longman's* readers
through a succession of novelistic engagements with Hodge and rural
culture that assume the shape of the investigatory practices that dominated the social sciences of the late nineteenth century. *Longman's*
readers' presumed stereotypes of 'the supposedly real but highly conventional Hodge [as] . . . a degraded being of uncouth manner and
aspect, stolid understanding, and snail-like movement' (*PW* 168) are
meant to be challenged by a series of descriptive observations of the
labourer at home, at the hiring fair, and on moving day. The primary
encounter with Hodge is narrativized, and the reader is cast as a field
worker who journeys into a remote region of Dorset to study 'Hodge in
his most unmitigated form':

> If one of the many thoughtful persons who hold this view [of Hodge] were to go by rail to Dorset, where Hodge in his most unmitigated form is supposed to reside, and seek out a retired district, he might by and by certainly meet a man who, at first *contact* with an intelligence fresh from the contrasting world of London, would seem to exhibit some of the above-mentioned qualities. The latter items in the list, the mental miseries, the visitor might hardly look for in their fulness, since it would have become perceptible to him as an *explorer* . . . that no uneducated community . . . could exist in an unchangeable slough of despond. . . .
>
>   Waiving these points, however, the *investigator* would insist that the man he had *encountered* exhibited a suspicious blankness of gaze. . . . But suppose that, by some accident, the visitor were obliged to go home with this man, take pot-luck with him and his, as one of the family. . . . [L]iving on there for a few days the *sojourner* would become conscious of a new aspect in the life around him. . . . Six months pass, and our gentleman leaves the cottage, bidding his friends good-bye with genuine regret. The great change in his perception is that Hodge . . . has become disintegrated into a number of dissimilar fellow-creatures, men of many minds, infinite in difference.   (*PW* 169–71; my emphases)

An interesting dynamic between reader-explorer and labourer-subject emerges here in the articulation of a 'first contact' with the farmworker. The reader vicariously enacts the process of social investigation, not in the impenetrable wilderness of the colonies detailed by nineteenth-century ethnographers, nor of the urban slums of Henry Mayhew or Charles Booth, but rather in the largely hidden social world of the late-Victorian countryside. Several scientific discourses intersect in this construction of a perception-altering encounter in which Hodge, under microscopic scrutiny by a social outsider, 'disintegrate[s]' into innumerable individuated fellow creatures. The politics of the relationship between reader and rustic is complicated by the irony deployed at the expense of 'our gentleman' 'sojourner' – by extension the *Longman's* reader himself – whose distinctly urban 'intelligence' has distorted his perception of Hodge in the first place. The encounter with the Dorsetshire workman is itself thematized, and the problems of knowledge and observation – the 'inability to see below the surface of things' (*PW* 173) – are foregrounded: 'the happiness of a class', Hardy notes, 'can rarely be estimated aright by philosophers who look down upon that class from the Olympian heights of society' (*PW* 172). The corrective to the reader's social myopia requires seeing Hodge as a 'friend'.

As the essay continues, however, the unmitigated Hodge viewed at close range turns out to be a transitional creature, one whose cultural features are filtered through the lens of Hardy's deep ambivalence about change in the village. That ambivalence would have resonated with the readers of *Longman's*, an audience whose ranks had been swelled by consumers with recently acquired cultural capital: the magazine in fact targeted 'that immense class . . . [that] has been largely reinforced in England since the passing of the Elementary Education Act in 1870'.[14] 'It is too much to expect [the labourers] to remain stagnant and old-fashioned for the pleasure of romantics spectators' (*PW* 181), admits Hardy, the novelist who 'disinterred' the name 'Wessex' 'from the pages of early English history',[15] even as he frequently laments that the folk of Dorset 'are, pictorially, less interesting than they used to be' (*PW* 176). Politics and aesthetics remain at odds, and Hodge as Hardy makes him known is a shifting palimpsest of recollected images laid over present conditions: 'Instead of the wing bonnet . . . cotton gown, bright-hued neckerchief, and strong flat boots and shoes . . . [rural Dorset women] wear shabby millinery bonnets and hats with beads . . . and boot-heels almost as foolishly shaped as those of ladies of highest education' (*PW* 176). The distinctly Dorset peasant is encountered even as he is losing his local character: 'it is only natural that, now different districts of them are shaken together once a year and redistributed, like a shuffled pack of cards, they have ceased to be so local in feeling or manner as formerly, and have entered on the condition of inter-social citizens' (*PW* 180). The picturesque is pictured but withdrawn, as the Dorsetshire dissolves into the 'inter-social citizen', who, in point of fact, is not yet a 'citizen' at all.

Four months after the Dorsetshire labourer appeared in *Longman's*, his Wiltshire counterpart was displayed, not, however, in the particularities of his habitats and habits, but rather in the 'general aspect' of his social condition and the housing and land tenure reforms that Jefferies advocated. Where Hardy's migratory Hodge was in motion, metamorphosing into a homogeneously 'inter-social citizen', Jefferies' 'Wiltshire Labourer' seems to have vanished from the countryside entirely, leaving readers to confront an unnerving vacancy in England's fields and meadows:

Some places among meadows appear almost empty. No one is at work in the fields as you pass; there are cattle swishing their tails in the shadow of the elms, but not a single visible person; acres upon acres of grass, and no human being. . . . Whole crowds might migrate into these grassy fields, put up shanties, and set to work. But set to work at what? . . . When ten or fifteen thousand acres of land fall out of cultivation, and farmers leave, what is to become of the labouring families they kept? What has become of them?[16]

Jefferies mobilizes his considerable descriptive powers to picture the mere shadows of vanished human labour in a haunted rural economy. Hodge slips from the reader's view, having migrated right out of the rural picture. The powerfully figured absence works to make urgent the need for Jefferies' proposed reorganisation of the rural social contract by instituting a reformed system of cottage leasing and allotments for labourers, which would guarantee both their 'fixity of tenure'[17] on the land and the future health of the nation.

'The Wiltshire Labourer' brings into the reader's line of sight, not an infinitely individuated assemblage of agricultural labourers, but rather a unitary 'race of men' whose investment in the land – in the rural 'home' – is vital to the well-being of the nation. In the article's closing passages, Jefferies offers up a bracing nationalistic vision of a reconstituted peasant workforce. The strong, 'manly' physical body of the labourer is mapped onto the body politic to become 'a rampart to the nation':

I should be in hopes that such a plan would soon breed a race of men of the sturdiest order, the true and natural countrymen; men standing upright in the face of all, without one particle of servility . . . men with the franchise, voting under the protection of the ballot. . . . The men are there. This is no imaginary class to be created, they are there, and they only require homes to become the finest body in the world, a rampart to the nation, a support not only to agriculture but to every industry that needs the help of labour. For physique they have ever been noted, and if it not valued at home it is estimated at its true value in the colonies. . . . It is acknowledged that the farm labourer is the most peaceful of all men, the least given to agitation for agitation's sake. Permit him to live and he is satisfied. He has no class ill-feelings, either against farmer or landowner. . . . He maintains a steady and manly attitude.[18]

Late Victorian attitudes towards the countryside and the rustics who peopled it were neither monolithic nor unambiguous, but as the century wore on, national identity became increasingly invested in an idea of

Englishness that relied upon an abiding affiliation with the agrarian 'sons of the soil' who were the living historical record of the ancient race of Britons.[19] *Longman's* readers' fears about unionist agitation and class unrest are assuaged by 'The Wiltshire Labourer's' burly but 'peaceful' worker on whose shoulders the future of English agriculture and industry rests.

The regional labourers embedded in the mass-market reading zone of *Longman's Magazine* contrast markedly with the politicized, partisan Hodge featured in a cluster of articles (1883, 1885) in the *Fortnightly Review* under the editorship of T. H. S. Escott, articles that orchestrated encounters with Hodge the incipient, and then official, voter. In 1883, the *Fortnightly* provided the vehicle for the circulation of 'The Radical Programme', the platform of reforms engineered by Joseph Chamberlain and the Liberal labour leaders. Jessie Collings's 1883 'The Agricultural Labourer' ran the same month as Jefferies' 'Wiltshire Labourer' and was one of four instalments of 'The Radical Programme', about which Chamberlain later claimed: 'I arranged with Escott . . . editor of the *Fortnightly* for the publication of a series of articles on Radical Politics and methods. These articles were all arranged with me beforehand and submitted to me in proof before publication'.[20] While pleading the cause of the agricultural labourer, *Fortnightly Review* articles were self-consciously engaged in the job of knowing the likely political leanings of 'the new voters', who were largely assumed to be conservative. 'Will the new and enlarged force act with the conservative part, or join the robust Liberal or radical cause led by Mr. Chamberlain and other advanced statesmen?'[21] was the leading question posed to readers by the 'robust' and 'advanced' radical *Fortnightly* writers themselves. Their resounding affirmation of the second alternative demonstrates how a social evolutionary paradigm was put to ideological uses in the domestic political sphere.

In contestation in all the encounters with Hodge in the periodical press is who possesses the knowledge to speak on behalf of the ploughman, and Collings frames this question of representational authority explicitly in terms of social class. Contemporary representations, specifically blue book accounts of the labourer as being 'better off . . . than he was years ago' are discredited, as Collings sets out to describe that agricultural 'section of the community so little known to the average Englishman':[22]

> Perhaps there is no section of the community so little known to the average Englishman as that of the agricultural labourer. . . . He is a cipher in rural society and a political pariah in this free country of

ours. . . . In Blue Books, agricultural newspapers, or at Farmers' Clubs, the position and standing of the labourer are described and descanted on by his masters. The descriptions of his flourishing condition invoke astonishment in the minds of those who know his actual status. Unfortunately in the battle of life, as in real war, it is woe to the vanquished, and in all communities . . . there is a tendency to accept, without sufficient investigation, the loud and oft-repeated statements of a dominant and influential class, respecting those who are condemned to silence and subjection.[23]

It was not necessary for Collings – the well-known former mayor of Birmingham, radical MP, and activist in Joseph Arch's agricultural workers' union – to defend to his *Fortnightly* readers the source or legitimacy of his knowledge of Hodge, any more than Hardy or Jefferies would have been called upon to identify to *Longman's* readers the source of their knowledge of rural England. However, in the next issue of the *Fortnightly* Chamberlain found it politically useful to point out that Collings's 'Agricultural Labourer' was written from first-hand knowledge.

In its closing exhortation to franchise and land reform, Collings's contribution to the 'The Radical Programme' invokes what was a growing fear of a deterioration of the workforce in the country. It mobilizes a set of tropes that construe the cultivators of the land as the foundation of the nation, not unlike Jefferies' high-pitched conclusion, though with different political inflections:

However much accumulated wealth may increase during spasmodic epochs of great commercial and manufacturing prosperity, yet the real safety of the nation, the permanence of its institutions, and the happiness and social condition of the people, are bound up in an inseparable manner with the condition and cultivation of the land. The fear is that reforms in this direction may come too late, and that the race of husbandmen – the hardy peasant class who constitute such a staying element, the 'backbone' of the nation – will have deteriorated or largely disappeared. . . . [However] [e]ducation, newspapers, and railways, the knowledge and example of America, and modern civilisation generally, are evolving forces which monopolies and privilege cannot withstand, and against which class efforts, prejudices, and angry assumptions will not avail.[24]

In this version of the function of the social body, the nightmarish eventuality of a race of husbandmen gone extinct is checked by the 'evolving forces' of civilization – a social evolutionist model of political progressivism that becomes the master narrative forwarded in the *Fortnightly* authors' efforts to persuade readers that 'the citadel of Toryism, enshrined as we are bidden to believe, in the bosom of every tiller of the soil' was not unassailable.[25] Collings's agricultural labourers are incipient liberals precisely because of cultural forces that cannot be withstood by the privileged and the prejudiced.

In the *Fortnightly*'s delineations of the ideas of the new voters, the ascendancy of liberal politics becomes a social-evolutionary inevitability. In this political vision of Hodge, evolution and revolution are entirely compatible. In the January 1885 leader, 'The Revolution of 1884' (published one month after the passing of the Franchise Bill and later reprinted as a part of 'The Radical Programme'), editor Escott acknowledges his liberal readers' anxieties that 'the rural population will remain in the long run what they now are, the strongholds of Conservatism [because] [i]n villages and hamlets matters move slowly. *Quieta non movere* is the motto engraved on the heart of the rustic, who is deaf to the allurements of the agitator'[26]. However, the demise of this Conservatism – incongruously phrased in the Latin motto – is guaranteed by a Spencerian, sociological 'law of progress':

> In the future Hodge will be brought within range of those quickening and revolutionary influences which the advance of knowledge, educational and political, and more frequent attrition with his fellow-subjects who live in towns, will supply. . . . But if like effects are generated by like causes, if there is any dynamic force in legislation, if the law of progress is not an imposture and the desire of self-improvement an unreality, the change of policy following the Reform Bill cannot fail to be yet more remarkable than the reduction of the numerical influence of conservatism. . . . unless the classes now enfranchised reveal an amount of Conservative immobility and obstruction to all change hitherto unsuspected . . . how is the onward movement to be arrested?[27]

The 'quickening influences' of cultural advancement 'cannot fail' to lead the new voters to Liberal affiliation in this political fantasy whose conceptual contours are indebted to Herbert Spencer's influential 1857 *Westminster Review* essay, 'Progress: Its Law and Causes'.

Published one month after Escott's 'Revolution of 1884', 'The Ideas of the New Voters', authored by Henry Broadhurst, William J. Davis (signed as 'A Trades Union Official'), and Alfred Simmons, espouses the same political narrative of the 'march of progress'[28] toward liberalism among the agricultural labouring classes. What is interesting about these discussions of the ideas and 'chief topics of interest to the peasantry'[29] are the ways that the teleology of this political evolution, which sees farm workers as future liberals, yields a set of analogies between present-day agricultural labourers and backward, primitive people. These analogies are the legacy of Tylorean social evolution, which posited a cultural proximity between British rustics and foreign primitive peoples: there is 'scarce a hand's breadth difference', claimed E. B. Tylor in *Primitive Culture* (1872), 'between an English ploughman and a negro of central Africa'.[30] Even as they campaign on behalf of the 'new voters', the *Fortnightly*'s authors advance a kind of domestic imperialism that figures Hodge as a cultural, political Other. Broadhurst, for instance, credits the labourers' unions with 'hav[ing] opened the windows of the hitherto dark mind of the farm labourer'.[31] Davis looks forward to a future when the inert, stolid labourers will become politically animated, claiming that their obeisance to 'the Church, the parson, and the squire [and] the ... farmer' cannot last long, 'as the quickening influence and fruits of a Socialistic treatment will act as a tonic on their low-beating pulse, and invigorate the political nerve which is even to be found with some degree of animation in what ought to be a bold peasantry'.[32] In the final section of 'The Ideas of the New Voters', Simmons analogizes the task of educating farmworkers to missionary work:

> Liberal and Conservative agents will scarcely appreciate the task of travelling about the wilds in search of stray labourers, and yet there are thousands of such men and they must be communicated with. ... [We must] employ ... intelligent men of their own class – men known to the labourers, and enjoying their confidence. ... By this means, and, I verily believe by this means only, we should achieve victory and educate the minds of the new voters to a higher level of political thought at the same time.[33]

While agents of neither party will relish canvassing votes in the 'wilds' of rural England, the political and cultural imperatives demand that liberal agents move to enlist and elevate the thousands of 'stray labourers' scattered in hamlets and villages across the English countryside.

Hodge as they thought they knew him was the product of various forms of interested, partial knowledge of a class of workers whose subjectivity remained a mystery. The problem of Hodge, intensified by the

Third Reform Bill and addressed by these periodical writers in the middle years of the 1880s, was by no means solved by century's end. Even as two successive Parliamentary Commissions scrutinized rural life and labour, writer Joseph Davies would complain, in an 1891 *Westminster Review* article entitled 'Hodge', that the labourer's story remained to be told:

> The history of the English farm-labourer remains to be written. Far less is known of him than of Saturn's rings; and as compared with our acquaintance with the intimate habits and thoughts of the sportive Ichthyosaurus, he is to us an almost undiscovered creature. The conventional Hodge of the novel and stage is a caricature, a semi-animated turnip surmounting a sartorial study in smock-frock and corduroys. Here and there an attempt at faithful portraiture has been made, but in no case with any degree of success . . . Hodge is a complex problem.[34]

Histories of the mundane Hodge have since been written; knowing the minds of the workers who 'left nothing identifiable behind them . . . no signature or mark'[35] remains, however, the complex crux of the problem.

Notes

1. Joseph J. Davies, 'Hodge', *Westminster Review*, 136 (1891), 301.
2. Davies, 'Hodge', 302.
3. T. H. S. Escott, 'The Revolution of 1884', *Fortnightly Review*, 37 n s (1885), 160.
4. Davies, 'Hodge', 302.
5. Jesse Collings, 'The Radical Programme. IV – The Agricultural Labourer', *Fortnightly Review*, 34 n s (1883), 610.
6. Collings, 'The Radical Programme', 610.
7. R. J. Olney, 'The Politics of Land', in *The Victorian Countryside* (ed. G. E. Mingay, London: Routledge, (1981), I: 58–70).
8. A not uncommon epithet for agricultural labourers (like 'tillers of the soil'), 'Folk of the Furrow' served as the title of a 1913 volume by Christopher Holdenby, a self-identified 'Oxford man writing of field labourers', (xiii). The book's opening chapter, 'The Challenge of Silence', attests to the 'mystery' of rural labourers and its persistence well into the twentieth century: ' "This is the mystery of the country I want to penetrate. Listen – look down at it. I want to know the meaning of it and to be right down there at the bottom of it. I want to see into those cottages and know the secret of their silence and the seclusion of their inmates". "Ah", burst in my friend, "there you will have a difficult task: there you have got the silence of suspicion to

combat, the legacy of centuries" ': Christopher Holdenby, *Folk of the Furrow* (London: Smith, Elder & Co., 1913), 4.

9. Quoted in Cyprian Bladgen, '*Longman's Magazine*', *Review of English Literature*, 4 (1963), 9.

10. The announcement ran as a footnote to the first article in the series, Justin McCarthy's 'The Irish Peasantry'. The other articles were James Purves's 'The Lothian Hinds', Hardy's 'The Dorsetshire Labourer', and Jefferies' 'The Wiltshire Labourer'.

    Though not officially part of the peasant series, it is possible to read Jefferies' 'After the County Franchise' that ran in *Longman's* in 1884 as an uncharacteristically explicit political epilogue to the 1883 peasant series. The editorial note that *Longman's* appended to the article *justifying* 'meddling' with politics bears consideration:

    'County Suffrage' is just now the counter with which the game of politics is being played. In meddling with this subject, the Editor may seem to be intruding into that Tom Tiddler's ground of politics on which, when this magazine was projected, he determined not to trespass. . . . It may be profitable to consider what changes this bill will work, when it becomes law, in the lives, and the social relations, of our rural population. In presenting to the readers of this magazine a forecast of those changes by a writer whose close acquaintance with the country is well known, the Editor believes he is not overstepping the limit which he laid down in undertaking to keep LONGMAN'S MAGAZINE free from the strife of party politics. 'After the County Franchise', *Longman's Magazine*, 3 (1884), 362.

11. For Jefferies' publishing career, see George Miller and Hugoe Matthews, *Richard Jefferies: A Bibliographical Study* (Brookfield, Vermont: Scolar 1993). Pearson's anthology of selected Jefferies essays, *Landscape and Labour* (Wiltshire: Moonraker Press, 1979), also provides a useful primary bibliography. With the exception of Raymond Williams's still provocative *The Country and the City*, literary studies of nineteenth-century rural writing have tended to treat political and historical contexts as secondary 'backdrop' to the literary analysis, though their surveys of the tradition of country writing are still useful. See: W. J. Keith, *Regions of the Imagination: The Development of British Rural Fiction* (Toronto: University of Toronto Press, 1988) and *The Rural Tradition: William Cobbett, Gilbert White, and Other Non-Fiction Prose Writers of the English Countryside* (Toronto: University of Toronto Press, 1975); Jan Marsh, *Back to the Land: The Pastoral Impulse from 1880 to 1914* (London: Quartet Books, 1982); Merryn Williams, *Thomas Hardy and Rural England* (New York: Columbia University Press, 1972); and Raymond Williams, *The Country and the City* (New York: Oxford University Press, 1973).

12. *Hansard* 285 (3 Mar. 1884), 403. Of the many studies on Victorian rural history and late-Victorian liberal reform, the following have informed my understanding of the politics and social history of the countryside: Alan Armstrong, *Farmworkers in England and Wales: A Social and Economic History 1770–1980* (Ames: Iowa State University Press, 1988); William Hayes, *The Background and Passage of the Third Reform Act* (New York: Garland Publishing, 1982); Pamela Horn, *Labouring Life in the Victorian Countryside* (Dublin: Gill and Macmillan, 1976); Alun Howkins, *Reshaping Rural England: A Social History, 1850–1925* (London: Harper Collins, 1991); T. A. Jenkins, *The Liberal*

Ascendancy, 1830–1886 (New York: St Martin's, 1994), Andrew Jones, *The Politics of Reform, 1884* (Cambridge: Cambridge University Press, 1972); G. E. Mingay, ed., *The Victorian Countryside*; K. D. M. Snell, *Annals of the Labouring Poor: Social Change and Agrarian England 1660–1900* (Cambridge: Cambridge University Press, 1985); F. M. L. Thompson, ed., *The Cambridge Social History of Britain, 1750–1950*, (3 vols; Cambridge: Cambridge University Press, 1990).

Discussions of Hardy's politics include Roger Ebbatson, *Hardy: The Margin of the Unexpressed* (Sheffield: Sheffield Academic Press, 1993); Snell, *Annals*, 1985 and Peter Widdowson, *Hardy in History: A Case-Study in the Sociology of Literature* (London: New York: Routledge, 1989), all of which offer commentary on 'The Dorsetshire Labourer'. Ebbatson's analysis of the ways that 'The Dorsetshire Labourer's' 'urbanely neutral prose' (129) effectively erases history is often shrewd, although I am wary of his conclusion that the 'underlying project of Hardy's overtly sympathetic text is to sustain and reinforce' the labourers' anonymity (129).

Dolin's online unpublished position paper, 'Hardy and the Decline of Victorian Liberalism, 1880–1900' (http://www.newcastle.edu.au/ department/ el/pages/dolin.htm), which I discovered near the completion of this essay, sets forth a highly informative discussion of the *Fortnightly's* 'Radical Programme' and Hardy's 'Dorsetshire Labourer'. Dolin persuasively argues that Hardy's essay was responding quite precisely 'to the terms of the land question, and the particular claims of the Radicals . . . and to specific Radical proposals' (11) like the franchise and the creations of smallholdings for labourers. Dolin concludes that Hardy was opposed to franchise. Nonetheless, 'The Dorsetshire Labourer' does remain exasperatingly silent about the franchise, and Millgate maintains that Hardy 'personally supported the Liberals in their undertaking to give agricultural workers the vote – or so it would appear from his sending copies of the published essay ['The Dorsetshire Labourer'] to Gladstone and John Morley'. See Michael Millgate, *Thomas Hardy: A Biography* (Oxford: Oxford University Press, 1985), 236. In that letter, Hardy compares his *Longman's* essay to Chamberlain's impassioned Birmingham speeches:

Dear Mr. Morley,
The Dorset Labourer, Mr. Joseph Arch, &c. are among the topics dwelt upon in the Birmingham Speeches; & M. Arch has just been attacked in the St. James Gazette. By a curious coincidence I have a paper on these identical subjects in the number of Longman's Magazine which appears to-day. Though a Liberal, I have endeavoured to describe the state of things without political bias; & my description so well harmonizes with what was said at Birmingham. (*Collected Letters*, I, 118–19)

13. Thomas Hardy, 'The Dorsetshire Labourer', *Longman's Magazine*, 2 (July 1883), 252–69. Reprinted and cited from Harold Orel, ed., *Thomas Hardy's Personal Writings* (Lawrence, Kansas: University of Kansas Press, 1966), 168–89 (168). My citations from 'The Dorsetshire Labourer' are from the Orel reprint, more readily accessible to readers, and are cited parenthetically in the text as *PW*.

14. Quoted in Bladgen, '*Longman's Magazine*', 10.
15. Thomas Hardy, 'Author's Preface', *Far From the Madding Crowd* (New York: Penguin, 1978), 47.
16. Richard Jefferies, 'The Wiltshire Labourer', *Longman's Magazine*, 3 (Nov. 1883), 54.
17. Jefferies, 'Wiltshire Labourer', 59.
18. Ibid., 63, 64–5.
19. Howkins, 'The Discovery of Rural England', in *Englishness: Politics and Culture 1880–1920*, ed. Robert Collsand P. Dodd (London: Dover; NH: Croom Helm, 1986), 62–88, offers interesting background on the 'ruralist version' of English culture that 'emerged within English politics and ideas in the 1880s' (63).
20. Joseph Chamberlain, *A Political Memoir, 1880–92* (Westport, Connecticut: Greenwood Press, 1975), 108.
21. William Davis, 'The Ideas of the New Voters–II', *Fortnightly Review*, 37 n. s. (1885), 158.
22. Collings, 'The Radical Programme', 611.
23. Ibid., 610.
24. Ibid., 625.
25. Ibid., 625.
26. Escott, 'The Revolution of 1884', 166.
27. Ibid., 167.
28. Davis, 'The Ideas of the New Voters–II', 160.
29. Alfred Simmons, 'The Ideas of the New Voters–III', *Fortnightly Review*, 37 n s (1885), 167.
30. E. B. Tylor, *Primitive Culture: Researches into the Development of Mythology, Philosophy, Religion, Language, Art and Custom* (New York: Henry Holt, 1889), I:7.
31. Henry Broadhurst, 'The Ideas of the New Voters–I', *Fortnightly Review*, 37 n. s. (1885), 149.
32. Davis, 'The Ideas of the New Voters–II', 160.
33. Simmons, 'The Ideas of the New Voters–III', 167.
34. Davies, 'Hodge,' 298.
35. Eric Hobsbawm and George Rudé, *Captain Swing* (New York, Pantheon Books, 1968), 12.

Part III
Urban Encounters

7

Encounters in the *Westminster Review*: Dialogues on Marriage and Divorce

Sheila Rosenberg

A series of important encounters on the subject of marriage and divorce, the position of women and relationships between the sexes took place in the pages of the *Westminster Review* (*WR*) between 1885 and 1891. These exchanges in the *Westminster* were crucially underpinned and influenced by the dialogues that occurred simultaneously outside the pages of the review among a close circle of *Westminster* contributors. Both sets of discourses shaped the different positions taken by the protagonists, influenced what would be published in the *Westminster* and made a major contribution to the debate nationwide. The history of this debate and the various confrontations which carried it forward are the subjects of this study.

John Chapman, editor of the *Westminster*, had a long tradition of personal commitment to feminist causes and encouraged the debate in the pages of his review. He was therefore delighted to accept for publication in August 1888 Mona Caird's article, 'Marriage' (page 129 below). Caird's attack on marriage created a great *succès de scandale* and prompted 27,000 letters to the *Daily Telegraph* on the question, 'Is marriage a failure?'[1] However, although Mrs Caird's is the best-known and most frequently-cited article on this issue from any journal of the period, her paper was not a singular achievement, a Halley's comet blazing a new trail across a darkened firmament. She was following a path which many, often her own friends, had opened up before her in the *Westminster*, and on a topic which was being actively discussed in a wide circle of supporters and contributors, above all by Eleanor Marx, Henry Havelock Ellis, Elizabeth Rachel Chapman, Jane Hume Clapperton, Elizabeth Cady Stanton, and herself. These writers belonged to the more extended *Westminster* circle that included members of the Men and Women's Club, initially called the Wollstonecraft Club, led by Karl Pearson. His

119

inaugural paper, 'The Woman's Question', given in July 1885, provoked much discussion and controversy. In this circle, and in a triangular emotional relationship with Ellis and Pearson, was Olive Schreiner.

From the very beginning of his editorship Chapman promoted the feminist cause. Two effective pieces by Caroline Cornwallis in October 1856 (*WR*, 66, 331–60) and January 1857 (*WR*, 67, 42–72) show how the inability to hold property affects women's education and employment opportunities, vitiates marriage and promotes male licentiousness. Cornwallis also attacks the English law of divorce. A number of other articles concentrated on attacking the English divorce laws, starting with one in April 1856 (*WR*, 65, 338–55) which analyses the injustice and anomalies of a system that first denies divorce and then grants it only to the wealthy and is unfair to women. Another notable piece is Helen Taylor's passionate support for 'The Ladies' Petition' in January 1867 (*WR*, 87, 63–79) in which she is following her mother and stepfather in advocating female suffrage.

John Chapman also wrote in support of feminist causes. His 'History of women in barbarism and among the ancients', October 1855 (*WR*, 64, 378–436), predates the pieces by Caroline Cornwallis as an early *Westminster* acknowledgement of the failure of contemporary English society to remedy the iniquitous position of women in relation to divorce and the ability to hold property, and the way the double standard over adultery punishes them unfairly. In his use of historical and anthropological surveys Chapman anticipates the approach which others would take in articles he would publish in the *Westminster* thirty years later. What, of course, is missing in his own earlier article is any personal statement about marriage and relationships between the sexes. These would be the focus of intense interest in the later period.

The *Westminster*'s long history of commitment to the feminist cause is praised by Sheldon Amos in his review in January 1870 of J. S Mill's *The Subjection of Women* (*WR*, 161, 63–9). Amos admires Mill's work apart from its failure to tackle the issue of divorce. Mill's support for the *Westminster*, founded by his father and Jeremy Bentham in 1824, covered his own editorship, 1835–40, and included writing a number of articles, most notably for this study 'The enfranchisement of women' by himself and Harriet Taylor in July 1851(*WR*, 55, 289–311), just before Chapman took over the editorship of the *Westminster*. Mill was actively involved in the writing of Chapman's Prospectus (page 122 below) and continued to support and influence him.[2]

However, Chapman's irregular personal life was not unknown[3] and this could, and did, militate against him as an editor and polemicist. It prevented a proper recognition of the powerful and courageous stand he took in the *Westminster* in 1869 and 1870 in support of Josephine Butler's campaign to repeal the Contagious Diseases Act (*WR*, 92, 179–234; 93, 119–79, 477–535). His analyses point forward to positions that would be widely adopted in the 1880s and 1890s. However, in 1870 his commitment was not valued. For his lengthy and well-argued statements, stressing equally the inefficacy and injustice of the Acts, Chapman earned, rather than Butler's thanks, a private statement of her personal distaste for him as being 'not of high character', as a 'man on whom a shadow sits'.[4]

This uncompromising judgement on Chapman's life foreshadows the later conflict between the public statements and private practices of many campaigners, whether those like Schreiner, Ellis, and Pearson in triangular relationships outside marriage, or those in 'free unions'. Though this conflict is reflected mostly in private letters and diaries, it surfaces explicitly in published articles, especially those by Elizabeth Rachel Chapman and Jane Hume Clapperton.

Although Chapman and the *Review* reaped no reward for his powerful championship of the repeal of the Contagious Diseases Acts, he persisted with the campaign. After his move to Paris in 1874, he published, in July 1876, a further article on the iniquitous position of prostitutes in England (*WR*, 106, 137–88). Then, in April 1883, he opposed the state regulation of prostitution in Paris (*WR*, 119, 494–521) in an article referred to by Havelock Ellis when discussing the subject with Olive Schreiner.[5] By then Chapman's stand had become more widely respected. He had represented England at the Congrès International du Droit des Femmes in Paris in July 1878, attending with his co-editor 'wife', and had presented a paper in French opposing the state regulation of prostitution. Also attending the conference were his friends and supporters Elizabeth Cady Stanton and her son Theodore Stanton,[6] who would become important members of the *Westminster* circle.

It has been important to establish Chapman's long-term commitment to the feminist cause, and that it pre-dated the period being considered here. It is also important to recognise that his unconventional private life was known and commented on[7] and that this coloured the responses of others to his work as the publisher of controversial papers on marriage and the relationships between the sexes. However, it will also be seen that he was cautious and knew his readership, and that, while privately he sympathised with the most radical views, publicly he demonstrated editorial prudence in choosing what he felt could be aired in the pages of the *Review*. Finally, as editor of a major quarterly, he also

had to balance the competing demands of the other financial supporters and well-wishers on whom he depended, and to support their different causes.[8]

The encounters on marriage and divorce between the chief protagonists – Chapman himself and a number of his main contributors – took
a number of different forms. As editor, Chapman had a long tradition
of communicating directly with his readers, dating back to the publication in 1851 of a Prospectus – a statement of editorial policy – as he
prepared to take over the *Westminster*. This prefaced the first number
under his editorship in January 1852 (*WR*, 57, iii–vi). Then throughout
his long editorship he used footnotes and rubric to communicate editorial views to his readers.

However, the most important device at his disposal was the Independent Section, whose potential value was clearly signalled in the 1851
Prospectus. The original wording was slightly modified to produce a
general format with which all articles in the Independent Section
between 1852 and October 1888 were introduced:

> Under the above title a limited portion of The Westminster Review
> is occasionally set apart for the reception of able Articles, which,
> though harmonizing with the general spirit and aims of the Review,
> may contain opinions at variance with the particular ideas or
> measures it advocates. The object of the Editors in introducing this
> department is to facilitate the expression of opinion by men of high
> mental power and culture, who, while they are zealous friends of
> freedom and progress, yet differ widely on special points of great
> practical concern, both from the Editors and from each other.

In this way the editors could tell the readers that, while they, the editors,
might disagree with the opinions expressed in an article, they nonetheless approved of their publication – a statement itself of limited editorial approval.

This introductory wording was not significantly changed until
November 1888. Then, in the preface to Mona Caird's article 'Ideal Marriage', which followed her much-discussed article, 'Marriage', Chapman
emended '*men* of high mental power' to '*writers* of high mental power'
(*WR*, 130, 617), communicating a clear, if belated, message to the
readership.

The writers themselves engaged in their own different encounters and
dialogues on marriage and divorce. Inside the *Review* they wrote articles
in direct response to views already expressed in its pages. Through the

copious use of internal reference, footnotes, and citations writers brought powerful allies to support their individual positions, and through these they also extended and consolidated the debate. They also engaged in exchanges with other serials.

Evidence for how these dialogues were simultaneously sustained and developed outside the pages of the *Westminster* is provided through the letters, diaries, and autobiographies of Chapman and the *Westminster* circle. These allow us to trace immediate responses to articles as they appeared, and show that these responses could, in their turn, affect what might next be published. They also provide information on the privately-held views of the editor, shared with only a few contributors and kept from the wider readership. They identify what it was felt could not be published and provide important insights into the constraints of editorship.

The conflict between a radical commitment to the feminist cause on the one hand, and editorial prudence on the other, is well illustrated in the encounters between Chapman and two influential and eminent contributors, the first being Karl Pearson.[9] On 23 September 1885 Chapman wrote to Pearson, warmly welcoming the pamphlet version of the paper he had given at the first meeting of the Men and Women's Club. Of this paper, 'The Woman's Question', Chapman writes,

> It represents more exactly and completely my views on that question than any other essay I remember to have read. To me the Woman's Question – What ought to be the relation of the sexes? is the most important question of our time. . . . Throughout the period of 35 years during which the Westminster Review has been in my hands it has been the advocate of (the) Woman's Cause in its various aspects; I am glad therefore to know that the Review has a greater claim (than) ever on your sympathies.[10]

Quite typically, Chapman then seizes the chance to urge Pearson to take out shares in the newly-established Westminster Review Company. Formed the previous year with support from a number of Liberal MPs and peers, this firmly allied the *Westminster* to the Liberal cause.

Chapman's enthusiastic response to Pearson's paper was not shared by most women members of the Men and Women's Club, and their dismay and anger are recorded in the club's minutes and in published correspondence.[11] However, whatever their reactions to his paper, all women writers on the topic would henceforward have to confront one issue which Pearson had now publicly tabled: the conflict he saw between women reaching educated independence on the one hand and their duty, on the other, to fulfil their biological and social functions of reproduction to ensure 'race predominance'.[12] Women writers too would have to consider the position of the child-less (i.e. unmarried) versus the child-bearing (i.e. married) woman, and whether sexual fulfilment was to be had only at the expense of intellectual development.

The warm relationship between Chapman and Havelock Ellis, whom Chapman had launched as a writer,[13] is revealed in Ellis's autobiography and correspondence with Olive Schreiner. These show that though privately Chapman and Ellis agreed on marriage and divorce and the relationships between the sexes, they differed on what they thought should be published, particularly in the *Westminster*.

Ellis paid generous tribute to Chapman's radicalism as

> a man of quiet solid ability, genuinely advanced in his ideas, once a courageous pioneer in various fields, and gifted with an insight that enabled him to recognise and assist some of the most daring and distinguished thinkers of his time.
>
> (*My Life* 154)

Ellis aimed to influence Chapman. 'I want to bring as many good & modernising influences on him as possible'.[14] However, he was not as powerful as he thought, and, despite some preliminary discussion, failed to persuade Chapman to join him in founding a new radical journal, which then never materialized.[15]

More significantly, Ellis also failed to persuade Chapman to publish in the *Westminster* in 1884, a daring consideration of marriage and sexuality by Caroline Haddon, sister-in-law of James Hinton, a controversial advocate of free unions and even polygamy. Caroline Haddon's work was published as a separate pamphlet, entitled 'The future of marriage: an Eironicon for a question of today by a Respectable Woman'. I have been unable to trace this publication to date. However, both Pearson and Ellis either quote from it or refer to it. Pearson quotes from it to illustrate his thesis on the two classes of women – childbearing and childless: 'the stifled cry of the unmarried woman, the Rachel-like appeal, 'Give me children, or else I die'.[16] Ellis gives more information in a letter to Olive Schreiner on 18 December 1884:

> I have just been going through Miss Haddon's paper which arrived again for the third time this afternoon. It is still more improved & is really a splendid paper. There are still points I don't agree with but

the sting has been taken out of them. It is no longer a mere plea for polygomy [*sic*]. She says, for instance, that some women need for their complete mental development not only a large amount of sexual indulgence, but *variety*. – I shall send it to the *Westminster* now.[17]

Publication of these views was clearly a step too far for Chapman. This was not because his private beliefs were offended. The following month Ellis reported to Olive Schreiner a conversation he had had with Chapman when they were discussing *The Story of an African Farm*:

He talked about his admiration for S.A.F (but 'very crude artistically') ... & expounded his views on marriage, that it ought to be quite free, permitting variations in the direction of polygomy [*sic*] and polyandry, which would soon die out if proved to be bad. I told him those were my sentiments. He says he hasn't expressed them yet but he means to.[18]

I have found no evidence that Chapman did express these views publicly. And a consideration of the *Westminster* articles shows that, while very powerful and wide-ranging dissatisfaction with marriage could be expressed, there could be no open support for sexual licence. Stable, long-lasting 'free unions' – privately practised by not a few members of the extended *Westminster* circle – could, however, be occasionally condoned.

The thesis of Ellis's own article, 'The changing status of women' (*WR*, 128, 818–28) was acceptable and accepted, and the article was placed in the main body of the review. After a survey of the position of women historically, drawing on, among others J. S. Mill and Mary Wollstonecraft, and citing his own (unattributed) article in the *Westminster* for June 1887, 'The form of capture in marriage ceremonies' (*WR*, 128, 283–94), Ellis identifies the main cause of women's subjection as economic. He believes that as women gain greater freedom economically there will be greater freedom in relationships between the sexes. Prostitution both within and outside marriage will disappear. The state regulation of marriage will become unnecessary. However, Ellis prudently acknowledges society has a continuing interest in sexual relationships by suggesting the state registration – undefined – of sexual unions freely entered into.

This article was originally submitted to Chapman in January 1886, the month in which Eleanor Marx's article appeared in the *Westminster* (below p. 127). A number of similarities in the positions taken in the two articles still remain. When Ellis's manuscript was submitted in 1886 there would appear to have been more duplications and Chapman asked him to remove some passages, including a consideration of *The Story of an African Farm,* which Marx had also drawn on. Ellis's article finally appeared in the *Westminster* in October 1887. In his introduction to the pamphlet version of the article published in 1888 (Ellis, *Women and Marriage*), Ellis states that excisions had been restored. One of these was a sharp attack on Frances Power Cobbe (7). Its original removal by Chapman could have been because Theodore Stanton, contributor to the *Westminster* and a member of the *Westminster* circle, had thought highly enough of Cobbe to prevail on her to write the introduction to his *The Woman Question in Europe,* 1884.

Ellis was a close and perceptive observer of the *Westminster* circle at this time, sharing what was being read and discussed – including August Bebel's *Die Frau in der Vergangenheit, Gegenwart und Zukunft* – and also monitoring the changing and complex attitudes of others to the position of women and the relationships between the sexes. This is seen very clearly in a letter to Olive Schreiner dated 30 July 1884:

> Have you got Bebel's book? Miss Haddon has mine. There are two articles in the 'Westminster' for July. I've just been reading them. One on the 'The Christian Harem' (it looks as if it might be by Miss Chapman) on equality of virtue, the same moral law for both sexes. That is a very ancient idea of mine. Only most or all (almost) of the people who preach it do not realise how fundamental a change that would be in the whole relationship between men & women. . . . I don't like your saying that 'manly' is the best epithet that you can apply to anything coming from a woman. It would be better to use a non-sexual word. It implies that there is some special secret in the possession of men, some mystery of development which it is the highest aim of women to attain. (This is Mrs Caird's &, to some extent, Miss Jones's feeling.)[19]

He goes on to encourage Schreiner to publish under her own name rather than use a male pseudonym. This sympathetic understanding of her tentativeness places Ellis in a very different position from Pearson, whose critical dominance of the Men and Women's Club probably contributed to its demise.[20]

Eleanor Marx was not tentative. She was a strong, committed, and able thinker. However, her article in January 1886, 'The woman question from a socialist point of view', (*WR*, 125, 207–22), was signed jointly by herself and Edward Aveling, a public announcement of their 'free union'. Since there is evidence that the first version published in the *Westminster* was more her work than his,[21] I shall concentrate on her. She was an active member of the extended *Westminster* circle. She was a friend of Olive Schreiner and Mona Caird[22] and was a guest at the Men and Women's Club in May 1886 in which L. Eckstein presented a paper on sexual relations in Rome (Pearson Papers 10/1, 66). Ellis was angry at the very thought that she might be refused full membership of the Club, but there is no evidence that she was ever accepted.[23]

In her article Eleanor Marx is reviewing and drawing on the first English translation by Harriet Walther of August Bebel's *Die Frau*. While identifying political, social and economic disadvantages facing women, she is following the main consensus of *Westminster* editors and reviewers. She attacks the Contagious Diseases Acts. She draws on J. S. Mill and Mary Wollstonecraft. She is angry at the despised state of the unmarried woman: 'How is it that our sisters bear upon their brows this stamp of lost instincts, stifled affections, a nature in part murdered? How is it that their 'more fortunate brothers' bear no such mark?' (212). She quotes from *The Story of an African Farm* Lyndall's despairing cry that equality between the sexes comes only in death (217). With the others in the *Westminster* circle she deplores the commercialisation of marriage and supports divorce. She cites with approval Stead's 'Maiden Tribute of Babylon' crusade in the *Pall Mall Gazette*[24] to support her attack on prostitution generally (219). Like Ellis she argues for unions freely entered into, but, unlike him, suggests they should be 'of a purely private nature, without the intervention of any public functionary' (222). However, she departs from the other writers being considered here in her belief that all injustices and inequalities will be redressed with the achievement of a socialist state. Such positive commitment to socialism would alone ensure that the article was placed in the Independent Section. But she goes on to deplore the dangers of the unfulfilled female sex drive, 'the slaying of sex is always followed by disaster' (218), and 'chastity is unhealthy and unholy' (218). Marx acknowledged privately that the editors of the *Westminster* had shown courage in publishing her article when the *Contemporary Review* had taken fright and refused it.[25]

The next article for consideration, 'Marriage ' (*WR*, 130, 186–205), by Mona Caird has already been noted as one of the best-known periodical articles of the late nineteenth century. Appearing in August 1888, its *succès de scandale* was not confined to the readers of the *Daily*

Telegraph. The article and its author have been extensively studied, particularly by feminist scholars in the last ten years. However, excellent though many of these studies are,[26] an important aspect of the article's significance is missed by not seeing it in the context of serial publication, and as on a topic being widely debated among a network of people who knew and were influenced by each other.

It is possible to trace some of Mona Caird's encounters with other thinkers and writers in the *Westminster* circle on the subject of marriage, the relationship between the sexes and sexuality. As has already been noted, she was a friend of Olive Schreiner. The Attendance Book of the Men and Women's Club (Pearson Papers 10/1, 319) shows she was a guest on 9 May 1887 at a discussion on birth control, though she was refused membership.[27] Elizabeth Cady Stanton records that Mona Caird was reading Karl Pearson's 'The Woman's Question' when they spent several days together in February 1888 (*80 Years*, 409). In March 1886 Olive Schreiner asked Pearson whether Caird was the author of the paper, 'Man's View of the Woman's Question', written to counter his paper, since 'the ideas are just like what she has expressed to me in speaking. It gives one hope to hear such brave free words from a woman'.[28] In fact the author was Henrietta Müller.[29]

Therefore it is not surprising that a close reading of Caird's article reveals very few ideas that had not already been expressed in the *Westminster* or within the *Westminster* circle. She was not, as some scholars seem to suggest,[30] simply influenced by, and replying to, Pearson. Her article responds both explicitly and implicitly to the different positions taken by many others, and assumes a core readership very familiar with the debate. She reacts to Pearson's identification of the two classes of women – childless and child-bearing – not by directly opposing him, but by emphasising the grinding miseries of constant child-bearing, the price paid by women for the prevention of men's sexual licence. She draws on the authority of Jane Hume Clapperton's *Scientific Meliorism* (195) and on Bebel (195) for the plight of the unmarried woman. She cites Theodore Stanton in identifying different but complementary intellectual qualities in men and women (199). Marriage by capture had been covered by Ellis in June 1887 (*WR*, 128, 283–94), marriage as legalised prostitution by Elizabeth Rachel Chapman in 'The Christian Harem' in July 1884 (*WR*, 122, 105–15). Her call for the removal of the state from the marriage contract echoes Eleanor Marx and Havelock Ellis. Caird is content to reiterate these views. She sees the need for social change but anticipates a gradual development through co-operation rather than Marx's social revolution. The tentativeness noted by

Havelock Ellis (page 126 above) has gone as she allies herself explicitly and with pride with these fellow thinkers and writers.

Though her views were not new to the *Westminster* circle, Mona Caird did make a unique contribution to the debate on marriage and divorce, and in two ways. The first is her ability to write with immediacy, passion and even humour – the talent of the populariser – to communicate with the widest audience. The second is her lively inclusion of men and their misery in her accounts of marriage:

> [W]e have well-meaning husbands and wives harassing one another to death for no reason in the world but the desire of conforming to current notions regarding the proper conduct of married people. These victims are expected to go about perpetually together, as if they were a pair of carriage horses; to be for ever holding claims over one another; exacting or making useless sacrifices, and generally getting in one another's way.   (196)

Even many supposedly happy marriages exact a terrible penalty as the pair withdraw from the world to become 'mere echoes, half creatures, ... (who) have let individuality die. There are few things more stolidly irritating than a very "united" couple. The likeness that may often be remarked between married people is a melancholy index of this united degeneration.' (197)

This ensured that the responses to the *Daily Telegraph* would come from both sexes.

Iconoclastic and provocative, few more lively articles graced the pages of the Independent Section in the whole history of the *Westminster*. The wider readership was electrified and the *Westminster* circle delighted. Elizabeth Cady Stanton recorded with satisfaction that Mrs Caird's article had 'stirred the press to white heat both in England and America' (*80 Years*, 409).

Having expressed such ideas, it was certainly not the case, as one writer seems to suggest[31] that Mona Caird had an unlimited choice in deciding on which journal would have the privilege of publishing them. On the contrary, in summing up as she does the consensus of the *Westminster* and its extended circle, it was the only journal she could approach. What ensured the article's place in the Independent Section, however, was that these well-rehearsed arguments were presented in such a way that the only conclusion to be drawn was that marriage is a failure. The *Daily Telegraph* certainly believed that this was the message.

Elizabeth Rachel Chapman – no relation of John Chapman – extended the debate further when, in the very next issue, September 1888, she directly confronted the *Westminster* consensus on support for divorce. She had not always been in opposition to the general *Westminster* approach. John Chapman had already published 'The Christian Harem' in the *Westminster* for July 1884 (*WR*, 122, 105–15). Dealing as it does with the double standard and the inequalities faced by women in marriage, it was consistent with mainstream *Westminster* opinion and was placed in the main body of the review. Her call in it for 'equality of virtue' between the sexes had been noted approvingly by Havelock Ellis.[32]

The new piece, 'Marriage rejection and marriage reform' (*WR*, 130, 358–77), was an altogether different matter. Writing before Caird's article appeared, Elizabeth Chapman expresses the most profound opposition to divorce. Before actually going to press there was time for an editorial footnote to inform the readers that 'This paper is not intentionally a reply to Mrs Caird's article on 'Marriage' in the August number of this Review: it was written some time before that article was published' (fn, 358). E. R. Chapman herself notes in the preface to *Marriage Questions in Modern Fiction* that the article 'chanced to follow ... the much-discussed attack on marriage by Mrs Mona Caird in the previous number' (vii). However, Elizabeth Chapman was able to draw on Mona Caird's article to support her own view of marriage as 'legalised inequity' by inserting a last-minute footnote of her own referring the reader to the earlier article (fn, 372). John Chapman must have been delighted with this fortuitous continuation of the debate. The piece was placed in the Independent Section.

In her article Elizabeth Chapman places those who currently criticise marriage into two groups: the rejectors and the reformers. Among the rejectors she cites Olive Schreiner with *The Story of an African Farm*, and Karl Pearson with 'The Woman's Question'. She regrets she is unable to name a single *Westminster* reviewer in the lists of the reformers! (368) However, she deals at some length, and with some sympathy, with the dissatisfaction with marriage expressed by Pearson, Schreiner and Caird. She acknowledges that both rejectors and reformers agree on the legal and social inequities of the current marriage system, and deplore the way it is underpinned by sordid economic considerations. She grants – possibly disingenuously given how well the members of the extended circle knew each other – that the rejectors are not cynical libertines but 'believe in a higher bond' (367). However, she is sceptical about the capacity of even the most high-minded members of free unions to sustain the relationship without the public commitment of marriage, and believes that for ordinary mortals such moral strength is unachievable.

She too cites *The Story of an African Farm*, not as illustrating the plight of women, but as evidence of the high-minded author's loss of faith in marriage and her misguided support instead for 'a union which shall be something higher, truer, and better than legal marriage' (365). Elizabeth Rachel Chapman, also a literary critic,[33] makes the perceptive observation that by ensuring that Lyndall makes an *informed* choice in preferring 'concubinage to marriage', and thus putting her heroine in a very different position from that of Effie Deans and Hetty Sorrell, Schreiner has marked a significant shift in the moral landscape of the Victorian novel.

> There is here no sense of something sacred violated, something white sullied, something whole fractured; there is an entirely new way of looking at the sexual relation – a view of sexual morality to which the better class of Victorian imaginative literature, at any rate, affords no parallel. (364)

However Lyndall suffers as severely as the most traditionally fallen woman – albeit that her creator lays the blame for this on society's failure rather than on her heroine's moral weakness.

Elizabeth Chapman's solution for the wellbeing of both society and the individual is to strengthen a reformed system of marriage. She quotes approvingly from two thinkers who influenced the *Westminster* strongly in the middle of the century, Herbert Spencer and August Comte. She draws on their teaching for her belief in the eventual evolution of a 'purified monogamy' (361) and completely rejects divorce, even for those who are totally miserable, for it would be 'the relief of the few at the expense of the well-being of the many' (376).

But what doubly ensured that the article would be placed in the Independent Section was the citing of George Eliot as the most illustrious example of the failure of free unions, with her pathetic clinging to the titles of 'husband' and 'wife' for herself and George Henry Lewes, and her headlong rush into marriage at the end of her life, after the death of Lewes.

This called forth an impassioned and direct attack on her in the next issue of the *Westminster*, December 1888, by Jane Hume Clapperton, novelist and socialist creator of *Scientific Meliorism* (1885). Clapperton attended at least one meeting of the Men and Women's Club in May 1888 (Pearson Papers 10/1, 142). Her fiery commitment is cited by Olive Schreiner in January 1888 when she attacks Havelock Ellis for his scholarly withdrawal: 'In time of revolution & war *you* will never be found, *you* will never be in the market place. Miss Capperton (sic) will, so will Eleanor Marx Aveling . . .'.[34]

In 'Miss Chapman's marriage reforms. A criticism' (*WR*, 130, 707–17) Clapperton shares Elizabeth Chapman's evolutionary approach, but criticises her 'airy faith in the sublime future' (713), though she substitutes one of her own that is scarcely less nebulous. She attacks Elizabeth Chapman for, on the one hand, powerfully describing all the inequalities and unhappiness in many marriages, and, on the other, pulling back from the logical conclusion that husbands and wives must be able to escape from their misery through divorce. She then quotes approvingly (713) from 'The Philosophy of Marriage', an article by Eliza Lynn Linton supporting divorce in the *Universal Review* for September 1888.[35] Clapperton, a fervent admirer of George Eliot, to whom she had dedicated *Scientific Meliorism*, then defends her heroine in a persuasive argument for free unions. This article, too, was placed in the Independent Section.

Elizabeth Chapman returned to the subject twice more in the *Westminster* at this period, in both cases responding directly to previous articles. The first article in February 1889, 'St Paul and the Woman Movement' (*WR*, 131, 135–147), was placed in the main body of the review. In it she analyses the responses to Mona Caird's 'Marriage' through the letters to the *Daily Telegraph* on 'Is Marriage a Failure?' She concludes: 'It was somewhat unexpected, and it was certainly depressing, to find that the modern reawakening of the sense of woman's claim to justice and to freedom had made so little way with the mass of the English nation' (136). She blames the teaching of St Paul for this.

Her paper is sharper and more focused than Mona Caird's own response to the *Daily Telegraph* letters. This article had appeared in the Independent Section in the previous November (*WR*, 130, 617–636) and was entitled, 'Ideal Marriage'. In it, Caird develops the arguments she had advanced in 'Marriage'. She characterises the general response of the English middle classes as the complacent pragmatism of 'Mr Brown of Tooting' (618) and attacks the *Daily Telegraph* correspondents for blaming the victims of marriage, the wives, for the failings of marriage (621). However, the piece is prolix, the tone hectoring, and the use of dialogue tedious. She clearly did not think well enough of it to reprint it in 1897 in *The Morality of Marriage*, alongside its much more successful predecessor.

Elizabeth Chapman's second article in April 1890, 'The Decline of Divorce' (*WR*, 133, 417–34) is a direct response to Jane Hume Clapperton's criticism of her opposition to divorce. This time the article was placed in the Independent Section. In it Elizabeth Chapman accepts the possibility of separation for truly unhappy spouses, but again rejects divorce. She then extends the debate, perhaps rather surprisingly given her own commitment to Comtism, by bringing to her support (425) Gladstone's recent article in the *North American Review* defending Christianity,[36] in which he opposes divorce.

Finally in January 1891 an important international dimension was added to the debate when Elizabeth Cady Stanton published her support for Parnell in the scandal over the O'Shea divorce case. Doyenne of the women's movement, secularist, and suffragist, Elizabeth Cady Stanton was in some ways the most far-seeing and courageous of all those discussed here. No insular American, she was familiar with the European women's movements through her own and her son's contacts, and she kept those contacts alive on her various visits to the UK and Europe. Her friendship with Mona Caird has already been noted (page 128 above). She liked John Chapman (*Diary*, 239), approved of the *Westminster*, and contributed to it when she was in London.[37]

Her defence of Parnell, 'Patriotism and Chastity' (*WR*, 135, 1–5), is short but effective. Five years earlier, in January 1886, Eleanor Marx had cited approvingly W. T. Stead's campaign in the *Pall Mall Gazette*, as she made her own general attack on prostitution (page 127 above). Now, in her article on Parnell, Elizabeth Cady Stanton takes a stance in direct opposition to Stead. She recorded in her diary her satisfaction with her assault on 'a little set of Social Purity people' and 'Stead and a set of canting saints' (*Diary*, 269–70). This provoked Stead to a counter-attack on her in the *Review of Reviews* for January 1891.[38]

Stanton's article has also been extensively studied. It is sufficient here to note her long list of examples of society's hypocrisy in relation to male sexuality, particularly of men eminent in public life, and her attack on the double standard, based as it is on civil and canon law, Blackstone and the Bible. She questions too the view that 'all legal relations of the sexes are chaste' (4) and contrasts unfavourably 'the family of twelve children and invalid wife' with 'a healthy and happy mother and child outside the bonds of wedlock' (4). She opposes the view that sexual morality is the exclusive responsibility of women within the domain of the home, particularly while women have no role in public life. There is no question of believing, as Karl Pearson did, that the education of women would undermine their sexuality and reproductive capacities.

Stanton, the loving mother and grandmother, believes that it is the 'education, elevation and emancipation' (4) of women – rather than the hounding of men – that will lead to the reform of sexual behaviour across society. As she says in her diary entry on the article, 'so long as women are slaves, men will be knaves' (*Diary*, 270). The article, with its arresting title, is clear and succinct. Chapman and his wife were delighted (*Diary*, 269), though 'the Editors' also appended a footnote (5) expressing their personal pain at the 'aberrations' of Parnell's savage response to being hounded. Chapman gave the article pride of place in the main body of the *Westminster*. It enabled him both to support Home Rule and to further the cause of sexual equality.

Conclusion

The woman question, the debate on marriage and divorce, and the reform of sexual relations had always been causes close to Chapman's own heart, causes for which he had in the past earned little support and no regard. He had now lived long enough to see them become national issues. Despite the inevitable price that had to be paid in terms of caution and prudence – no public advocacy of sexual licence or even some of those more limited freedoms which he privately supported – he was in a position, as editor of the *Westminster Review*, to make a major contribution to the debate.

The *Review's* reputation for openness to the discussion of such radical topics pushed the debate forward. Havelock Ellis, writing to Olive Schreiner in February 1886, recounts happily how he had told Chapman that 'the reactions of the *Westminster* were nowadays considered a form of socialism & called Anarchism and that if he wanted to be at the front he must recognise this.'[39]

Nonetheless, a radical editorial policy alone was not enough, however strongly it was encouraged by supporters like Ellis. It was the series of encounters within the *Westminster* and its wider circle that formulated and promoted the debate nationwide.

The main protagonists in this circle were avid readers of each other's works, especially articles in the *Westminster,* responding to them both in its pages and outside. Most knew each other personally. They spent time together socially, even intimately. They carried the discussions into new and even more radical areas of debate, particularly those writers who were involved in discussions at the Men and Women's Club. There can be few better illustrations of the importance of dialogues in serial publications in encouraging, and testing new ideas. The articles in the

Westminster encouraged immediate responses. They kept readers and contributors alike keenly attuned to the issues, eagerly anticipating the next riposte, the following counter-thrust and the subsequent parry, the very stuff of serial publication.

Notes

1. Harry Quilter, ed., *Is Marriage a Failure? The most important letters on this subject in the Daily Telegraph, a paper on the philosophy of marriage by Mrs Lynn Linton* . . . (London: Swan Sonnenschein Co., [1888]).
2. Sheila Rosenberg, 'The Financing of Radical Opinion: John Chapman and the *Westminster Review*', in *The Victorian Periodical Press*, ed. J. Shattock and M. Wolff (Leicester and Toronto: Leicester University Press and Toronto University Press, 1982), 167–92.
3. Gordon Haight, *George Eliot and John Chapman, with Chapman's Diaries* (Yale: Archon Books, 1969), passim.
4. I am indebted to Ms Jean L'Esperance for this quotation from a letter from Mrs Josephine Butler.
5. Yaffa Claire Drazin, ed., *'My Other Self': The Letters of Olive Schreiner and Have-lock Ellis* (New York: Peter Lang, 1922), 321.
6. The British Library copy of the proceeding of the Congrès international du droit des femmes, 25 juillet–9 août 1878 is bound in the volume of collected issues of *Le droit des femmes, revue mensuelle*, for 1879–80, the eleventh year of a review that started as *L'année des femmes*, both edited by Leon Richer. Chapman's paper is in the 'section de Morale', 129–136. Theodore Stanton is identified as 'le fils de la courageuse mistress Elizabeth Cady Stanton' (35).
7. Havelock Ellis speculates on the real relationship between Chapman and his 'wife' and 'daughters' and records that Mrs Chapman 'had a defiant air which suggested an uncertainty of position' (Henry Havelock Ellis, *My Life* [London: William Heinemann,1940], 154). There is still conflicting evidence on whether Chapman married Hannah MacDonald after his wife Susannah's death in 1882 (Haight, 116). What is clear is that 'Pres', as Chapman called Hannah MacDonald, was involved in the day-to-day running of the *Westminster* (four letters dated 20, 29 January and 5, 10 February in the George Eliot Collection, Yale University Library) and continued to edit the *Westminster* after Chapman's death in 1894 (Haight 118).
8. Rosenberg, 'The Financing of Radical Opinion'.
9. Pearson wrote two articles: April 1883, 'Humanism in Germany' (*WR*, 119: 315–33) and January 1884, 'Martin Luther: His Influence on the Welfare of Germany' (*WR*, 121: 1–44). In a letter dated 20 November 1883 (University College London: Pearson Papers, 892/9) Chapman asked Pearson to under-take the reviews of German works in the Theological Section. There is no evidence that Pearson did so, but in June 1889 Chapman published Emma Pearson's article 'Henrik Ibsen: his Men and his Women' (*WR*, 131, 626–49), one of the first studies of the dramatist in the English periodical press. See Judith Walkowitz, *City of Dreadful Delight* (London: Virago Press, 1992), 167.
10. Pearson Papers 656/9. Corrected for obvious typing errors.

11. Olive Schreiner was angered that Pearson seemed to be suggesting that the only purpose of the club seemed to be to discuss women, and Henrietta Müller (a *Westminster* writer) was stung to written refutation with 'The other side of the question' (Walkowitz, 149–52).

12. Karl Pearson, *The Ethic of Free Thought: A Selection of Essays and Lectures* (London: T. Fisher Unwin, 1888), 389.

13. In April 1883 Chapman had published Ellis's first publication, an article on Thomas Hardy (*WR*, 119, 334–64) and Ellis went on to write several more: the Theological Sections for July 1886 (*WR*, 126, 231–40); October 1886 (*WR*, 126, 520–4); January1887 (*WR*, 127, 191–201). 'Thomas Ashe's Poems', April 1886 (*WR*, 125, 416–29); June 1887, 'Forms of capture in marriage ceremonies', (*WR*, 128, 283–94) as well as October 1887, 'The changing status of women' (*WR*, 128, 818–28) discussed in this paper.

14. Drazin, 416.

15. Ibid., 406.

16. Pearson, 373.

17. Drazin, 268.

18. Ibid., 295.

19. Ibid., 116.

20. Walkowitz, 164.

21. Yvonne Kapp, *Eleanor Marx*, 2 vols (London: Virago Press, 1979), 2: 3–4.

22. Richard Rive, ed., *Olive Schreiner Letters 1871–1899* (Oxford: Oxford University Press, 1988) and Drazin, both passim.

23. Drazin, 404–5.

24. *Pall Mall Gazette* 6, 7, 8, 10 July 1885.

25. Kapp, 83.

26. Lucy Bland, *Banishing the Beast: Sexuality and the Early Feminists* (New York: New Press, 1995); Florence Boos, 'A History of Their Own: Mona Caird, Frances Swiney, and *fin de siècle* Feminist Family History', in *Contesting the Master Narrative*, ed. Jeffrey Cox and Shelton Stromquist (Iowa City: University of Iowa Press, 1990), 19–32; Ann Heilmann, 'Mona Caird (1854–1932)', *Women's History Review*, 15 (1996), 67–95; Walkowitz, *City of Dreadful Delight*.

27. Heilmann, 72.

28. Rive, 74.

29. See note 11.

30. Bland, 126–7; Walkowitz, 167.

31. Heilmann, 71.

32. Drazin, 116.

33. Elizabeth Rachel Chapman was both a bellettrist, and a Comtist social commentator, writing *The New Godiva* (London: T. Fisher Unwin, 1885), *A Comtist Lover and Other Stories* (London: T. Fisher, Unwin, 1886), *A Companion to In Memoriam* (London: Macmillan and Co., 1888) as well as *Marriage Questions in Modern Fiction* (London and New York: John Lane, 1897).

34. Drazin, 441.

35. *Universal Review*, 2, 21–37. The editor, Harry Quilter, reprinted this piece, with minor changes, in *'Is Marriage a Failure?'* (see note 1), the volume he put together to evaluate the *Daily Telegraph* readers' responses to Mona Caird's 'Marriage'. Mrs Lynn Linton, noting the controversial debate, but not

naming Mona Caird, takes a cautious, pragmatic approach but grants the need for divorce: 'When the essential meaning of marriage and the good of the family are lost, the form may well go, and divorce is a better state of things than domestic unhappiness' (35).

36. 'The indissolubility of marriage', *North American Review* 146, 481–508 (at 499). Gladstone was engaged in a theological dispute with Robert T. Ingersoll which covered several issues of the journal.

37. September 1890 'Wyoming Admitted to the Union' (*WR*, 134, 280–4); November 1893, 'Emma Willard' (*WR*, 140, 538–44). Theodore Stauton was also a contributor to the *Westminster*. He wrote a series of articles on Abraham Lincoln (*WR*, 135, 635–47; 136, 1–13; 124–31; 255–67); June 1893 'American Dictionaries' (*WR*, 139, 610–15); February 1894 'A Franco-American's Notes on the United States' (*WR*, 141, 195–204). *References to Elizabeth Cady Stanton's Diary are to T. Stanton and H. Stanton Blatch, as Revealed in her Letters, Diary and Reminiscences*, ed. (New York and London: Harper & Bros., 1922).

38. *Review of Reviews* 3, 60.

39. Drazin, 406.

8
Urban Encounters and Visual Play in the *Yellow Book*

Mark W. Turner

Remembering the 1890s

In his recent collection of poems, *The Yellow Book* (1997), the Irish poet and journalist Derek Mahon draws on the literary culture and decadent spirit of the 1890s to comment on the weariness of postmodern cosmopolitanism he perceives a century later. In the opening poem, 'Landscape', Mahon positions himself as a Baudelairean metropolitan observer, peering out from an attic and deciphering the cityscape:

> Chastely to write these eclogues I need to lie,
> like the astrologers, in an attic next the sky
> where, high among church spires, I can dream and hear
> their grave hymns wind-blown to my ivory tower.
> Chin in hand, up here in my apartment block,
> I can see workshops full of noise and talk,
> cranes and masts of the ocean-going city,
> vast cloud formations dreaming about eternity.[1]

So begins a collection of poems that takes us to Dublin, Paris, London, New York, and elsewhere – weaving together the cultural histories of these cities with the present day, contrasting the exuberance of the late nineteenth century with the less satisfying, fragmented global urbanism of the present. In a later poem, 'Remembering the '90s', the speaker recalls the 1890s and passes judgment on the 1990s; he finds 'those desperate characters of the previous '90s/slaves of the Siren, consorts of the Sphinx/like Dowson, Johnson, Symons and Le Gallienne' (Mahon, 28) to be the heroes of modernity. In the speaker's recollection of literary life in the 1890s:

The most of what we did and wrote was artifice,
rhyme-sculpture against the entangling vines of nature –
a futile project since, in the known future,
new books will be rarities in techno-culture,
a forest of intertextuality like this,
each one a rare book and what few we have
written for prize money and not for love,
while the *real* books like vintage wines survive
among the antiquities, each yellowing page
known only to astrologer and mage
where blind librarians study as on a keyboard
gnomic encryptions, secrets of the word,
a lost knowledge; and all the rest is lit(t)erature.

(Mahon, 29)

In the symbolism and impressionism of the Rhymers' Club and others, in the yellowing pages of the experimental 1890s *Yellow Book*, Mahon identifies the *real* that contrasts with the postmodern *unreal*. As he writes in '"shiver in your tenement"', 'Those were the days; now patience, courage, artistry,/solitude things of the past, like the fear of God,/we nod to you from the pastiche paradise of the post-modern.' (Mahon, 19) The art-for-art's-sake sensibilities of the 1890s, the Baudelairean construction of the detached artist who locks himself away *'to build my faeries palaces in the night'* (Mahon, 11), the Paterian aesthete – these are things Mahon finds lacking in his own *fin-de-siècle*, in which 'Everything aspires to the condition of rock music' (Mahon, 35).

There is certainly a nostalgic romanticization at work in Mahon's incorporation of *The Yellow Book*, but one thing that his return to the 1890s and the cultural milieu of the original *Yellow Book* reminds us of is the centrality of the city in much of the literature and art of the period. In fact, in revisiting the 1890s through the *Yellow Book*, Mahon takes for granted what I take to be one of the defining characteristics of the periodical – its metropolitan pose. While critics writing on the *Yellow Book* have noticed in passing the variety of urban expressions in the periodical, no one has yet emphasized the extent to which the city was a primary subject for contributors. Furthermore, the link between the periodical's 'modernness' and its urbanism has largely been undiscussed. So it is the *Yellow Book*'s contribution to the development of an urban aesthetic that I wish to explore here, an aesthetic in which multiple, sometimes overlapping, points of view capture the diverse nature of the city of modernity.

The *Yellow Book*, officially edited by the expatriate American Henry Harland and Aubrey Beardsley (both posing dandies), was the centre of the 'new art' and 'new literature'. It emerged out of the culture of the experimental, provocative 1890s and was largely a joint effort from men and women writers – including most notably the New Woman writer Ella D'Arcy – connected to the publisher John Lane. In many ways, the *Yellow Book* was a collaborative project, a coterie periodical with numerous contributors, rather than the work of a single editor or editors.[2] Its character and form are notable for their transgressive hybridity: it was a quarterly, but one that was artistic and literary rather than based on weighty review journalism; it was a periodical that called itself (and was bound as) a book; it was a journal that insisted on the merit of the art within and so challenged the assumption that illustrations were merely decorative and that periodicals were essentially ephemeral. As the editors tell us in advance of the first issue in April 1894, 'We feel that the time has come for an absolutely new era in the way of magazine literature. . . . Distinction, modernness – these, probably, so nearly as they can be picked out, are the two leading features of our plan'.[3] A new era, daring to be different and self-consciously embracing the modern is what the *Yellow Book* aspired to encapsulate and in some part define.

Whether or not the *Yellow Book* was quite as daring as it proposed to be has been debated since the publication of the very first number. The *Athenaeum*, for example, commented that it 'evidently aims at novelty, and yet it is not unlike in appearance the annual volumes of *Chatterbox* and other periodicals for young people'.[4] The *Critic* found its contents more challenging, suggesting of illustrator Beardsley that 'his genius is so grotesque that it is beyond the understanding of ordinary mortals',[5] and in reviews of subsequent volumes they called the periodical 'A Yellow Impertinence'.[6] Richard Le Gallienne, a poet identified with the New Literature and one published in the *Yellow Book*, was measured about its outrageousness:

> The *Yellow Book* was certainly novel, even striking, but, except for the drawings and decorations by Beardsley, which, seen thus for the first time, not unnaturally affected most people as at once startling, repellent, and fascinating, it is hard to realize why it should have seemed so shocking. But the public is an instinctive creature, not half so stupid as is usually taken for granted. It evidently scented something queer and rather alarming about the strange new quarterly, and thus it almost immediately regarded it as symbolic of new movements which it only partially represented. Even the compromise, which,

after the first four or five numbers, was to rob it of any disquieting originality, was already present in the first issue. This was the shrewd [John] Lane's doing. He was afraid to let its editors, Henry Harland and Aubrey Beardsley, be as daring as they wished to be, and so with such representatives of 'modernity' as Max Beerbohm, Arthur Symons, George Egerton, Hubert Crackanthorpe, John Oliver Hobbes and George Moore, he sandwiched in such safe and even 'respectable' writers as Henry James, Arthur Christopher Benson, William Watson, Arthur Waugh, Richard Garnett, and Edmund Gosse, while he sought to break the shock of Beardsley with a frontispiece by Sir Frederic Leighton.[7]

As publisher of the venture, John Lane was keen to promote writers and artists associated with the 'new literature' and 'new art', many of whom were on his booklists at the Bodley Head, alongside solidly established, and in some cases, establishment figures.[8] This was, after all, a commercial publishing venture, so well-known figures like Henry James were as necessary for publicity as the young newcomers who championed the 'new' discourses of the modern and modernity.[9]

Hide and seek

Both the form of the *Yellow Book* and the content – which one critic reviewed as 'a combination of English rowdyism and French lubricity'[10] – shifted assumptions about periodicals. Most notably, as the critical comments quoted above indicate, the illustrations were presented for their own sake, rather than being merely incidental, decorative, or linked directly to the literature, as was conventional in periodicals hitherto. More significantly for the modern pose of the *Yellow Book*, the illustrations also helped to establish one of the dominant discourses in the periodical – having to do with vision and how to interpret what we see. Beardsley's illustrations are the most playful of the visual images, destabilizing notions of gender and sexuality in particular, with their depiction of androgynes, imps, prostitutes, and New Women. His visual language was mischievous, so much so that Le Gallienne recalled:

> Poor Lane had rather a nerve-wracking time with Beardsley, who, for the fun of it, was always trying to slip some indecency into his covers, not apparent without close scrutiny, so that Lane used to go over them with a microscope and submit them to a jury of his friends before he ventured to publish. Even so, I remember that one issue

had gone to press before a particularly audacious impropriety was discovered, with the result that the whole binding had to be cancelled. It was quite a game of hide-and-seek between Lane and Beardsley, in which Beardsley took a boyish delight.

(Le Gallienne, 133)

The notion of a hide-and-seek game encapsulates nicely the sort of visual play at work in virtually all Beardsley's images, and the visual scrutiny Lane feels necessary is appropriate given the visual scrutiny at work in the images themselves. Take the cover illustration to Volume I (Figure 6). Here, the contrast between light and dark and the use of masquerade demonstrate the inquisitive visual play in Beardsley's images, which often ask questions about what it is we are seeing, and about the nature of sexual and gender identity generally. The sexually open central figure, assumed to be woman, suggests a prostitute (note the iconic beauty mark on her cheek and her open bosom) who gazes out at the viewer; the other figure is more androgynous and could just as easily be a man in drag as a woman. He or she is positioned behind the central figure, perhaps seductively, perhaps predatorily, perhaps already engaged in a sexual act – we cannot quite tell, and the masks prevent us from deciphering with complete certainty the 'real' story. Another Beardsley image in Volume I, 'Night Piece', presents us with a city street scene that again presumably depicts a prostitute walking the streets at night. The image is almost entirely black, with the woman's bosom and neck providing the focus of contrasting light against dark. She is decoratively dressed, almost overdressed, and the reader/viewer is positioned fairly unequivocally as voyeur or consumer. We remain detached, observing the woman walk the street without any direct visual engagement by her, unlike the front cover image that invites readers in. Beardsley's 'Night Piece' precedes the poem 'Stella Maris' by Arthur Symons, about the speaker's love for a prostitute:

> Why is it I remember yet
> You, of all women one has met
> In random wayfare, as one meets
> The chance romances of the streets,
> The Juliet of a night?[11]

While Beardsley's 'Night Piece' does not quite illustrate Symons's poem, there is clearly an intertextual relationship between the two,[12] not only in whom they seemingly depict (prostitutes), but also in the discursive

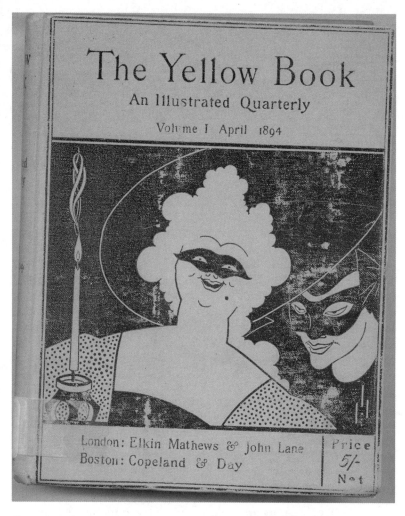

Figure 6   Aubrey Beardsley, Cover, *Yellow Book,* I, April 1894.

formation each text is a part of – the gendered encounters and visual play of the city that are central to representations of urban experience.

Whether it is browsing, staring in the mirror, parading on the street, taking to the stage – the dynamic between spectator and spectacle (both in the content of the image and in the viewer/image relationship) is of central interest. Often, the spectacle is woman and the spectator is

positioned as male, suggesting the prominence of male-gendered discourses in the periodical,[13] and images in the *Yellow Book* such as Beardsley's 'The Comedy Ballet of Marionettes' (Volume II) appear to depict
a man's initiation of a woman into sexual play.[14] However, there *are*
other ways of seeing offered and the dynamic is not always as straightforward as male/objectifier, female/objectified, not least because of the
indeterminacy of the figures. As Linda Zatlin has demonstrated, the
artist was interested in challenging conventions regarding Victorian sexuality and gender, although the evidence appears more often outside
the *Yellow Book* than within its covers. Beardsley's cover to Volume III
of the *Yellow Book* (Figure 7), in which we watch a woman in her boudoir
making herself up presumably for an evening out, captures precisely the
ambiguity of the illustrator's play on vision. The woman stares at herself
in the mirror, applying cosmetics, as we stare at her. Her dress is typically exaggerated, and the drapery in the background suggests the sexual
motif of genitalia common in a number of Beardsley's images. Another
Beardsley trope, the gaslights which light the mirror and metaphorically
bring the external world of the street into the boudoir, suggests the prostitute – although we cannot be certain, and they may more generally
represent the urban world in which women occupy the streets, in a con-
fident, self-fashioning (or made-up) way. This cover could be compared
to another Beardsley image from Volume III (October 1894), 'La Dame
aux Camélias', in which an actress similarly looks into the mirror.
Actresses were a significant category in Beardsley's *Yellow Book oeuvre*, at
least in reviewers' eyes.[15] The cover to Volume II certainly suggests male
voyeurism, but it might equally be read as an expression of sexual
freedom, and the performativity of sexual and gender identities.

Beardsley's images, then, hinge on a complex, often indeterminate
play of vision that, at the very least, questions our assumptions about
how we see and interpret the world, unsettling seemingly stable categories such as male/female, exterior/interior, light/dark. In short, there
are many ways of seeing and being seen at play in the *Yellow Book*. The
emphasis on observation and display that Beardsley develops through
a unique visual language is, however, related to the discursive formation of the *Yellow Book's* metropolitanism and does not sit in isolation.
The urban encounters of observing and being observed in the metropolis that we see in Beardsley's images can be read alongside a number of
other illustrations in the *Yellow Book* that also emphasize urban spec-
tating. Walter Sickert's depictions of music halls, for example, in
Volumes II and III, are precisely aligned with the periodical's wider interest in display, artifice, spectacle and urban pleasure. Sickert's painting

Figure 7   Aubrey Beardsley, Cover, *Yellow Book*, III, October 1894.

of a Camden music hall, *Little Dot Hetherington at the Bedford Music Hall*, was published in the *Yellow Book* (Volume II) as 'The Bedford Music Hall' (Figure 8). As a number of critics have observed,[16] Sickert's visual play in the painting relies on unsettling the viewer through the use of mirror reflections, which forces us to question precisely what we are looking at and how we make sense of the visual encounter. In discussing *Little*

Figure 8   Walter Sickert, 'The Bedford Music Hall', reproduced in *Yellow Book*, II, July 1894.

Dot, Anna Gruetzner Robins points out that 'real and reflected images create spatial ambiguities' that work against absolute definition and precision. Similarly, Lisa Tickner suggests that Sickert's work was often in dialogue with other forms of representing urban scenes, including illustrated journalism, reportage, and realist narrative painting, so that his paintings 'offered morally and narratively ambiguous scenes of contemporary life, open to a range of interpretations and solutions.' And as Sickert explained in 'The Language of Art' in 1910, 'pictures, like streets and persons, have to have names to distinguish them. But their names are not definitions of them, or indeed, anything but the loosest kind of labels that make it possible for us to handle them, that prevents us from mislaying them, or sending them to the wrong address'.[17]

Sickert, then, is no less teasing in his way than Beardsley. He offers us scenes of urban entertainment and locates those places specifically, but also engages the viewer in a process of defamiliarization. While the nature of the ambiguities in Beardsley and Sickert are very different in their execution, both suggest the complexity of the relationship between stage and audience, between reader and text, in the city of modernity.

The city of modernity

The *Yellow Book*'s focus on urban experience owes a debt to Charles Baudelaire, the poet of Bohemia for whom the urban and the poetic were synonymous, and his shadow is cast in the periodical in significant ways, although critics have hitherto not explored in great detail the obvious connections. Baudelaire emphasizes distinct kinds of urban experiences, ways of inhabiting city space that have come to define modernity for many critics. In the 'Tableaux Parisiens' section of *Fleurs du Mal*, in his prose poems and especially in his essay on the painter Constantin Guys, 'The Painter of Modern Life', Baudelaire explores fragmented ways of seeing, addressing over and over the glimpsed stranger and the unexpected encounter. For Baudelaire, 'modernity is the transient, the fleeting, the contingent',[18] and 'the observer', he proclaims, 'is a prince enjoying his incognito wherever he goes' (Baudelaire, 400). In a general way, the focus on urban visions in the *Yellow Book* – the theatricality and indeterminacy of Beardsley and Sickert, for example – can be seen in a line of urban cultural production back to the French dandy whose understanding of modernity was related to voyeuristic, see-and-be-seen urban practices in an atmosphere of transformation. But Baudelaire's urban vision appears more obviously between the lines of the first volume of the *Yellow Book*, in Max Beerbohm's polemical manifesto for the 1890s, 'A Defence of Cosmetics', which echoes Baudelaire's 'In Praise of Cosmetics', section 11 of 'The Painter of Modern Life'.[19] Baudelaire champions artifice over nature, and it is through women that the artificial finds its most potent expression:

> Woman is well within her rights, we may even say she carries out a kind of duty, in devoting herself to the task of fostering a magic and supernatural aura about her appearance; she must create a sense of surprise, she must fascinate; idol that she is, she must adorn herself, to be adored. It follows, she must borrow, from all the arts, the means of rising above nature, in order the better to conquer the hearts and

impress the minds of men. It matters very little that the ruse and the artifice be known of all, if their success is certain, and the effect always irresistible.   (Baudelaire, 427)

Despite what nineteenth-century realists might tell us, beauty, according to Baudelaire, comes from making-up rather than from imitating nature. Beerbohm's 'Defence of Cosmetics' makes similar claims, and artifice, perhaps even to a greater degree in Beerbohm, is what makes 'the modern' modern. Indeed, the rise of artifice sounds the death toll for the Victorian era:

> The Victorian era comes to its end and the day of sancta simplicitas is quite ended. The old signs are here and the portents to warn the seer of life that we are ripe for a new epoch of artifice. Are not men rattling the dice-box and ladies dipping their fingers in the rouge-pots?
>
> No longer is a lady of fashion blamed if, to escape the outrageous persecution of time, she fly for sanctuary to the toilet-table; and if a damosel, prying in her mirror, be sure that with brush and pigment she can trick herself into more charm, we are not angry.[20]

Men have become chancers (another motif in Baudelaire, in fact) and women have been artificial: such is the modern way. For Beerbohm, Baudelaire offers a prophetic way of seeing; he is a dandy whose urban vision gets articulated into a satirical, playful defense of the modern over a generation later. The poet of urban modernity, Baudelaire finds his way into the *Yellow Book* through his emphasis on what we see, and how the object is presented for our visual consumption. It is all a performance, like the women making up in Beardsley's images, or the women on stage in Sickert's music halls. The urban world – modernity – offers new sights for the sore eyes of the Victorian era.

That the city should be such a prevalent focus for the *Yellow Book* is not all that surprising, given the prominence of urban interests at the end of the century. In the first two volumes alone, a range of contributors variously address ideas of vision and the city: as we have already seen, Beardsley and Symons, but also John Davidson, 'George Egerton' (pseudonym of Mary Chavelita Dunne Bright), Charlotte Mew, Henry Harland, Katharine de Mattos, Dauphin Meunier, Francis Forster and others. As Le Gallienne suggests, the 'interest in the town and urban things' was one of the defining characteristics of the 'general revolutionary Time Spirit' of the 1890s, when a 'cult of London and its varied life, from coster to courtesans' emerged (Le Gallienne, 122). In his cultural history of London in the 1890s, Karl Beckson suggests that 'the city became for writers of the decade, as it had not been for the mid-Victorians, the symbol of one's soul with implications of spiritual and psychological turmoil.'[21] The *Yellow Book* did not initiate the interest in all things metropolitan, but many of the writers associated with the cult of London certainly converged in the magazine's pages. In this way, the *Yellow Book* is one of the sites where the focus on urbanism can be gleaned. The influence of the artist James McNeill Whistler, in whose paintings of London at twilight and writings about art we can see a distinctly modern urban aesthetic being developed, was felt throughout the *Yellow Book* circle.[22] Consider this well-known passage from Whistler's 'Ten O' Clock Lecture' delivered in London in 1885:

> And when the evening mist clothes the riverside with poetry, as with a veil, and the poor buildings lose themselves in the dim sky, and the tall chimneys become campanili, and the warehouses are palaces in the night, and the whole city hangs in the heavens, and fairy-land is before us – then the wayfarer hastens home; the working man and the cultured one, the wise man and the one of pleasure, cease to understand, as they have ceased to see, and Nature, who, for once, has sung in tune, sings her exquisite song to the artist alone, her son and her master – her son in that he loves her, her master in that he knows her.
>
> To him her secrets are unfolded, to him her lessons have become gradually clear. He looks at her flower, not with the enlarging lens, that he may gather facts for the botanist, but with the light of the one who sees in her choice selection of brilliant tones and delicate tints, suggestions of future harmonies.[23]

Like Baudelaire confronting the limitations of Nature, Whistler positions his artistic vision against realism ('purposeless copying'), which erupts in his great feud with Ruskin, but what is significant here is that the city is the muse, the source of artistic and poetic inspiration. Whistler's urban aesthetic combines many of the tropes of nineteenth-century urban literature and art – the transformative mist, the urban wanderer, the sense of wonder and hidden mystery – which, by the 1890s, are almost the stuff of cliché. Still, well-trodden territory though it was, the city, and in particular London, was one of the great subjects for the 'new literature' and 'new art' at the end of the century, and as

Derek Mahon detects a century later, the *Yellow Book* positioned itself as one of those places where a contemporary urban aesthetic was being defined and explored.

The city of many encounters

Significantly, there is no single urban vision offered in the pages of the *Yellow Book*, and it is this feature – its wide-ranging exploration of urban encounters – that makes the periodical appear so modern. While the *Yellow Book* looks back to Baudelairean ways of encountering the city, the periodical offers more multiple and overlapping accounts of the city which raise questions about gender and sexuality in the representations of the city, in particular. At the same time as it seems to promote Baudelaire's fragmented vision of the city, it also provides fundamental challenges to the gendered nature of Baudelaire's *flâneur*. This dialogic quality in the periodical makes its presentation of the urban all the more vibrant, but also more ambiguous and tentative.

We could examine, for example, the city as place of unexpected, random but significant encounters as one of the dominant visions of nineteenth-century urban literature and it is captured in Charlotte Mew's story 'Passed' in Volume II. The narrator, who craves space, leaves her home and wanders the streets of London, as the dusk descends and the boundary between night and day blurs. Her exploration of the transformative period between night and day is reminiscent of Baudelaire (see his poem 'Dusk', for example) and also of Whistler's mysterious nocturnes. She happens upon a church where she encounters a young girl whose misery touches the narrator:

> My will cried: Forsake it! – but I found myself powerless to obey. Perhaps it would have conquered had not the girl swiftly raised herself in quest of me. I stood still. Her eyes met mine. A wildly tossed spirit looked from those ill-lighted windows, beckoning me on. Mine pressed towards it, but whether my limbs actually moved I do not know, for the imperious summons robbed me of any consciousness save that of necessity to comply.
>
> Did she reach me, or was our advance mutual? It cannot be told. I suppose we neither know. But we met, and her hand, grasping mine, imperatively dragged me into the cold and noisy street.[24]

This chance encounter – 'the magnetism of our meeting', as the narrator later calls it – leads her to a squalid room where the young girl's dead siblings rest. This confrontation with immortality that literally stares at the narrator – 'those dark eyes unwillingly open reached mine in an insistent stare' (Mew, 130) – sends her into a phantom reverie, and eventually she flees:

> My sole impulse was flight; and the way, unmarked in the earlier evening, was unknown. It took me some minutes to find a cab; but the incongruous vehicle, rudely dispersing the haggling traders in the roadway, came at last, and carried me from the distorted crowd of faces and the claims of pity to peace.
>
> (Mew, 136)

Disoriented and lost in an urban land of the unknown (poverty, death), the woman returns home, where her brothers are laughing with friends and a waltz is taking place in the rooms upstairs. In the concluding scene, four months after the encounter in the church, the narrator finds herself among the throng of the crowd at a department store sale:

> The place presented to my unfamiliar eyes a remarkable sight. Brilliantly lit windows, exhibiting dazzling wares, threw into pro-minence the human mart.
>   This was thronged. I pressed into the crowd. Its steady and opposite progress neither repelled nor sanctioned my admittance. However, I had determined on a purchase, and was not to be baulked by the unforeseen. I made it, and stood for a moment at the shop-door preparing to break again through the rapidly thickening throng.
>
> (Mew, 139)

The 'human mart' and the thickness of the crowd suggests 'Virtue's very splendid Dance of Death', and as 'sickening confusion of odours' assails her senses, she recalls the night four months previously when she confronted death and fled. It is only through memory that the narrator makes sense of the unexpected urban encounter which gradually comes to take on a deeper significance, almost to a religious degree.

In Volume III, Henry Harland's story 'When I am King' similarly explores the outcome of a chance urban encounter. The narrator here explores the labyrinthine city of unknown streets – 'I had wandered into a tangle of slummy streets, and began to think it time to inquire my way back to the hotel'[25] – when he turns a corner and is forced to confront his past. As in Mew's story, a kind of magnetism draws the speaker forward, and the sound of a piano playing lures him into a dive bar where he sits enraptured, undistracted by female attentions:

> I don't know why, but from the first he drew my attention; and I left my handmaid to count her charms neglected, while I sat and watched him, speculating about him in a melancholy way, with a sort of vicarious shame.   (Harland, 72)

The sound of the music is the catalyst for memory:

> The tune he was playing now, simple and dreamy like a lullaby, and strangely at variance with the surroundings, whisked me off in a twinkling, far from the actual – ten, fifteen years backwards – to my student life in Paris, and set me to thinking, as I had not thought for many a long day, of my hero, friend and comrade, Edmund Pair . . .
> (Harland, 72)

Pair is an old friend of the speaker's; indeed, he is the object of hero-worship, but a figure now tragic and fallen. He tells his story – of his marriage to a lower class wife who dies (formerly she had been abused by her tailor husband) – but refuses to maintain his friendship with the speaker, preferring to remain detached and apart from such sympathy as figures from the past can offer. In Mew and Harland, chance encounters in the city are revelatory, exposing both the layers of harshness of urban life and the difficulties we have once the urban margins have been revealed. John Davidson's poem, 'Thirty Bob a Week', in Volume II, similarly points out that the city is a place of struggle for a worker whose life is viewed as a cycle of drudgery:

> For like a mole I journey in the dark,
>   A-travelling along the underground
> From my Pillar'd Halls and broad suburban [sic] Park
>   To come the daily dull official round;
> And home again at night with my pipe all alight
>   A-scheming how to count ten bob a pound . . .[26]

Reading through the early, defining volumes of the *Yellow Book*, what we notice is the range of approaches to depicting the city, an almost kaleidoscopic attempt to show the modern metropolis as multiple, shifting and uncertain. There is a celebratory, exultant tone in George

Egerton's story 'A Lost Masterpiece: A City Mood, Aug. '93' (Volume I), in which a woman returns from the country to the city, eager to bathe in the multitude of the crowd: 'The desire to mix with the crowd, to lay my ear once more to the heart of the world and listen to its life-throbs, had grown too strong for me; and so I had come back . . .'[27] Her engagement with the city takes the form of the common pose of the detached onlooker for whom the rush of undeciphered images, sights and sounds lead to reverie:

> The coarser touches of street-life, the oddities of accent, the idiosyncracies of that most eccentric of city-dwellers, the Londoner, did not jar as at other times – rather added a zest to enjoyment; impressions crowded in too quickly to admit of analysis, I was simply an interested spectator of a varied panorama.   (Egerton, 190)

For the narrator, the congested, chaotic imagery of the city is the raw material of poetic vision:

> The tall chimneys ceased to be giraffic throats belching soot and smoke over the blackening city. They were obelisks rearing granite heads heavenwards! Joints in the bricks, weather-stains? You are mistaken; they were hieroglyphics, setting down for posterity a tragic epic of man the conqueror, and fire his slave; and how they strangled beauty in the grip of gain. A theme for a Whitman!
>   (Egerton, 191)

Whitman, of course, was one of the greatest writers of the city in the nineteenth century, a poet for whom the streets of Manhattan offered multitudinous opportunities to encounter the teeming mass of humanity. In Whitman's urban vision, encounters with others are more significant than remaining coolly detached, and in Whitman there is a desire to connect with the objects of the urban gaze. For the narrator in Egerton's story, to engage with the contradictions of the external world of the city streets is, as in Whitman, to engage with the internal world of the self; the seemingly insignificant gets transformed into the deeply meaningful through the imaginative power of the self to (self-)create.

Egerton's streetwalker takes us back to Baudelaire, as so many urban rambles in the nineteenth century do. Baudelaire's figure of the *flâneur* has dominated discussions of the city, at least since Walter Benjamin's exploration of *flânerie* as a defining, alienating experience of modernity. Certainly, Benjamin's reading of Baudelaire, and other urban writers such as Poe, is imaginative and suggestive; the problem is that his reading of the *flâneur* is partial and is often too general a concept to be strictly applicable, either to literary texts or to historical moments. Joachim Schlor makes precisely this point in his book, *Nights in the Big City*:

> Different authors, following Walter Benjamin, have tried to capture the 'socio-historical profile' of this figure, its behaviour and its 'reasons for movement', to link it to a specific historical background, and to trace the changes in the 'type' in the succeeding period. I do not always find the results of such studies convincing, and I believe one of the reasons for this is the fact that the concept is too broad: far too much is to be read into the *flâneur*, is attributed to him.[28]

A great deal of critical energy has been spent measuring Benjamin's understanding of the Baudelairean *flâneur* against figures in literature. A central problem of this approach is that by placing Benjamin's conceptualization of the *flâneur* on top of a literary text, say, the critic simply reproduces the blind spots in Benjamin. One of the most problematic blind spots, as many feminist critics in particular have noted, is that the *flâneur* is a gendered category.[29] Were women *not* a part of street culture in the nineteenth century? Or was there a *flâneuse* who can be identified alongside the *flâneur*? Or, are these simply not the right questions to ask? I prefer not simply to revise Benjamin's category, to prove that women as well as men occupied the streets in similar ways. This approach still holds a rigid binary opposition in place – that there are *male* ways of inhabiting the streets, and there are *female* ways. Simply put, *flânerie*, whether male or female, can ultimately be a reductive way of thinking about the city, because it is set up as an overarching, totalizing way of understanding urban movement which precludes other, different ways of experiencing the city. Again, as Schlor warns us:

> It makes no sense to try and bring all these forms together under the concept of the *flâneur*, and it is worth putting the question more precisely. Who walks, when, where, why, and how? The *functions* of walking in the city are as varied as its forms. For us, one characteristic is particularly important: some – certainly not all – walkers distinguished themselves as *good observers of the urban scene*, and it is this, not the name we give them, that makes their texts interesting.[30]

It is a straightforward point, but one that critics have often been reluctant to make: there are as many ways of walking the streets as there are walkers in the streets. Rather than unify urban experience, we must attend to its multiplicity.

The *Yellow Book*, as I have been suggesting, is one such site where different points of view (some more familiar than others) get explored. Henry Harland's story, 'A Responsibility' (Volume II), challenges the binary grip of male/female street-walking and offers a different way of reading the urban encounter, through the figure of the *cruiser*, rather than the *flâneur* (more Whitman than Baudelaire).[31] If the *flâneur/flâneuse* is the anonymous wanderer who remains detached from individuals in the crowd, and who objectifies the world around him/her through a penetrating gaze, the cruiser is the anonymous wanderer who enters the crowd in order to seek out another individual – to find that other whose gaze meets his own. Cruising is another way of walking the street and producing meaning – another kind of urban practice altogether – and it is a type of urban *function*, erotically charged, that has to do with mutual understandings between individuals.

'A Responsibility' is a simple story – two men meet on holiday in Biarritz; there is an attraction of some sort which never gets explored; they meet again on the street in London, where they remain separated despite their attraction; one of the men, Richard Maistre, commits suicide. The reader knows of Richard's death from the beginning, so the story is set up as the narrator's recollection of their encounters, in an attempt to determine the level of responsibility he must take for the suicide. In this way, it is a very Jamesian story, in which what does not happen has larger moral ramifications than what might have happened.

Like so many other stories in the *Yellow Book*, 'A Responsibility' relies on a dynamic of vision, whether on the city street or not. The narrator and Richard exchange glances and stares over the dinner table in Biarritz, always catching each other's eye. The narrator says that Richard was:

> . . . the only member on whom the eye was tempted to linger. The others were obvious – simple questions, soluble 'in the head'. But he called for slate and pencil, offered materials for doubt and speculation, though it would not have been easy to tell wherein they lay. What displayed itself to a cursory inspection was quite unremarkable: simply a decent-looking young Englishman, of medium stature, with square-cut plain features, reddish-brown hair, grey eyes, and clothes and manners of the usual pattern. Yet, showing through this

ordinary surface, there was something cryptic. For me, at any rate, it required a constant effort not to stare at him. I felt it from the beginning, and I felt it till the end: a teasing curiosity, a sort of magnetism that drew my eyes in his direction.[32]

In many ways, this is a definitive *flâneur*'s point of view, adopting the external world around him as a place to be deciphered – as a mystery in need of interpretation as in Poe's 'Man of the Crowd'. The narrator objectifies Richard, finds him curious, interesting to watch, appealing; yet, he tries (not very successfully) to remain as distant as possible: 'I tried to appear unconscious of him as a detached personality, to treat him as merely a part of the group as a whole. Then I improved such occasions as presented themselves to steal glances at him, to study him *à la dérobée* [on the sly] – groping after the quality, whatever it was, that made him a puzzle – seeking to formulate, to classify him.' (Harland, 'A Responsibility', 105)

The point here, however, is that the narrator is simply unable to remain detached and aloof from his object because Richard continues to return the gaze, making stolen glances *à la dérobée* futile:

As I looked up, our eyes met, and for the fraction of a second fixed each other. It was barely the fraction of a second, but it was time enough for the transmission of a message. I know as certainly as if he had said so that he wanted to speak, to break the ice, to scrape an acquaintance; I knew that he had approached me and was loitering in my neighbourhood for that specific purpose. I *don't* know, I have studied the psychology of the moment in vain to understand, why I felt a perverse impulse to put him off. I was interested in him, I was curious about him; and there he stood, testifying that the interest was reciprocal, ready to make the advances, only waiting for a glance or a motion of encouragement; and I deliberately secluded myself behind my coffee-cup and my cigarette smoke. I suppose it was the working of some obscure mannish vanity – of what in a woman would have defined itself as coyness and coquetry.

(Harland, 'A Responsibility', 105–6)

The narrator's anxiety here is created through an act of reciprocal vision. It is one thing to stare at someone to whom you are attracted, but it is quite another thing to have that person stare back, especially when their eyes seem to suggest longing. This is similar to other urban encounters we have seen in the *Yellow Book*. When the narrator in Charlotte Mew's story 'Passed' comes face to face with the pitiful young girl in the church, she asks: 'Did she reach me, or was our advance mutual?' (Mew, 126) The urban encounter with the other is a fraught exchange, precisely because it *breaks* the rules of the city, forcing connection, rather than reinforcing separation. In 'A Responsibility', the message transmitted between the two men is untranslatable; the content of the stare remains undeciphered and so unspoken, and the visual never becomes the verbal. There is a clear spatial metaphor indicated – Richard *loiters* – a word resonant of casual sexual encounters – in the neighbourhood for a specific reason the narrator fails to understand. Finally, he understands his anxiety, comparing it to that of a flirtatious woman, and thus making the sexual tension of the passage explicit through an act of imaginative gender reversal. Later, the narrator tells us that:

> I was among those whom he had marked as men he would like to fraternize with. As often as our paths crossed, his eyes told me that he longed to stop and speak, and continue the promenade abreast. I was under the control of a demon of mischief; I told a malicious pleasure in eluding and baffling him – in passing on with a nod. It had become a kind of game; I was curious to see whether he would ever develop sufficient hardihood to take the bull by the horns.
>
> (Harland, 'A Responsibility', 111–12)

The phallic imagery of the bull's horns is obvious enough; what is more revealing is that the narrator understands Richard's isolation and alienation from others, but views it all as a game. He knows that he can redeem Richard, can offer hope through mutual recognition by making the visual expressions of desire verbal, but he finally refuses.

The story ends with both men back in London, where they pass each other in St James in the West End. They stop and stare, as is their wont, but the narrator chooses once again not to act and acknowledge the unspoken desires between the two men. The suicide note that Richard leaves is a simple one: '"I have no friends . . . Nobody will care. People don't like me; people avoid me. I have wondered why; I have tried to watch myself, and discover; I have tried to be decent. I suppose it must be that I emit a repellent fluid; I suppose I am a "bad sort"'' (Harland, 'A Responsibility', 115). Harland's story, I suggest, is a different kind of urban encounter than others in the *Yellow Book* and than overly simplified accounts of the *flâneur* are able to elucidate. 'A Responsibility' is a cruising narrative, in which the 'cruise' is unsuccessful because the narrator refuses to acknowledge the true nature of the visual interaction. The psychology of the moment of urban modernity that so puzzles the narrator is a common one, but it is less about alienation than thwarted connection, less about detachment than a longing to be with another.

For the *Yellow Book*, the project to be 'modern' was significantly bound up with the exploration of an urban aesthetic which numerous contributors were a part of. Beerbohm with his Baudelairean, dandiacal pose in praise of artifice; Beardsley with his gender reversals and emphasis on urban vision; George Egerton and Charlotte Mew's accounts of women alone on the streets of the metropolis; Henry Harland's tragic tale of young men visually craving but never connecting — all of these were a part of the kaleidoscopic representation of the city that the *Yellow Book* presented to readers. There is no total visual or urban encounter which serves as a paradigmatic way of understanding the city and its inhabitants, just as there is no one way of representing the city in its pages. On the contrary, what the *Yellow Book* suggests in its bid to encapsulate urban modernity, is that the city is multiple and ambiguous, and many different ways of imagining the city are required in order to express that vision. Rather than trying to locate a central, focal urban experience, in the way readers have sometimes tended to do, we need to walk down all the varied streets of the metropolis. There is no single way of seeing and experiencing the urban world – that is the truly modern aspect of those early volumes.

Notes

1. Derek Mahon, *The Yellow Book* (Loughcrew, Ireland: Gallery Books, 1997), 11.
2. Margaret Stetz and Mark Samuels Lasner, *The Yellow Book: A Centenary Exhibition* (Cambridge: Houghton Library, 1994), 12–18.
3. Anon., 'What the "Yellow Book" is to be', *The Sketch*, 5 (11 Apr. 1894), 557.
4. Anon., 'Our Library Table', *Athenaeum* (21 Apr. 1894), 509.
5. Anon., 'The Yellow Book', *Critic*, 21 n.s. (5 May 1894), 300–1.
6. Anon., 'A Yellow Impertinence', *Critic*, 21 n.s. (26 May 1894), 360 and Anon., 'A Yellow Bore', *Critic*, 22 n.s. (10 Nov. 1894), 316.
7. Richard Le Gallienne, *The Romantic '90s* (first publ. 1926; London: Robin Clark, 1993), 132–3.
8. On the Bodley Head, see James G. Nelson, *The Early Nineties: A View from the Bodley Head* (Cambridge: Harvard University Press, 1971) in addition to Stetz and Samuels Lasner.
9. Critics have frequently suggested that after the trials of Oscar Wilde, the periodical was greatly tamed, necessarily so because the periodical was directly connected in the public imagination with the Wilde scandal. Among other things, it was believed that Wilde was carrying a copy of *The Yellow Book*

when he was arrested – in fact, it was another yellow book altogether, a French novel. (See Laurel Brake, *Print in Transition 1850–1910: Studies in Media and Book History* (Basingstoke: Palgrave, 2001), 154; Katherine Lyon Mix, *A Study in Yellow: The* Yellow Book *and its Contributors* (Lawrence, Kansas: University of Kansas Press; London: Constable, 1960), 140–7). However, as Stetz and Samuels Lasner have recently shown, the *Yellow Book* did not radically alter after the Wilde trials, and when the periodical came to a close in 1897, it was more of a natural ending that a post-Wilde backlash. 'Thus, contrary to myth,' Stetz and Samuels Lasner tell us (38), 'the *Yellow Book* entered its last phase of existence with much of its intellectual vigor and distinctive character intact, still a site of fusion and collaboration across cultural and artistic divides.'

10. Anon., Review of The *Yellow Book*, *The Times* (20 Apr. 1894), 3.
11. Arthur Symons, 'Stella Maris', *Yellow Book* I (Apr. 1894), 129.
12. See, for example, Karl Beckson, *London in the 1890s: A Cultural History* (London and New York: W. W. Norton, 1992), p. 243.
13. Laurel Brake, *Subjugated Knowledges: Journalism, Gender and Literature in the Nineteenth Century* (Basingstoke: Macmillan, 1994), 155 and Laurel Brake, *Print in Transition*, 154.
14. Linda Gertner Zatlin, *Aubrey Beardsley and Victorian Sexual Politics* (Oxford: Clarendon, 1990), 189.
15. Bridget J. Elliott, 'Sights of Pleasure: Beardsley's Images of Actresses and the New Journalism of the Nineties', in *Reconsidering Aubrey Beardsley*, ed. Robert Langenfeld (Ann Arbor and London: UMI Research Press, 1989), 75–6. As Elliott notes, 'La Dame aux Camelias' was previously published in *St Paul's* as 'Girl at her Toilet', which further aligns the image with the cover to Volume II, and suggests the interchangeability of 'actress' for 'woman', 76.
16. See Anna Gruetzner Robins, *Walter Sickert: Drawings. Theory and Practice: Word and Image* (Aldershot, Hants: Scolar Press, 1996), 17–18, and Lisa Tickner, *Modern Life and Modern Subjects: British Art in the Early Twentieth Century* (New Haven: Yale University Press, 2000), 30–1.
17. Quoted in Tickner, 12.
18. Charles Baudelaire, *Selected Writings on Art and Literature*, trans. P. E. Charvet (first publ. 1972; London: Penguin, 1992), 403.
19. John Felstiner, *The Lies of Art: Max Beerbohm's Parody and Caricature* (London: Victor Gollancz, 1973), 9–10.
20. Max Beerbohm, 'A Defence of Cosmetics', *Yellow Book*, I (Apr. 1894), 65 and 67.
21. Beckson, *London in the 1890s*, 266.
22. Whistler was also tremendously influential on Sickert's indeterminate vision. See, for example, discussions in Wendy Baron, *Walter Sickert* (New York and London: Phaidon, 1973), 24 and David Peters Corbett, *Walter Sickert* (London: Tate Publishing, 2001), 15–16.
23. James McNeill Whistler, *The Gentle Art of Making Enemies* (orig. pub. 1890; London: Heinemann, 1929), 144–5.
24. Charlotte Mew, 'Passed', *Yellow Book*, II (July 1894), 126.
25. Henry Harland, 'When I am King', *Yellow Book*, III (Oct. 1894), 71.
26. John Davidson, 'Thirty Bob a Week', *Yellow Book*, II (July 1894), 99.

27. George Egerton, 'A Lost Masterpiece: A City Mood, Aug. '93', *Yellow Book*, I (Apr. 1894), 189.

28. Joachim Schlor, *Nights in the Big City: Paris, Berlin, London 1840–1930*, trans. Pierre Gottfried Imhof and Dafydd Rees Roberts (London: Reaktion Books, 1998), 244.

29. On the debate about women in the city and the figure of the female *flâneuse*, see: Janet Wolff, 'The Invisible *Flâneuse*: Women and the Literature of Modernity,' *Theory, Culture and Society*, 11, 3 (1985); Elizabeth Wilson, 'The Invisible *Flâneur*', *New Left Review*, 195 (Sept.–Oct. 1992), 90–110; Sally R. Munt, *Heroic Desire: Lesbian Identity and Cultural Space* (London: Cassell, 1998). Deborah Parsons usefully re-reads Baudelaire and suggests that his vision of street-walking is much broader than has often been suggested; see Deborah Parsons, *Streetwalking the Metropolis: Women, the City and Modernity* (Oxford and New York: Oxford University Press, 2000). For examples of the insistence of some literary critics to read urban literature rigidly through the image of the *flâneur*, see Dana Arnold, *Re-presenting the Metropolis: Architecture, Urban Experience and Social Life in London 1800–1840* (Aldershot: Ashgate, 2000). Arnold (26–7) unproblematically uses the Baudelairean *flâneur* as the only significant way of walking the streets, with almost no regard for the ways gender, sexuality and other social determinants impact upon urban street movement.

30. Schlor, 245.

31. For a reading of Harland's 'A Responsibility', in the context of late nineteenth century cruising discourses, see Mark W. Turner, *Backward Glances: Cruising the Queer Streets of New York and London* (London: Reaktion Books, 2003), chapter 3. For a more extended discussion of the way the cruiser poses a challenge to the Baudelairean construction of the *flâneur*, see Turner, chapters 1 and 2.

32. Henry Harland, 'A Responsibility', *Yellow Book*, II (July 1894), 104–5.

9

'Atlas' and the Butterfly: James McNeill Whistler, Edmund Yates and the *World*

Patricia de Montfort

For the American-born artist James McNeill Whistler, the pursuit of an audience for his art was central during the years 1878–88. Whistler's artistic credo was based on the romantic notion of the artist as detached outsider; art was 'selfishly occupied with her own perfection only – having no desire to teach.'[1] Having distanced himself from didactic currents in Victorian art, he attempted to explain his views. His pamphlet 'Harmony in Blue & Gold: The Peacock Room' (1877) defined the strictly formal relationship between each element of his celebrated decorative scheme for the Liverpool ship-owner Frederick Leyland.[2] In November 1878, his libel suit against the critic and social reformer John Ruskin placed him firmly in the public spotlight and highlighted his controversialist status. Despite Ruskin's absence from the courtroom due to illness, it brought into focus the most contentious issues in Victorian art – pictorial content versus aesthetic value; labour and finish versus artistic effect. A middle-class Victorian public became intrigued with the personalities and aura of celebrity about the case, and the press coverage was overwhelming.[3] The press provided a ready platform for Whistler's views, and journalistic context became a significant factor in projecting his modernist aesthetic on a middle-class audience puzzled by the abstract qualities of his art. Bankrupted by the Ruskin case, exiled to Venice from 1879 to 1880, and having quarrelled with Leyland, his most important patron, Whistler aimed to exploit the acerbic public persona known to audiences from the trial. The trial, as Whistler later privately agreed, had been a valuable 'advertisement'[4] upon which he hoped to capitalise.

Whistler carved out his career during a period in which entertainment became an important element of the newspaper's function. Along with art magazines, art columns (such as the *Athenaeum's* 'Fine Art Gossip') and columns of social gossip were well established by the 1870s and the successful Whistler became a celebrity. He recognised that by capitalistically exploiting the appetite of the press for news and gossip, he could project the image of a vanguard artist. In an age when celebrity was dependent upon printed word, photographic *carte de visite* and engraver's line, it was the society papers[5] – chiefly the *World*, the *Pall Mall Gazette* and *Truth* – that provided a window for Whistler's views and witty persona. All fell broadly within the framework of the New Journalism. So-called 'personal journalism' was a keynote of its style – intimate, entertaining, crusading – which served the tastes of a middle-class public in a concise and easily digestible form. Both the *World*, a weekly founded in 1874 by Edmund Hodgson Yates and E. C. Grenville Murray, and Henry Labouchère's *Truth*, founded three years later, regularly found space to publish Whistler's letters and report his social doings. The *World* was cosmopolitan and iconoclastic in style. Yates described his formula as 'all the light and gossipy news of the day together with good political and social articles written in a bolder, freer and less turgid style than that in which such topics were commonly handled.'[6] The *World* was progressive in outlook and claimed to be Liberal-independent in politics. While it did not proclaim itself the house journal of London society nor of the educated and media literate, the critical tone of its writing did foster that perception.

Truth aimed at a similar audience, eager for the social and political gossip of the day. A former financial editor of the *World*, Labouchère aimed to rival the paper with his 'Entre Nous' gossip column but *Truth* became particularly known for its hard-hitting investigative journalism. Writing in 1882, Joseph Hatton described *Truth* as 'bitter, personal, brilliant, chatty, impudent, sometimes reckless, always amusing. People bought *Truth* with a desire to see who was 'going to get it'.[7] *Truth* was characterised by an iconoclastic radicalism that was governed by Labouchère's free-thinking politics and personal wealth. This contrasted with the softer tone and well-established formula of the *World*. While the *World* started its life with a reputation for investigative financial reporting during Labouchère's brief tenure (1874–76), the pace of its journalism gradually became more relaxed. As Yates declared, the *World* was intended to be an 'amusing chronicle of current history' (Yates, II, 319).

It is Whistler's encounter with Yates (who quickly became sole editor-proprietor of the *World*), that is the focus of this essay. While both *Truth* and the *World* provided important mouthpieces for Whistler, a distinct relationship developed between the two men through 'What the World

Says', Yates's column of social and political gossip, written under the pseudonym 'Atlas'. The impact of their encounter will be explored in the context of Whistler's volume of collected writings and reviews, *The Gentle Art of Making Enemies* (1890).[8] Most of his appearances in the *World* are reproduced in *The Gentle Art* with each arranged for maximum impact through disingenuous editing, typography and wide margins. I would like to suggest that ultimately, Whistler's posturing in the press set the tone of *The Gentle Art* and made it a publishing success.

Whistler was well acquainted with Yates. Both men were of similar age and frequented bohemian clubland. They probably met through George Sala, a mutual acquaintance, or possibly through shared theatrical connections such as Henry Irving. Indeed, Yates was a minor dramatist. Yates claimed that one of his favourite books was Henri Murger's *Scènes de la vie de Bohème* (Yates, I, 289), the book that Whistler always professed had inspired his student days in the Latin Quarter in Paris during the 1850s. In addition, Yates owned works by Whistler and was a regular guest at Whistler's celebrated Sunday 'breakfast' parties in Chelsea. He was brash, energetic and cosmopolitan by temperament. He was a capitalistic polymath who, like the art critic Tom Taylor, had a long career as a civil servant and wrote novels, plays, and journalism. He knew Thackeray and Dickens, revelled in luxury and kept influential political company. Yates's deputy at the *World*, T. H. S. Escott, wrote of him in 1894:

> In its strenuous and aggressive energy, in its demonstrative ambition, its love of glare, glitter, luxury and material comfort, its undaunted resolution to push its fortune and to proclaim its cleverness and merits, Edmund Yates was in harmony with, and was a favourable type of, the epoch in which he lived and died.[9]

The artist Louise Jopling observed that, like Whistler, Yates could be a 'bitter enemy'.[10] A lecturing stint in America and a period as correspondent for the *New York Herald* encouraged Yates to seek out new formats and readerships. The dramatic critic Clement Scott thought that Yates should be called 'without exaggeration . . . the pioneer of "personal journalism"'.[11] Hatton, Yates's journalistic contemporary, suggested that he may have been aware of the success of a 'Celebrities at Home' feature in the American *Harper's Magazine* (Hatton, 89). Yates also wrote the 'Flâneur' column in the *Morning Star* during the late 1860s, later admitting that its proprietor was in the habit 'of toning me down'. In an interview in 1893 we are told that 'he frequently wires a full-stop, or a semi-colon to the office when on his way home on press nights, should he think such would improve a sentence or make its meaning more apparent!'[12] All these qualities would have appealed to Whistler, whose obsession with fine-tuning his prose is documented in draft after draft letter in the Whistler Archive[13] at the University of Glasgow.

The appeal of Whistler's acerbic, often controversial literary style in his sparring matches with journalist critics with Ruskinian sympathies like Taylor, Harry Quilter, and – later on – Oscar Wilde, was mirrored in the sensationalism and entertainment value demanded of the journalistic trade. Joseph Hatton commented: 'society is cruel. It enjoys the misfortunes of its neighbours' (Hatton, 104). To Francis Phillimore, in the world of the New Journalism in 1888, Whistler seemed 'a singularly able . . . literary man . . . witty in his ideas, clever in his choice of words, brief and full of "touch" – in a word, a model journalist of the new school'.[14] Indeed, Sheridan Ford, Whistler's one-time collaborator on *The Gentle Art*, related that Whistler used to brag that 'he could have been a great newspaper man if he had so chosen'.[15]

Hatton suggests that the traditional links between the press and clubland gossip were formalised by the society papers (Hatton, 104). The society papers enabled Whistler to reach a specific readership (including many of his patrons) via Yates's 'What the World Says' column. Whilst monthly art periodicals such as *Art Journal* and the more progressive *Magazine of Art* sprung up to accommodate middle-class aesthetic taste, their sober tone and editorial structure of long articles, exhibition reviews, and notes were not really compatible with Whistler's persona. Above all, their lack of immediacy did not allow Whistler the same free rein for his polemic. The *Magazine's* editor Marion H. Spielmann (a former contributor to the *Pall Mall Gazette*) recognised this, as he explained to Whistler in 1888: 'I'm not, like you, a full-lance tilting only for yourself & (I don't blame you) getting all the allies & reinforcement you can.'[16] In the *World*, Whistler could 'tilt' for himself. As with the Ruskin trial, he postulated the image of a vanguard artist-Mephistopheles. With his epigrammatic style and veiled allusions to personalities known, Whistler created a rapport with a closely-knit society readership to which he was socially and economically bound. He knew that his acerbic remarks and witty repartee would be heard and repeated in its salons and drawing rooms.

By November 1878, the date of the Ruskin trial, Whistler's first substantial appearance in print had already taken place.[17] On 22 May 1878, he was interviewed for the series 'Celebrities at Home' in the *World*.[18] 'Celebrities at Home' was then a novel and highly successful journalistic format later repeated in such papers as the *Pall Mall Gazette*.[19] As their 'Celebrity No. 92', Whistler was interviewed alongside politicians, royalty and other prominent figures of the day. The interview theme centred upon subject matter and the necessity for the artist to understand his materials. Given his approaching clash in court with Ruskin (who had been featured in the series the previous October), Whistler saw the interview as a useful means of vindicating his cause. Yates stressed at the outset that 'in no case has an article been written without the full consent and authority of its subject'.[20] While the extent to which the interview subject held editorial control is arguable, the illusion of it was maintained. Indeed, a metaphorical microphone has been passed over to Whistler in the opening passage of the interview. Wearing an expression of 'intense earnestness' (we are told), he declares: 'Why not? . . . [W]hy should not I call my work symphonies, arrangements, harmonies, nocturnes, and so forth? I know that many good people . . . think my nomenclature funny and myself eccentric. Yes, eccentric is the best adjective they find for me. . . .'[21] He insists that as music is the poetry of sound, so is painting the poetry of sight.

The intimacy created around the interview subject and the musical-abstract shorthand associated by Whistler with his picture titles correlated with the cosmopolitan style of the paper – knowing, razor-sharp. Whistler's modernist stance is heightened by the uncluttered visual impact of the *World*'s pages. Well-spaced paragraphs float on the page and contrast with the densely packed columns of the *Daily Telegraph* and the *Athenaeum*. Column headings for an issue from July 1878 indicate its style and preoccupations. They included 'Under the Clock' (a parliamentary sketch), 'Celebrities at Home', 'The Genesis of Jingo' (comment on the Eastern Question), 'Beauty's Husband' (witty social comment), 'The Inventor of the Phonograph' (on Thomas Edison), 'The Season' (a satirical poem on the society Season), and 'Feuilleton' (a literary serial).[22] A series entitled 'People You Know' from December 1880 featured caricature sketches of such personalities as Gladstone, Henry Irving, Ruskin, and Lillie Langtry, often accompanied by a satirising rhyme.[23] The aesthetic tastes of the *World*'s readership were reflected in advertisements for the Grosvenor Gallery, Messrs M. A. Lock's Artistic Pottery, Maple & Co's furniture, and Japanese screens.

Between 1878 and 1888, Whistler featured in Yates's 'What the World Says' column. His social events, including his Sunday breakfasts (attended by artistic and literary luminaries of the day such as Wilde) were reported by Yates, a frequent guest. Yates also seized upon gossip about events such as Whistler's controversial resignation from the presidency of the Royal Society of British Artists.[24] This was an echo of Yates's approach in an earlier column for the *Illustrated Times*, 'The Lounger at the Clubs' (1855–63). While it depended upon the bohemian clubs of Yates's own circle of writers, artists, and theatrical people for stories rather than the smarter corners of West End society, it did enable Yates to create a rapport with his readership. In the 1870s Yates's own *nom de plume* 'Atlas' became rapidly known and associated with 'What the World Says'. As Peter D. Edwards has said:

> 'What the World Says' is in every sense the most 'personal' of Yates's gossip columns. By adopting 'Atlas' as his *nom de plume*, in a paper called *The World*, he virtually renounced the anonymity that he had hidden behind, ostensibly at least, as the Lounger at the Clubs and the Flâneur.[25]

The regular appearance of Whistler's letters on artistic and social topics meant that they became immediately recognisable. Yates also valued Whistler's own trademark butterfly signature, with its sting-like tail. Its appearance amidst the spacious paragraphs brought editorial colour and notoriety to his column. Indeed, Whistler's correspondence suggests that a die – a metal printing block of the butterfly – circulated between the offices of the *World*, *Truth* and the *Pall Mall Gazette* on a more-or-less constant basis.[26]

Whistler's butterfly may perhaps be allied with the journalistic world of banner headlines in which, by the 1870s, the identity of the author was being increasingly trumpeted. John Morley believed that to reveal the authorship of an article gave credence to its assertions, especially if the author was an authoritative figure upon the subject.[27] The amplifying profile of the author, in parallel with diversifying journalistic formats in the press, meant that celebrity became a definitive norm in art, literature, and the theatre. The decline of anonymous journalism and abundance of pictorial advertising meant that one's public identity was paraded along with one's views. It is pertinent to note the critic Harry Quilter's complaint about the New English Art Club during the 1880s:

> The art of pictorial advertising has, chiefly owing to the recommendation of the Press, fallen almost entirely into the hands of artists of this new Anglo-Gallic school. Indeed, several of the New English Art Club men are prominent designers of street posters, play-bills, and other advertisement placards [. . .] They are also rapidly coming to

the front as book illustrators [. . .] some of the signatures to these pictures are wholly fanciful ones and occasionally in the same paper
there may be two drawings of which one is signed by the artist's real
name and the other by some *nom de plume* assumed for that occasion only.[28]

Signatures and identities were being affected and rejected, interchanged,
in the pursuit of a marketplace and an audience. Reducing the complexity of this public identity to its essence via the shorthand label of
a signature became a crucial tool. Responding to a comment from Yates
about Quilter, Whistler replied loftily, 'Atlas – In spite of the Kyrle
Society, I don't appeal to the middle-classes.'[29] A large butterfly signature boldly emblazoned the text of his reply. For Whistler, the butterfly
became an imprecise extension of the insult. Its spiky graphic style
and the manner in which it hovers insect-like on the page leaves the
intended 'victim' (and the reader) nervously looking around for the next
Whistlerian barb. What will happen next?

Whistler's sense of dramatic timing and of the importance of presentation runs through his press letters of the late seventies and eighties.
The lessons of the Ruskin trial in 1878 remained with him. In July 1877,
writing about the Grosvenor Gallery exhibition, the most important
new *avant garde* venue of the day, Ruskin had made some serious accu-
sations against Whistler. The review was published in *Fors Clavigera*
(itself conceived in a letter format) and became the subject of the libel.
Ruskin's tone is highly charged:

> For Mr Whistler's own sake, no less than for the protection of the
> purchaser, Sir Coutts Lindsay ought not to have admitted works into
> the gallery in which the ill-educated conceit of the artist so nearly
> approached the aspect of wilful imposture. I have seen and heard,
> much of cockney impudence before now; but never expected to hear
> a coxcomb ask two hundred guineas for flinging a pot of paint in the
> public's face.   (Whistler, 1)

One is deliberately presented with the full force of Ruskin's public personality. As he himself acknowledged in his two-volume collection of
letters, *Arrows of the Chace* (1880), 'All these letters were written with
fully provoked zeal [. . .] expressed with deliberate precision.'[30] Ruskin
harangued the conscience of his audience, claiming that 'I never was
tempted into writing a word for the public press, unless concerning

matters which I had much at heart' (Ruskin, 1880 in Cook & Wedder-burn, 470–1). Always conscious of his role as public controversialist, Whistler displays a certain Ruskinian zeal in his letters. But in the *World* he also dresses up his message as entertainment. His targets are vividly personified: he harangues yet he entertains. When the critic and drama-tist Tom Taylor[31] complained that he had been quoted out of context in Whistler's anti-art criticism pamphlet 'Art & Art Critics', Whistler concocted an elaborate, provocative letter in reply. Parodying Polonius, giver of useless advice in *Hamlet*, he declared:

> Dead for a ducat, dead! my dear Tom: and the rattle has reached me by post.
> 'Sans Rancune,' say you? Bah! you scream unkind threats and die badly.
> Why squabble over your little article? You *did* print what I quote, you know, Tom; and it is surely unimportant what more you may have written of the Master. That you should have written anything at all is your crime.[32]

The effectiveness of Whistler's performances in the press was often dependent upon some form of comic foil – the players must be dressed up as well as the stage. His knowing jibes deliberately poked fun at their professions. Francis C. Burnand was editor of *Punch* and a popular creator of burlesque and light comedy, notably the three-act 'The Colonel' (1881), which satirised aestheticism. To Burnand's views on his aesthetic manifesto, the 'Ten O'Clock Lecture,' Whistler replied in elab-orately mocking tones:

> O! grand Roi des farceurs – [. . .] Nothing could be kinder and nicer than the way in which you would help me – but what will you? – I who had thought my 'Ten O'clock' a scientific writing – the outcome of my work and wisdom – and you, who see in it the success of the Three Act farce.[33]

Yates played Whistler's comic advocate in these kinds of exchanges, publishing Taylor's follow-up letter and other correspondence together in the *World*.[34]

Whistler's jibes against Taylor, Quilter, and others loosely identified with the Ruskin camp together represent a kind of gross caricature of art criticism. All wrote for prominent papers and the ponderousness of Taylor's criticism and Quilter's characteristically hectoring tone was well known to his audience. But ultimately their individual 'sins' fade into the background alongside the persiflage that Whistler creates around them as in, for example, his vivid personification of Quilter as ''Arry'. The character probably has its roots in a music hall song, but may also be connected to the satirical figure of that name that flourished in *Punch* from the late 1870s. Most likely, Whistler had both in mind.[35] As Patricia Marks describes, he represented *'Punch's* anti-hero'. 'Arry is 'brash, vulgar and Tory down to his toes, he provides a witty and thought-provoking gloss on social and political issues.'[36] In 1881, 'Arry was portrayed by Harry Furniss in *Punch* as 'The Cheap Aesthetic Swell'.[37] Quilter had become well known for his public attacks on aestheticism that he portrayed as vacuous and morally corrupting in his essay 'The New Renaissance: or the Gospel of Intensity' (1880).[38] The association between Whistler's nickname for Quilter with 'Arry must have stung the unfortunate art critic.

Under his *nom de plume* 'Atlas', Yates, devotee of the stage, had the histrionic instincts to heighten the impact of his interjections with Whistler. If he did not see a contribution forthcoming from Whistler, Yates would encourage him to join the fray. In December 1883, parodying his own gossip-mongering, he provoked Whistler with the report:

Mr Whistler's last Sunday breakfast of the year was given on Sunday last. The hospitable master has fresh wonders in store for his friends in the new year; for, not content with treating his next-door critic after the manner that Portuguese sailors treat the Apostle Judas at Easter-tide, he is said to have perfected a new instrument of torture. This invention is of the nature of a camera obscura, whereby a craft 'arrangement' of reflectors, he promises to display in his own studio, to his friends, ''Arry at the White House', under all the appropriate circumstances that might be expected of a 'Celebrity at Home'.[39]

In writing the story, Yates knew that Quilter had purchased Whistler's studio house the White House, after his bankruptcy in 1879, much to Whistler's great injury. So did many of Yates's society readership. A reply from Whistler was bound to amuse them. On 27 December, far away in Cornwall on a painting trip, he wrote his reply:

I have read here, to the idle miners – culture in their manners curiously, at this season, blended with intoxication – your brilliant and graphic description of 'Arry at the other end of my arrangement in telescopic lenses.

The sensitive sons of the Cornish caves, by instinct refined, revel in the writhing of the resurrected 'Arry.

Our natures are evidently of the same dainty brutality. Cruelty to the critic after demise is a revelation, and the story of 'Arry pursued with post-mortem, and, for Sunday demonstration, kept by galvanism from his grave, is to them most fascinating.[40]

Once Whistler became associated with the *World*, a kind of expectation of future instalments rapidly established itself. In this Yates played a part, enticing his readership to follow the story in a manner akin to a fiction serial. When Harry Quilter set himself up as a candidate for the Slade Chair of Fine Art at Cambridge, this was Yates's invitation to Whistler:

Please to take note my dear Mr James McN. W., that your 'dearest foe' 'Arry is a candidate for the Slade Chair in the University of Cambridge! This is said to be the age of testimonials. A few words from you, my dear James, addressed to the distinguished trustees after the manner of your Ten o'Clock, with which you recently so delighted [. . .] would not fail to give 'Arry a lift. His competitors are, I fear, likely to be a sorry lot. What say you, my dear James? 'Why don't you speak for yourself sir?'[41]

On 24 February Whistler replied, 'Atlas you provoke me!' and claiming 'Now, in truth, 'Arry is dead – very dead. Did I not, from between your shoulders, sally forth and slay him? Thereby instructing – and making history – and avenging the beautiful?'[42] Weeks later Whistler, having managed to obtain a copy of the testimonial used by Quilter to canvass for the Professorship, sent Yates a mocking parody of it. 'Read, Atlas,' he urged 'and seek in your past for a parallel.'[43] In the final letter of the sequence, Whistler presented heavily edited extracts of Quilter's testimonial in the form of a dialogue with Yeats, 'Had Alma [Tadema] the classic aught in common with this 'Arry of commerce? Believe him not, Atlas!' The incident perhaps represents the culmination of the encounter between Whistler and Yates in the *World*. It has all the familiar elements – dialogue, arch wit, wide spacing within the page for maximum impact. In his guise as Butterfly-scorpion, Whistler removed himself a pace or two from his readership. The extraordinary and ethereal Butterfly, a motif with well-rooted theatrical and artistic associations, was pitched opposite the so-called pedantic and vulgar – the unfortunate Quilter.

In the early 1880s, Oscar Wilde, rising poet and lecturer on aesthetic matters, became a contributor to the *World*. He also joined Whistler and Yates on stage in 'What the World Says.' Whistler and Wilde were well aware of their paired reputation as wits and exploited any opportunity to spar publicly. It was prudent to join forces. The *World* printed their most celebrated exchange of telegrams in November 1883:

> From Oscar Wilde, Exeter, to J. MacNeill Whistler, Tite Street –
> Punch too ridiculous – when you and I are together we never talk about anything except ourselves.
> From Whistler, Tite Street, to Oscar Wilde, Exeter –
> No, no, Oscar, you forget – when you and I are together, we never talk about anything except me.[44]

A 'performance' between Whistler and Wilde would often be rehearsed in private before the carefully composed exchange would find its way to an appropriate editor. It became a kind of game. Wilde wrote to Yates's deputy, T. H. S. Escott, at the *World:*

> There is an ominous silence from 'Jimmy' over the way; if he sends my letter to the World, I wish you wd. not publish it till I can write my answer. There is no delight unless both guns go off together.[45]

Years later, Quilter would accuse both Yates and Wilde (who was identified closely with Whistler for a much of the eighties), of being 'mixed up' in his row with Whistler. He claimed that Yates 'not only admitted their [Whistler and Wilde's] attacks, which always took the form of personalities, but identified himself with them whenever occasion served'.[46] Yates, the *agent provocateur*, had become part of the 'game.'

However, as the 1880s progressed, Whistler grew resentful of his younger rival and their paths began publicly to diverge. With Yates' collusion, the *World* became a platform for his increasingly bitter attacks on Wilde. Wilde, self-declared Professor of Aesthetics, asserted: 'I differ entirely from Mr Whistler. An Artist is not an isolated fact; he is the resultant of a certain *milieu*. . . .' The poet 'is the supreme Artist,' Wilde argued, 'for he is the master of colour and form, and the real musician besides.'[47] Whistler's reply was swift and caustic: 'I have read your exquisite article,' he wrote, 'Nothing is more delicate, in the flattery of "the Poet" to "the Painter," than the *naïveté* of "the Poet," in his choice of his Painters – Benjamin West and Paul Delaroche.' Wilde's rejoinder warned Whistler against explaining himself away by lecturing on art: 'remain as I do, incomprehensible'. Yates, always quick to seize the moment, joined in and published both letters together under the gently mocking heading 'Tenderness in Tite Street'.[48]

Through the 1880s, Whistler had struggled to assert his specialist status and artistic originality in an atmosphere of multiplying technologies in which such notions were being questioned, yet at the same time, increasingly valued. By November 1886, irked by what he saw as Wilde's 'amateur' status and borrowing of his aesthetic ideas, Whistler asked: 'What has Oscar in common with Art? except that he dines at our tables and picks from our platters the plums for the pudding he peddles in the provinces.'[49] Wilde's reply, addressed to Yates, was brief: 'Atlas, this is very sad! With our James vulgarity begins at home, and should be allowed to stay there.'[50] Aided by new journalistic formats and Yates's sharp editorial skills, the *World* echoes two different strands of aestheticism in which Whistler's isolationist stance distances him from Wilde's more socially engaged model.[51]

By 1890, the columns of 'What the World Says,' through which Whistler and Yates had carried on much of their dialogue, were transposed to the pages of *The Gentle Art*. Included were his quarrels with Ruskin, Wilde, Taylor, Quilter and others. Like a frame within a frame, Whistler presented an artfully conceived construction of his career in *The Gentle Art*. In the *World*, Yates developed a journalistic style that was abrasive yet compelling, intimate yet of the modern-day urban world. These qualities enabled it to command an estimated readership that jumped from 6,000[52] to an eventual average weekly sale of 22,000.[53] Whistler and Yates had common commercialising instincts for entertainment and the commodification of personal trademarks. This enabled Whistler to engage with a specific upper-middle-class audience of aesthetic tastes, from which many of his supporters derived. Sparring matches with Quilter, Taylor, and Wilde in which Yates often acted as impresario intensified the entertainment value of the *World*. Ultimately, society journalism inspired *The Gentle Art* and Whistler's reputation as a nineteenth-century wit and modern-day celebrity, a reputation that lingers today.

Notes

1. James McNeill Whistler, *The Gentle Art of Making Enemies* (London: Heinemann, 1892), 136.
2. The contents of the leaflet filtered through the press reports (see 'Notes on Art & Archaeology', *Academy*, 250, 17 Feb. 1877, 147).
3. Reports appeared in *The Times*, the *Daily Telegraph* and at least a dozen other newspapers. For an authoritative account of the trial, see Linda Merrill, *A Pot*

of Paint: Aesthetics on Trial in Whistler v Ruskin (Washington DC: Smithsonian Institution Press, 1992), 2.

4. Whistler to James Anderson Rose, 6 December 1878 (Library of Congress, Manuscripts Division [hereafter LCMS], Pennell-Whistler Collection, Box 4).

5. Society journalism should perhaps be related to developments in America such as Joseph Pulitzer's *New York World*. Early-nineteenth-century British models are typified by Theodore Hook's *John Bull* and the *Age*. For a useful account of the genre, see Laura Smith, 'Society Journalism,' *Newspaper Press Directory* (London: C. Mitchell, 1898), 80–1.

6. Edmund Yates, *Edmund Yates: His Recollections and Experiences* (2 vols; London: R. Bentley, 1884), II, 308.

7. Joseph Hatton, *Journalistic London* (London: Sampson Low, 1882), 96, 104.

8. A second expanded (now standard) edition was published in 1892. The book ran to more than six editions and remains in print.

9. T. H. S. Escott, Obituary, *New Review*, July 1894, 88.

10. Louise Jopling, *Twenty Years of My Life* (London: John Lane, 1925), 271.

11. Clement Scott, Obituary, Edmund Yates, *Mitchell's Newspaper Press Directory* (London: C. Mitchell, 1895), 84.

12. Harry How, 'Illustrated Interviews. no. XXIV – Mr Edmund Yates', *Strand Magazine*, July 1893, 86.

13. Some 7,500 documents are housed in the Department of Special Collections, Glasgow University Library, Glasgow, Scotland.

14. Francis Phillimore, 'Mr Whistler', *Merry England*, X, Jan. 1888, 588.

15. Mary Humphrey and Don C. Seitz, 'The Story of Sheridan Ford – International Critic', *Detroit Free Press*, 30 April 1922, 8.

16. Glasgow University Library (hereafter GUL), MS Whistler M102, 20 June 1888. Having been forced to resign the presidency of the Royal Society of British Artists, Whistler sought Spielmann's help to attack his successor Wyke Bayliss in the press.

17. Whistler had already published two letters clarifying picture titles in the *Athenaeum* (5 July 1862 and 22 Nov. 1873). However, I regard these briefer excursions into print as belonging to an earlier and separate period in his career.

18. 'Celebrities at Home no. XCII: Mr James Whistler at Cheyne Walk', *World*, 22 May 1878, 4–5.

19. Discussed further in Anon., *The Progress of British Newspapers* (London: Simpkin, Marshall, Hamilton, Kent, n. d., [1901]), 17.

20. Edmund Yates, Preface, *Celebrities at Home*, first series (3 vols, London: Office of 'The World,' 1877–9), I, 1.

21. *World*, Celebrities at Home.

22. *World*, 31 July 1878.

23. *World*, 22 Dec. 1880, 15–19.

24. A colourful report appeared in the column 'Gossip from Paris', *World*, 20 June 1888, 22.

25. Peter D. Edwards, *Dickens's 'Young Men': George Augustus Sala, Edmund Yates, and the World of Victorian Journalism* (Brookfield, VT: Scolar Press, 1997), 146–7.

26. F. G. A. Whistler to H. E. Morgan, [Feb. 1885], Freer Gallery of Art, Washington DC, Freer, 189.

27. John Morley, 'Anonymous Journalism,' *Fortnightly Review*, VIII, Dec. 1867, 287.

28. Harry Quilter, ed. Mary Quilter, *Opinions on Men, Women and Things* (London: Swan Sonnenschein, 1909), 367–8.

29. *World*, 17 May, 1882, 14. Whistler was mocking the philanthropic aims of the Kyrle Society, founded in 1877 in memory of John Kyrle (1637–1724), an English philanthropist. It promoted the idea of art as a means of social improvement.

30. John Ruskin, *Arrows of the Chace* (1880) in *The Works of John Ruskin*, ed. E. T. Cook and Alexander Wedderburn (39 vols; London: George Allen, 1903–12), XXXIV, 470–71.

31. Tom Taylor (1817–80) was art critic of *The Times* from c.1857–80.

32. Whistler was paraphrasing the line 'How now! A rat? Dead for a ducat, dead!', from Shakespeare's *Hamlet*, III. iv. 23. Whistler's letter is dated 8 January 1879 (see note 34).

33. Whistler to Frances Cowley Burnand, [Feb. x Mar. 1885], GUL, MS Whistler P699.

34. Whistler-Taylor correspondence dated between 6–10 January 1879. Published together in the *World*, 15 Jan. 1879.

35. 'Arry's long association with the paper commenced in *Punch's Almanack for 1874*.

36. Patricia Marks, ' "Love, Larks & Lotion": A Descriptive Bibliography of E.J Milliken's " 'Arry" Poems in *Punch*', *Victorian Periodicals Review*, 26 (1993), 67.

37. 'The Cheap Aesthetic Swell', *Punch*, 81 (30 July 1881), 41.

38. Quilter, *Opinions*, 339–76.

39. *World*, 26 Dec. 1883, 10.

40. *World*, 2 Jan. 1884, 17.

41. *World*, 17 Feb. 1886, 14.

42. *World*, 24 Feb. 1886, GUL, Whistler Press-cuttings.

43. *World*, 24 March 1886, 17.

44. *World*, 14 Nov. 1883, 16.

45. Wilde to T. H. S. Escott [c. late February 1885], British Library, Department of Western Manuscripts, Escott Papers, WiL. 4.

46. Quilter, *Opinions*, 136

47. 'Mr Whistler's Ten O'Clock,' *Pall Mall Gazette*, 21 Feb. 1885, 1–2.

48. *World*, 25 Feb. 1885, 14. Tite Street, Chelsea, home to Whistler and Wilde, through which the street had gained currency as the home of aestheticism (an image popularised by George du Maurier's *Punch* cartoons).

49. *World*, 17 Nov. 1886, 16.

50. *World*, 24 Nov. 1886, GUL, Whistler Press-cuttings.

51. See Regenia Gagnier's useful discussion of Wilde and consumer culture in Regenia Gagnier, *Idylls of the Marketplace: Oscar Wilde and the Victorian Public* (California: University of California Press, 1986; Aldershot, Hants, 1987), esp. 14.

52. Edwards, 143.

53. Although it was admittedly overtaken by *Truth* (see Gary Weber, 'Henry Labouchère, *Truth* and the New Journalism of Late Victorian Britain,' *Victorian Periodicals Review*, XXVI, 1, Spring 1993, 36).

Part IV
Political Encounters

10
The *Dart* and the Damning of the Sylvan Stream: Journalism and Political Culture in the Late-Victorian City

Aled Jones

In the centre of Birmingham, England's 'Second City', stands a piece of public sculpture by Dhruva Mistry entitled 'The River'. Erected in 1993 as part of the pedestrianisation of Victoria Square, it comprises a monumental female figure (the 'life force') who reclines on a series of mountain peaks and holds in her hand a bowl out of which flows a fountain of water which descends by gravity down a series of steps to another pool, in which kneel two youthful and healthy figures, emblems of a young and vigorous city. Carved on the rim of the upper pool is a line from T. S. Eliot's 'Burnt Norton', 'And the pool was filled with water out of sunlight . . .'.[1] Mistry's monument celebrates the city's nerve and vision in capturing, a century earlier, a plentiful supply of fresh water from the first of a series of dams erected by the city's founding fathers 73 miles away in the highlands of the Elan Valley in Radnorshire, central Wales. It assumes a natural and organic connection between the city and those distant hills, its 'hinterland', that improved the health of Birmingham's people, increased the prosperity of its urban economy and underpinned its urban growth and its political status.

A radically different set of images of the engineered 'river' that connected Birmingham to Wales, however, may be seen elaborately articulated, in words and visual images, in the pages of Birmingham's late-Victorian satirical press. The most forceful oppositional readings of the city's water scheme, and of the notion of civic progress it symbolised, are to be found in the pages of the *Dart*. Started by Robert Simpson

Kirk[2] in October 1876 as a Liberal 'journal of sense and satire', and positioned in relation to Birmingham much as the *'Illustrated London News,* the *Graphic* and the *Sketch* are to national history',[3] its 16 pages included four full pages of advertisements, but with adverts also squeezed into the margins, the total advertisement content came closer to 50% of the printed page space, including virtually the entire front page (Figure 9). A further six pages were devoted to gossip, comment and travel, four pages to theatre news and reviews, and one weekly cartoon.[4] The last issue appeared in September 1911.

For the *Dart*, the idea of drawing water from the mountains of Wales for consumption in Birmingham was bizarre, expensive and unnecessary. It provides evidence that there were at least some voices in late-Victorian Birmingham that contested the values that were a century later to be embedded in Mistry's monument to triumphant Victorian urban progressivism. Yet while their view of the world has been sidelined by the story of the city's modernisation, the positions adopted by the 'antis', and the ways in which they were expressed, suggest much about the multi-layered and conflictual political culture of the city at a formative moment in its history. Those positions structure an alternative set of readings of the political and technological processes that legitimated the damming of the headwaters of the river Wye, Wordsworth's 'sylvan stream',[5] from the 1890s. At the same time, they also point to a differently imagined relationship between Birmingham and its Welsh 'hinterland' that connects and overlaps notions of geography, cultural difference and power in the late-Victorian city.

In terms of the uses made of it by twentieth-century historians, the *Dart* must rank among Michael Wolff's 'sub-minor documentation . . . a representatively unknown Victorian serial' which, when raised 'from obscurity to accessibility', is a pearl that undoubtedly shimmers in the waters of Wolff's 'golden stream'. However, arranging the periodical's transition from 'submerged existence' to a position where it might cast a 'broader light . . . on the Victorian world' involves two substantial difficulties, both of which were addressed by Wolff in his 1982 study of the *British Controversialist.*[6] One involves the description of 'something as complex and extensive as the file of any journal . . .', the other refers to the question of representation and the point at which 'the periodical becomes representative only of itself'.[7] Both are pertinent to the examination of the *Dart* that follows, and both are partly resolved by conclusions drawn from Wolff's collaboration, first with Celina Fox and later with Joanne Shattock, that conceptualised the Victorian press as 'essential' cultural forms 'both in the creation and the revelation of a

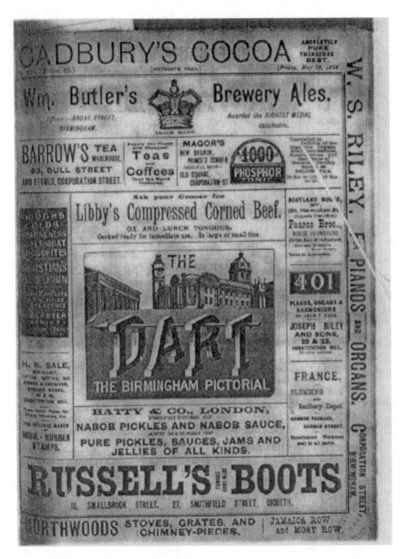

Figure 9 Title page, *Dart*, 13 May 1892.

general urban culture'[8] and as 'the verbal equivalent of urbanism'.[9] The close study of that journalism, they went on to argue, would enable historians to engage with the 'self-consciouness' of the city, and with types of evidence 'which told the city-dweller about himself as well as telling the historian about the reader'.[10] The historical approach to the Victorian periodical press in its urban contexts that follows has also been informed by two other groups of insights. One, closely associated with the urban context of journalism, emanates from the debates around the idea of the transformation of the bourgeois public sphere in nineteenth-century Britain.[11] The other turns around the ways we theorise our engagement with the language of the past, and how we read the subjectivities of voice, register and dialect.[12] Reading periodicals as discourse also raises the problem of illustration, and of how words and pictures interact to produce meaning. Here, the work of Patricia Anderson, Roy Porter, Brian Maidment, and Peter Sinnema have been particularly germane and influential.[13] The *Dart* and other satirical Birmingham publications, like the *Owl* and the *Town Crier*, no less than the ubiquitous city dailies, spoke to their contemporary readers, and now speak to us, through the line as well as the word, and Brian Maidment has rightly urged us to focus attention on the interaction of word and image 'at the level of the page'.[14] I shall attempt to read the *Dart* also at the level of the periodical, both as an issue and as a serial, and at the level of what Peter Sinnema calls, in relation to the first decade of the *Illustrated London News*, the 'moment'. The *Dart*'s moment, for my purposes here, was its engagement with its world through and around its response to the arguments that raged over Birmingham's Welsh water scheme in the spring and summer of 1892.

Much, though by no means all, of our work as students of periodicals has in one way or another been influenced by arguments around the public sphere and the so-called linguistic turn. Furthermore, Jon P. Klancher's development of the idea of the late eighteenth-century periodical as a coloniser of 'social groups previously excluded from it' has been particularly fruitful.[15] However, a case can also be made for adding a spatial dimension to Klancher's reading of the press, especially during the Victorian period. We are familiar with the notion that the periodical press, particularly the newspaper press, as a product of industrial capitalism is, in its very periodicity, a means of imposing order on time. It might also be helpful to think of periodicals as instruments for the ordering of geographical space, or as a form of territorial mapping. The territories they survey, and report, and distribute copies to, and take advertisements from, can sometimes appear remarkably well-defined and yet startlingly strange, their boundaries conforming to no very obvious political or demographic borderlines. And the ways in which those borders change over time can be mapped in much the same way as political boundaries may after wars, say, or, and this is possibly a better analogy, the way the geographical distribution of occupational or language groups may change from one census to the next. The *Dart*, as a non-metropolitan, midland periodical, defined its own space, its own area of operation, in relation to the hierarchies of power that it observed operating in the very large region that surrounded its own city. Seen in this way, a reading of the *Dart* in 1892 not only disturbs the city's own preferred progressive historical narrative, but it can also suggest different ways of reading the history of Britain in the nineteenth-century, in particular in relation to the tensions generated between cities, regions and the British state.

The *Dart* in its moment of political opposition to the city authorities in 1892 operated within a very particular set of circumstances. It is important to recall that Birmingham in 1892 was a relatively new city, having acquired city status by royal charter only in 1889. But it was a new city too in terms of its social policy. Under Joseph Chamberlain's leadership as Mayor, Birmingham in the 1870s successfully experimented with the corporate municipalisation of its basic utilities, in a locally driven initiative that was to become known as gas and water socialism. The Welsh water scheme, which gestated slowly during the 1880s, was regarded by its advocates not only as a continuation of that enlightened social policy, but as its culmination, the final guarantor of the city's long-term viability, in particular of its public health and its economic prosperity. After Chamberlain had moved on to the national political stage as a Birmingham MP, the local supporters of the scheme included the city's most prominent elected representatives. Thomas Martineau, nephew of Harriet Martineau and Mayor of Birmingham from 1884 to 1887, who, from 1891, served as chairman of the city's Water Committee, was a leading proponent of the Welsh water scheme. Lawley Parker, Mayor from 1891 to 1893, was equally committed. Together, with the aid of the civil engineer James Mansergh, whose idea it originally was,[16] they stepped up their campaign in 1890 and 1891, winning a Liberal majority in the Council chamber in support of the venture, and seeking the approval of Parliament to proceed with their purchase of the Welsh water-catchment area early in 1892. There they faced two significant forces of opposition. One was London, concerned that Birmingham's principal motive was to steal a march on the capital by preventing it from getting its hands on Welsh water. Birmingham's need, it was argued, was less physical than political. Birmingham disagreed, insisting on the inadequacy of its supply, and opposed any further delay. Other opponents put the Welsh case. In March, T. E. Ellis, the MP for Merionethshire who shortly afterwards was appointed Gladstone's Chief

Whip, argued that it was Welsh water, and should be used for the economic improvement of Wales itself, pointing to the needs of the rapidly expanding coalfields and iron industries of Wales's south and south east. Following a bravura performance in the Commons by Joseph Chamberlain in defence of the scheme, Birmingham won the day against both the London and the Welsh MPs. As a result, the city began on its largest and most expensive collective project, enclosing 70 square miles of central Wales, an area larger than Birmingham itself, paying substantial sums in compensation to landowners, railway companies and fishery interests, and resettling the inhabitants of some 390 small farms. The use by Birmingham of scientific expertise, particularly that of its chief engineer and most talented propagandist, James Mansergh, in support of its case had been crucial to its success. It was he, personally in committee, as well as through advice to supportive MPs on the floor of the House of Commons, who rebutted criticisms that the scheme would desiccate the Wye, and poison the people of Birmingham with impure water drawn from the bogs of mid-Wales. He also argued that higher rates would be offset by other savings, such as the £60,000 a year that would be saved on soap because of the natural softness of the water.[17]

Birmingham's victory thus followed some very effective political management, locally as well as nationally. In a sophisticated public relations exercise, leaders of the City Council employed every means possible to win support. Lectures, public meetings, magic lantern shows, and exhibitions were held across the city for months on end, all of which was reported in and further promoted by the daily and weekly press. The scheme's advocates had to win four arguments: firstly, that the scheme was necessary in terms of the future of the city; secondly, that it was the only valid option; thirdly, that water from that source was safe and clean for domestic as well as industrial consumption; and finally, that it was worth the cost in increased rates. The city's most powerful newspaper proprietors and editors pounded out the Council's case, day by day, week by week, for several months, and then continued to justify it for several years afterwards. Those newspapers were, after all, closely tied to the city's ruling Liberal elites. John Thackeray Bunce, proprietor of the *Birmingham Daily Post*, had in the 1860s been a member of the Shakespeare Club, which also included such figures as George Dawson, who in the post-Chartist years had grasped the importance of the local forms of government, captured the City for the Liberals, effectively created Joseph Chamberlain and guided his path to the Mayorship, and thereby virtually invented the modern city of Birmingham.

The publicity drive also took place in the run-up to a General Election, which further intensified media activity in the city, and increased the political stakes in a year that saw a further swing to the Liberal Party nationally. On 8 July 1892, the *Dart* complained that

> newspaper enterprise in Birmingham is outdoing all previous record. Election editions at 11.30, 12.30, 1.30, midnight, and at 5.0 in the morning, besides the score or so of usual editions during the day, are too much for endurance by ordinary humanity. Life is too short to permit of careful reading.

In this high pressure atmosphere, the *Dart* alleged that Birmingham, and the country, was being bulldozed into supporting the Welsh water scheme. Paradoxically, it argued, the daily press was producing too much information – geological maps, microbiological analyses of different water sources, engineering plans – which the majority of its readers were incapable of understanding. Furthermore, approved Liberal newspapers became by proxy the city's official historians. Asked by opponents of the water scheme about its projected cost, Mayor Lawley Parker affected ignorance and advised them to 'look it up in the newspapers in the Public Library'.[18] This prompted the *Dart* to ask whether elected city politicians or the editors of newspapers were in control of the city. Even more significant was the decision taken by the Council to chronicle the entire history of the water scheme, from its inception through to the Royal opening of the first of the dams in 1904. This chronicle fills two thick volumes, which consist wholly of cuttings from the key Liberal newspapers.[19] Newspaper coverage was thus re-edited into a second redaction that told the linear story of battle and triumph the way the Council leadership and its allies in the press themselves saw it.

For the *Dart*, these were all agents of an interfering and arrogant city government. In the face of their physical as well as ideological dominance, the *Dart* offered a different reading, an unofficial version of Birmingham's history. Donald Gray has pointed out that 'scandal is potentially unsettling, for it is not an amusing or denigrating addition to the news. It is rather an invitation to a dark reading of the news itself'.[20] From Roman Polanski's dramatisation of the politics of water in inter-war California in his film *Chinatown* to Arundhati Roy's ongoing protests against dam construction in northern India, it is apparent that where some see cleanliness, improved public health, and industrial growth as results of big hydrological schemes, others see conspiracy, official arrogance, and corruption. The *Dart* provides precisely such a 'dark reading' of the doctrine of urban improvement through the use of technology in late Victorian Britain. It was not alone. In 1894, William Michael Rossetti decried Birmingham's drowning of the Elan Valley, which in 1812 had been Shelley's home, and where he had written his 'The Retrospect: Cwm Elan 1812', 'The Tombs', and 'On Robert Emmet's Grave', and where he had lived with Harriet Westbrook. Observing how Shelley had drowned in the Mediterranean, and Harriet in the Serpentine, Rossetti mourned the drowning of the site of their lost love, 'a world of waters, a world of death', striking a tone markedly at variance with the modernist assumption that water was a life-giving substance.[21]

But in 1892, largely devoid of such gloomy sensibilities, the problem for the scheme's opponents in Birmingham was primarily one of expense. Economist opposition to the water scheme was complicated by the presence in Birmingham of three satirical weeklies, each of which in their different ways reported on and pursued the story. The oldest was the *Town Crier*, founded in 1860 by progressive allies of George Dawson and the Shakespeare Club in the interests of good city government. While attacking 'incompetent and pretentious' councillors, its main role was to ridicule and outflank the retrenchment instincts of the more obdurate ratepayers and to advocate cautious 'improvement'. Its approach to the water scheme in 1892 was thus typically nuanced: while scorning the penny-pinching of the ratepayer opponents, it also questioned the motives of councillors in supporting that particular scheme. The youngest journal was the *Owl*, a Gladstonian Liberal serio-comic paper started in 1879. Though never fully in sympathy with the ratepayer opposition, it nevertheless ruthlessly pursued the turncoat Chamberlainite tendency wherever it was imagined to be. Of the three, it was the *Dart* that associated itself most closely with the anti-water scheme faction, both in terms of its politics and in the column inches that it devoted to the issue. If, then, as some in the city believed, 'the opposition [had] got into bad hands', and that 'the agitation [had] been left to a few cranks',[22] then one of the most vocal yet at the same time the most reclusive of those cranks was Robert Simpson Kirk, proprietor and editor of the *Dart*. His very public conversion from Liberalism to Conservatism prompted his rivals on the *Owl* to dismiss him on 25 August 1879 as the 'disestablished and disendowed Scotch Kirk'. No obituary, or much in the way of other extraneous evidence about him, has to date been found. More is known about its first illustrator, George Henry Bernasconi, who produced a weekly cartoon for the *Dart* from its launch in 1876 until the end of 1878. Bernasconi had earlier worked with Matt Morgan, illustrator of the *Tomahawk* in London,[23] then in

1879 went on to the *Owl*, and, from 1880, began to contribute illustrations prolifically to the *Town Crier*. In the early 1890s, the *Dart*'s weekly illustrator was Ernest Chesmer Mountfort, whose cartoons were sold annually for a guinea a set in limited cloth-bound editions.[24] In 1886, Mountfort was contracted by W. T. Stead to illustrate the Christmas number of *Review of Reviews* with some 40 drawings of the Gladstone-Chamberlain split over Home Rule. He later produced Chamberlain's campaign posters for the Tariff Reform League.[25]

A few extracts make clear the *Dart*'s approach to the water scheme. On 19 February 1892 it claimed that 'opposition to the water scheme is gaining ground daily. The impression is that the scheme is the latest product of officialism . . . (which) feeds on great schemes, and grows fat. . . . When a ratepayer asks the simple question it is not enough to refer him to files of the daily papers.' On 11 March 1892 it noted that 'The *Daily Post* gave an elaborate defence of the new Water Scheme on Monday, but touches very lightly on the financial aspect of the question. Now, this is what is bothering everybody. Why not tell us clearly how much will be added to the rates when the Welsh water is on tap?' On 13 May 1892, 'Welsh water is full of lead and arsenic . . . In fact, it seems to be dangerous stuff this Welsh water, and not at all safe to drink without Scotch whisky'. And on 1 July 1892, it greeted the election of the opposition ratepayer leader Samuel Lloyd to the Council as 'a protest against the extravagant policy . . . of the Town Council. The union of the Liberal-Chamberlain party and the Tories has removed all opposition on economic grounds to big schemes. But the suffering ratepayers in Central Birmingham are determined to have a word. . . . The *Dart* was the only paper which backed up Mr Lloyd and hoped he would win, and *voted* for him too.' The following week, in the middle of the election campaign, the *Dart* declared that 'we are firmly of the opinion that the Conservatives are a vital preserving, and upholding force in the State, and we never admired the Liberalism of Bright and Chamberlain when they used to insult the Conservative citizens and deny them civil rights because they denied them all the patriotic virtues', thus nailing its party colours firmly to the mast at the national level, despite its criticisms of the Tories for falling in line behind the water scheme locally. On 5 August 1892, complaints from Liverpool that their Welsh water supply from Lake Vyrnwy was 'being continually cut off, and when it is on, it is full of sand' were gleefully reported.

In the course of this relentlessly negative campaign against the scheme, the loyalties of other journals in the Birmingham periodical constellation began to shift. The Gladstonian *Owl* of 5 August 1892 caught a whiff of corruption in the payment of £1,000 by the Council to Orton Smith, the Town Clerk, for 'engineering the (Welsh Water Scheme) Bill through the House of Commons', calling the payment a 'scandalous misappropriation of the public funds', and suggesting that

> Folks are beginning to regard the water Scheme in its real light. [While] they cannot affirm that Birmingham is built upon the top of Amazons or Mississipi (sic) as some would have us believe, [a reference to the *Dart*] . . . they do think that the Scheme has been 'rushed' just to flatter the ambitious aspirations of a few aldermen. The Town Council have never attempted to discover alternative schemes. They have produced a proposal which does credit to their ingenuity, but it is imprudent on their part to say that their pet project is the only one deserving of consideration.

For the *Dart*, however, the scheme was not only corrupt in practice but wrong in principle. Studies by E. P. Hennock, Geoffrey Crossick, Norman McCord and others have vastly improved our knowledge of Victorian ratepayer's movements, and Birmingham's was not dissimilar to those of nineteenth-century Liverpool, Newcastle and elsewhere.[26] It was characterised by the *Birmingham Post* principally as a movement driven by the greed of landlords who objected to paying the additional water rates on behalf of tenants living in 'small-house property, precisely the kind of property which most needs looking after by the sanitary authorities, and which would derive most benefit from a full and plentiful supply of pure water'. A survey of some 300 large shopkeepers in the city centre revealed that only 2% of them supported the Elan scheme.[27] It was among this social constituency that the *Dart*'s opposition to the water scheme found its resonance.[28] Personified by Mountfort as the serious-faced Jester (Figure 10), his quiver full of arrows, sobering up a Council, drunk on social reform plans and wretchedly suffering from the delirium tremens caused by its addiction to the 'rate craze', the *Dart* insists on the possibility of building a clean, healthy, and prosperous city at little or, preferably, no cost to the ratepayer.[29]

The *Dart* of 1892 had thus positioned itself precisely around economism, cleanliness, practicality, a rejection of 'officialism' and 'big schemes', and an attachment to the powerful myth of individual self-sufficiency. But there is more to the *Dart* than a political movement in print. Taking the periodical as a whole, at the level of the 16-page individual issue, and at the level of the serial run, at least in our 'moment'

THE SLAVERY OF THE RATE CRAZE!

Figure 10   'The Slavery of the Rate Craze!', *Dart*, 11 March 1892.

defined by its preoccupation with the Welsh water scheme, we can read
in the *Dart* a fundamentally different way of imagining the city. And it
is not only the city's internal arrangements that are being imagined differently here, but also its position in relation to its adjacent territories.
It looks outwards as well as inwards. Like the Liberal city newspapers
that are ranged against it, it looks westwards. Where the *Post* and
the *Mail* construct the mountains of central Wales as the vital and

scientifically verifiable source of the city's future prosperity, health and public order, the *Dart* looks to a different hinterland.

Some 60–70% of the editorial content of the *Dart* in 1892 is concerned with the affairs of individuals in a cluster of streets in the city centre. Its overwhelming preoccupation is with reviews of, and behind the scenes gossip from, the theatres, music halls and the Council House. The other 30–40% of content, however, covers forms of amusement and leisure in towns and villages some 150 miles distant on the north and west coasts of Wales. When it is not criticising city councillors for their mad infatuation with Wales, the *Dart* prints stories about Wales, the very source of all that troublesome water, and the unhappy cause of its rate increases. By eliding leisure in the city with leisure on the beach, Wales is being read and imagined as if it were part of the city. It was continuing a long tradition of English writing about Wales, from the reports of tours in the late eighteenth century to the huge commercial success in the 1850s of George Borrow's *Wild Wales*. Artists such as Turner and Wilson travelled Wales in search of the picturesque, and found a landscape which they conceptualized as both exotic and not too distant from the English cities. The railways, ruefully accused by Thomas Carlyle in 1850 of having 'set all the Towns of Britain a-dancing . . . confusedly waltzing, in a state of progressive dissolution',[30] further opened up the north and west coastlines to urban tourists. They also extended and accelerated distribution networks for periodicals, including those from Birmingham. Throughout 1892 (though the process actually begins much earlier), the *Dart* regularly printed descriptions of Welsh seaside villages,[31] reviewed their best beaches, walks, seaside attractions, and social activities, profiled their 'characters', and advertised their hotels.[32] Having damned the damming of Welsh water for consumption in Birmingham, the *Dart* praised Welsh seaside towns for the excellence of their drinking water, and their health-giving properties. It also actively promoted the development of these towns. On 5 August 1892, it refers to the 'lively suburb of Birmingham, called Rhyl. You know I have set Llandudno a-going, and it is getting on pretty well. Now I am putting Rhyl on its legs.' It presses for gas lighting and other improvements to Rhyl's amenities, and even criticises the authorities there for not raising sufficient rates to pay for them. Seen in this light, the *Dart* also operates as a travel agency, which may be explained by its commercial connection with railway companies and their excursions.[33]

But if the *Dart* targets a different Wales from the one that was endlessly being discussed in the Birmingham dailies, the languages of their respective approaches are remarkably consistent. Both sought to improve the Welsh landscape, to civilise its people and to extend the English language. The ridiculing of the Welsh for the unreasonableness of their language was as commonplace in the satirical weeklies as in the daily newspapers. The following excerpt is by no means untypical:

> Llandudno, which the stupid Welshers will persist in calling 'Clandidno', after the manner of their consonantal language, which baulking all etymological rules, continually pops up in an inconsequential way and with but the slightest apparent reason, was all agog last Saturday resulting from a descent upon her, in force, of a novel Brummagem contingent.[34]

While encouraging readers to imagine Wales as part of their own city, the *Dart* was anxious that cultural influence should not flow in the other direction. 'I noticed a small house in a new row at King's Heath has been christened "Cader Idris". What next? They will be calling their homes "The Himalayas", and why not "Asia" or "Africa"?'[35] News that R. W. Dale, who owned a second home at Llanbedr, a village 'almost untouched by English influence' some eight miles from Barmouth on the Welsh coast,[36] had by the early 1890s started to learn Welsh aroused general amusement.

> Dr. Dale is learning to speak Welsh. Well, it's a good language to speak, for . . . if a man can speak Welsh he can speak anything. We are glad to hear that Dr. Dale can speak in any language; his ill-health and his inability to set his loyalty to Liberalism above his idolatry of Mr. Chamberlain have of course kept him out of public life, and perhaps some had begun to fear that he had grown unfamiliar with his native tongue.[37]

In their different ways, then, both sides of the water debate valorized Wales as a source of enjoyment, health, and the city's general well-being. Both regarded these territories as an under-developed estate in the city's own back-yard that was ripe for development. At the same time, both sides ridiculed, homogenized, and essentialized the Welsh as irrational opponents of modernity as represented by the city and its culture. 'Taffy is jealous', wrote another leader writer in another Birmingham newspaper, the *Rural World*, on 5 August 1892, 'over English townspeople getting their water from Wales. . . . Taffy has no use for the water himself.' But how was it that both sides in the water-scheme controversy were so fixated by the Welsh territories to their west? There are two closely related explanations, both of which return us to the idea of the periodical as the verbal equivalent of urbanism, to the connection between the press and the city.

The first is that the City Council and the *Dart* were imagining, articulating and consuming Wales in two very different ways. Whereas the former advocated the collective incorporation of a part of Welsh land as a public resource and utility, the latter advocated its private consumption through commercial tourism. One is tempted to see them as the Welsh seaside faction against the Welsh mountain faction. In Mountfort's cartoons, the sea often makes fools of the water schemers[38] and in 1902 it may be seen washing away the childish plans of the Council, which were nothing more than sand castles.[39] Secondly, though, the tensions generated by the playing out of these two very different ideologies of the city during the spring and summer of 1892 find a resolution of sorts in the notion of the city as an imperial entity, as a centre that reaches out to claim, in one form or another, its estate to the west. The *Birmingham Post*, for example, had announced that at Elan they were 'proposing to make one of the remotest and wildest districts of Mid Wales . . . an outlying and yet integral and essential portion of Birmingham'.[40] Years later, looking back at the achievements of 1892, Lawley Parker remarked that in the intervening years the city had not only 'learnt how to manage an estate of 43,000 acres one hundred miles away . . . (but) we have founded a colony. . . . What would Birmingham be to-day without its Welsh water'.[41] That control of space had not only happened on the ground, it occurred also, albeit in very different ways, in the pages of Birmingham's newspapers and magazines, at the level of print and the imagination as well as in the form of dams and pipelines.

Welsh response to the scheme, at least amongst Liberals in the Commons, was outspoken. Swansea Liberal MP Hussey Vivian, protested in 1892 'against the Principality being regarded as a carcass, to be divided according to the wishes and the wants of Birmingham and London'[42] while an alarmed T. E. Ellis argued that 'water supply is . . . a national question',[43] meaning both that it was a Welsh national question (he argued that the rapidly expanding industrial areas of south-east Wales needed the water of the Elan more urgently than did the urban planners of Birmingham) and a matter of British state planning, an issue which might only properly be decided by the national Parliament, not by individual city corporations. By calling for a Royal Commission on water resources he was taking refuge in the constitution, insisting in the supremacy of the nation over the city, of Britain over Birmingham.[44] Yet, in time, Welsh fear of the power wielded by the large English city corporations fuelled national consciousness and, in the 1960s, led to the only serious nationalist political violence in twentieth-century Wales.

In conclusion, this exploration of the satirical journal as a textual 'equivalent of urbanism' has sought to position the *Dart*, at a certain moment, in relation both to a formative urban political issue, and to the structure of journalism, the periodical economy, of the city. Both approaches identify the *Dart* is an irritant in the city's dominant narrative of modernisation since it projected an altogether different idea of how the city should be organised internally, and on what terms it should reach out externally. By mobilising one Victorian urban identity against another, pitching the private world of the self-sufficient middle-class, with its commercialized leisure, economism, and retrenchment, against the public vision of a corporate politics allied to scientific and engineering knowledge, the *Dart* complicates the city's history, and asks different questions about its conduct. But while, in terms of its own self-image, it claimed to speak for the 'people' against the 'officials', it nevertheless speaks also for the city as a whole, the city as an identity, as a centre that competes with other centres for land and resources. In its own peculiar way, the *Dart* too addressed an imagined 'Greater Birmingham' that extended as far as the north and west coasts of Wales. At a time when historians are becoming increasingly interested in a history of Britain which reconceptualises Britishness in terms of conflicts and negotiations between its diverse nations and regions, it might be considered pertinent to extend beyond Birmingham a study of the ways in which periodicals imaginatively mapped the internal and external territories of the Victorian city. Comparative studies of the *Dart* and satirical magazines in other British towns and cities might in future allow the courses of such 'submerged' Victorian periodicals to be charted in novel and productive ways.

Acknowledgement

An earlier version of this article was delivered as the Michael Wolff Lecture at the annual conference of the Research Society for Victorian Periodicals, Birkbeck College, University of London, 21 July 2000, and published in *Victorian Periodicals Review*, 35 (2002), 2–17. The title, along with so much of my work on periodicals, is deeply indebted to Professor Wolff's critical paper on 'Damning the Golden Stream', delivered at the Research Society for Victorian Periodicals Conference ('The

Periodical Press: production, bibliography, theory') held at Aberystwyth, 19 July 1987. See also his earlier, seminal article, 'Charting the Golden Stream', *Victorian Periodical Newsletter*, n. 13 (1971).

Notes

1. For a brief illustrated history of the monument, known locally as 'the floozie in the jacuzzi', consult the Birmingham City Council website at *www. birmingham.gov.uk/history* ('Statues and Public Art'). The verse is from T. S. Eliot, *Four Quartets*.
2. For Kirk, see the *Owl*, 28 Aug. 1879. I am grateful for the kind assistance of Mr Stephen Roberts and Mr Lewis Jones in tracking down this elusive journalist.
3. *Dart*, Oct. 1876.
4. John S. North, *The Waterloo Directory of English Newspapers and Periodicals 1800–1900* (5 vols; Waterloo: North Waterloo Academic Press, 1997), II: 1381.
5. William Wordsworth, 'Lines composed a few miles above Tintern Abbey, on revisiting the banks of the Wye during a tour, July 13, 1798', *Complete Poetic Works* (1888).
6. Michael Wolff, 'The British Controversialist and Imperial Inquirer, 1850–1872: A Pearl from the Golden Stream', in Joanne Shattock and Michael Wolff, eds, *The Victorian Periodical Press: Samplings and Soundings* (Leicester and Toronto: University of Leicester Press, 1982), 369.
7. Shattock and Wolff, eds, 391–2.
8. Celina Fox and Michael Wolff, 'Pictures from the Magazines' in J. Dyos and M. Woolf, eds, *The Victorian City* (2 vols; London and Boston: Routledge and Kegan Paul, 1973), II: 59.
9. Shattock and Wolff, eds, *The Victorian Periodical Press*, xiv.
10. Dyos and Woof, eds, *The Victorian City*, II: 197.
11. Many of these debates have emerged from Jürgen Habermas's *The Structural Transformation of the Public Sphere*, trans. Thomas Burger (London: Polity Press, 1989).
12. Most significantly in the work of Patrick Joyce, especially *Visions of the People: Industrial England and the Question of Class 1848–1914* (Cambridge: Cambridge University Press, 1991) and *Democratic Subjects: The Self and the Social in Nineteenth-Century England* (Cambridge: Cambridge University Press, 1994).
13. Patricia Anderson, *The Printed Image and the Transformation of Popular Culture 1790–1860* (Oxford: Oxford University Press, 1991), Brian Maidment, *Reading Popular Prints 1790–1870* (Manchester: Manchester University Press, 2001), Roy Porter, 'Seeing the Past', *Past and Present* (1988), 186–205, Peter Sinnema, *Dynamics of the Pictured Page: Representing the Nation in the Illustrated London News* (Aldershot: Ashgate, 1998).
14. Brian Maidment, '*The Illustrated Exhibitor* (1851–52): John Cassell and the Artisans', unpub. RSVP conference paper delivered at Yale University, 17 September 1999.

15. Jon P. Klancher, *The Making of English Reading Audiences, 1790–1832* (Madison: University of Wisconsin Press, 1987), 25.
16. For Mansergh, see *Birmingham Daily Gazette*, 21 July 1904.
17. Andre Anderson, 'A Magnificent Sequcel": Birmingham, the Elan Valley and the Politics of the Exploitation of Welsh Water Supply in the 1890s' unpub. Ph. D. (University of Wales Ph.D., forthcoming); T. Barclay, *The Future Water Supply of Birmingham* (1898), passim.
18. *Dart*, 19 Feb. 1892.
19. 'Newspaper cuttings relating to the Birmingham Water Scheme', vol. I, 1891–97, Birmingham City Library, 115557. See, for example, cutting from *Birmingham Weekly Post*, 19 Mar. 1904 on 'Birmingham's Niagaas'.
20. Shattock and Wolff, eds, *The Victorian Periodical Press*, 327.
21. William Michael Rossetti, 'Shelley at Cwm Elan and Nantgwilt', in R. Eustace Tickell, *The Vale of Nantgwilt, a Submerged Valley* (1894) 17–35. See also *Birmingham Gazette and Express*, 21 July 1904.
22. *Owl*, 26 Feb. 1892.
23. *Birmingham Faces and Places*, vol. v, 1893, 83.
24. *Dart*, 13 May 1892.
25. Obituary, *Birmingham Mail*, 2 June 1922.
26. E. P. Hennock, *Fit and Proper Persons: Ideal and Reality in Nineteenth-Century Urban Government* (London: Edward Arnold, 1973), Geoffrey Crossick, ed., *The Lower Middle Class in Britain, 1870–1914* (New York: St Martin's Press, 1977), Norman McCord, *North East England: An Economic and Social History* (London: Batsford Academic, 1979).
27. Lewis William Jones, 'Aspects of Birmingham Community Power around 1900. A Study in Decision-Making', unpub. M.Phil., University of London, 1992, 163–5.
28. A comparison between the *Dart* in Birmingham and the *Porcupine* in Liverpool might prove highly suggestive. For the *Porcupine*, see Sally Sheard, 'Water and Health: The Formation and Exploitation of the Relationship in Liverpool, 1847–1900', *Trans. of the Historic Society of Lancashire and Cheshire*, 1993, 143 (1994), 141–59.
29. *Dart*, 11 Mar. 1892.
30. Thomas Carlyle, *Latter-Day Pamphlets. VII Hudson's Statue* (1850), 226.
31. Examples include 'Sketches of Llandudno' and 'Whitsun-week at Barmouth', *Dart*, 17 June 1892. 'Views at Pwllheli, North Wales', 12 Aug. 1892, 'Sketches around Barmouth', 3 Sept. 1897.
32. *Dart*, 10 June 1892 and 17 June 1892.
33. For example, *Dart*, 3 June 1892, on the 'North Wales Passenger Service'. See also advertisement for 'Tours in Wales' in the *Moseley Society Journal, Holiday Guide Supplement*, May 1898.
34. *Birmingham Owl*, 27 May 1892.
35. *Dart*, 24 June, 1892. Cader (properly Cadair) Idris is a mountain of 2,928 ft in south-west Merionethshire.
36. There, according to his son, he 'kept open house – open to all; and his friend-liness went far to break down the barrier of suspicion and reserve that kept the two races strangers and apart', A. W. W. Dale, *The Life of R. W. Dale of Birmingham, by his Son* (1898), 588. For an account of Dale's contribution to the municipal politics of Birmingham, see Gill Conrad, Asa Briggs, et al,

History of Birmingham (2 vols; Oxford: Oxford University Press, 1952), II: 69.

37. *Birmingham Owl*, 2 Sep. 1892.

38. *Dart*, 5 Aug. 1892.

39. *Dart*, 7 Mar. 1902.

40. *Birmingham Post*, 11 Dec. 1891.

41. Conrad Gill and C. G. Robinson, *A Short History of Birmingham* (Birmingham: Corporation of the City of Birmingham, 1938), 71.

42. *Birmingham Daily Mail*, 9 Mar. 1892.

43. See, for example, the report of Ellis's speech in the 1892 Parliamentary debate on the Elan scheme in Barclay, 104.

44. Ellis proposed that 'the appropriating (of) gathering grounds . . . should be an Imperial matter', quoted in Jones, 'Aspects of Birmingham Community Power', 129.

11
Islam, Women, and Imperial Administration: Encounters and Antagonisms between British and Colonial Authors in the Victorian Press

Julie F. Codell

> The voice of certain alterities, kept silent by the valorized culture, begins to enter the dialogue, thereby complicating the meanings and contextual fabrics of the art objects and disrupting inherited historiographic legacies.
>
> Zeynep Çelik, 'Colonialism, Orientalism, and the Canon'[1]

The above quote by Çelik assumes several points that have dominated studies of orientalist discourses. One is the dichotomous nature of this discourse between the colonial power and the colonized peoples. Another is that entry of the colonized speaker into this discourse is an entry as 'Other', or as an alterity, into the discourse. In this paper I will interrogate and explore these assumptions through several contentious debates between British and Indian authors in the Victorian press. These exchanges defy a simple dichotomy between a 'valorized culture' and a valorized alterity; all the Indian authors I will examine claim authority/identity as British, *and* as 'native'. Neither British nor 'other' is monolithic, and scholars following in the wake of Edward Said's landmark study have increasingly investigated these interstices and multiplicities to question the identity/alterity dichotomy. Many argue that nations are heterotopias in which identities blend or overlap, crossing the discourse with divergent views and political antagonisms.

Indian authors wrote on behalf of British values and culture, as well as on behalf of their native cultures, as the Victorian press offered

Indians living in Britain a platform. These authors re-presented British and colonized cultures to British readers, redefining, criticizing, and juxtaposing Enlightenment ideals and orientalisms. Looking at debates between British and Indian authors published in the press, on the three most debated topics – Islam, colonized/native women, and imperial policy – I will explore a series of antagonistic encounters in which colonized speakers responded to hostile attacks. These authors undercut their British antagonists by juridical and judicious arguments and claimed authority by virtue of their own participation in British culture, as well as by their colonial identity.[2]

Antagonistic debates present some unique textual situations. Gayatri Spivak applies the term 'worldling' to the inscription by the West on what the West perceives as uninscribed territory (e.g., colonies as 'uninhabited' or 'discovered'). Spivak calls this 'a texting, textualising, a making into art, a making it into an object to be understood'[3] which contained and foreshadowed 'the planned epistemic violence of the imperialist project'.[4] Dominated by Orientalist discourses *and* by their desire to reach a British readership, colonial authors re-texted and re-textualized their cultures as both 'native' and British to generate discourses of resistance and modification. As native informants living in Britain, they were distanced from indigenous subaltern forces and sometimes represented their 'people' in Orientalist terms as anti-progressive and superstitious. However, they were just as often sympathetic to resistance which they employed rhetorically to perform their own elastic subjectivity stretched between Anglicised hegemony and indigenous subalternity, neither of which they fully inhabited. As Mrinalini Sinha and others have argued, colonizer and colonized were both unstable terms defining heterogeneous groups constructed out of historical 'alliances across various axes of power' and subject to changing material conditions and identities.[5] As native informants, Indian authors argued that their insights were vital to the successful continuation of the British Empire because the Empire was always precariously poised among natives ever ready to resist and rebel. Political instability in the Empire empowered native informants' recommendations as means for protecting the Empire, making them invaluable allies of the British. Indians arranged themselves on all sides of these issues, pro- or anti-British, reformist or anti-reformist.

Colonial authors embodied multiple selves as intermediaries arguing for greater autonomy under British imperial administration. They described their native (or 'native') countries as manageable and progressive and demanded restraints on imperial authority. They saw the

British from a native perspective and understood well the orientalizing discourse, applying oriental stereotypes to the British themselves in rhetorical reversals. But they also saw themselves through British eyes. Their English education and privilege led them to measure their native cultures by European standards.

Authors understood their opportunity to use the press as a platform to educate the British public about what was 'real' in their cultures and to revise stereotypes they knew British readers harboured. Protap Chunder Mozoomdar, newspaper editor and apologist for British rule, praised England for the 'freedom of public opinion'[6] that allowed for and encouraged lively encounters between Britons and Indians. In one case, an editor even jumped into the debate, increasing its sensationalism. The most compelling rhetorical device was colonial authors' appeal to British readers against the civil servants whom these authors accused of failing to uphold British ideals. For these authors the British reader became the hope and the site of Enlightenment ideals of fair play against which were pitted 'bad' British imperial administrators. Indian authors wrote *to* the British public in order to de-textualize British rule, interrogate its political and legal policies, and turn their own cultures from textualized to discursive. Colonized authors sought to re-inscribe their 'native' cultures as historical to make possible changes in native cultures. This historicity offered British readers knowledge of the material conditions of native populations that de-universalized British laws and policies and thus made it possible to conceive of change in the colonies and the conditions under which those changes could occur.

Christianity versus Islam

The three most popular debated topics were not discrete. One frequent defence of Islam was that Islamic women were better off than British women and had more rights.[7] Comments on issues relating to imperial policy often defended and explained Muslim or Hindu religious beliefs. The most contentious debate was over the nature of Islam, its historicity and practice as opposed to an essentialized, 'medieval' theology. Canon Malcolm MacColl, in his anonymous 1895 *Quarterly Review* book review of several volumes on Islam, described Islam as carrying 'the seeds of inevitable decay', modified by Westernization, as when the Spanish taught Muslims to inhibit the 'licentiousness . . . of harem life', while the Spaniard learned the 'dignified deportment and magnificent air of the Arab'.[8] But these exchanges only temporarily concealed Muslims' 'vices', including hostility to learning. Citing 'impartial' historians, both British and Muslim, MacColl claims the Moors were 'utterly corrupt', unable to 'amalgamate with the native population and thereby receive that regeneration which the mixture of races so often imparts' (233). MacColl, morphing religion into race, described Muslims as having a barbaric 'native character' (231–2). Once they gave up the manly discipline of warfare, Muslims, synonymous with Arabs for MacColl, began their 'process of dissolution' to 'become utterly effete, . . . decomposing germs' against Christian and Jewish 'antiseptic spray' (233–4). This scientized medical vocabulary of hygiene brought Islam into late Victorian degeneracy discourse.

MacColl orientalised Islam as identical to the Arab who was 'not only useless but pernicious', despite 'a fine and subtle brain with rare powers of acquisition and assimilation', talents which increased as 'he recedes from the heart of Islam'. Causes of Islamic degeneracy were '1, intellectual bondage inherent in the Musulman [sic] system; 2, the moral teaching and example of Mohammed; 3, the inflexibility of Islam as a social and political system, making progress impossible to its votaries' (234). MacColl attacked what he considered dogmatic adherence to the Koran, exemplified by Khalif Omar sanctioning the burning of the library at Alexandria (supported with citations from Islamic historians). Islam was incompatible with 'civilization and free thought', and incapable of science (242). He attacked Mohammed as a power mad, licentious, womanizing, incestuous autocrat, and of the Islamic 'type' – rigid, rule bound, tied to religion not nation, society, or language, within a 'cosmopolitan militant Papacy' (243).[9] His exemplum of Islamic faults was Turkey, 'a military theocracy . . . condemned by its constitution to remain immutable' (251) and impermeable to reform, making the Ottoman Empire 'an anachronism in the midst of modern civilization', whose end was inevitable, as Europeans would eventually liberate it (253).

MacColl's identity as the writer of this book review was revealed in his article in the *Fortnightly Review*, October 1895.[10] Justice Syed Ameer Ali, prominent Islamic jurist and one of the authors of the books MacColl attacked, responded to MacColl in two essays.[11] Ameer Ali was a frequent contributor to *Nineteenth Century* and a critic of imperial policies throughout the 1880s and 1890s. In 'Islam and its Critics' in *Nineteenth Century* his rhetoric orientalized MacColl, whose essay was typical of 'wicked and immoral attempts of inferior men to stir up religious animosities . . . and passions . . . by his malignant onslaught' against Turkey, 'leading to mischievous consequences' by stirring up 'feelings of the uneducated and ignorant masses'.[12] In 'Islam and Canon MacColl' in November 1895, he characterised MacColl as a 'vulgar and disgrace-ful' fanatic whose 'seeds of dissension and discord, encourage discon-tent and agitation', which might lead to 'murderous reprisals', portraying MacColl as hysterical and diabolical.[13] In both of his essays he peppered his prose with Latin quotes and with the pronoun 'we' that eradicated differences between him and his British readers, and he insisted on the loyalty of Indian Muslims to the Crown (Nov. 1895, 785).[14]

Above all, Ameer Ali historicized Islamic law and culture. He described the Koran's content and compared Muslim cultural rises and falls to European ones, due in both cases to circumstances of invading hordes, as well as periods of peace, learning, and progress. He cited changing practices in post-Koranic texts over centuries, citing Islamic law's prin-ciple of precedent that is also fundamental to English law. He cited English jurists to support his views, argued for Turkish civility toward Christians in its law courts, and corrected misinterpretations of Arabic legal terms by English authors (Nov. 1895, 783).

Ameer Ali separated law from morality – 'sometimes the moral sense of the people is in advance of their laws, as in the case of slavery and woman's property in England' – to sarcastically remind British readers of their own 'backwardness' only recently corrected by the Married Women's Property Act, 1882. He also distinguished morality from reli-gion and religion from progress (Sep. 1895, 374): Muslim communities practising polygamy did so against its condemnation by the Prophet and Imams. True Muslims advocated monogamy and exhibited toler-ance for other cultures, while Christian history was marred by genocidal rampages. His sarcastic tone met MacColl's attack with a survey of Chris-tian hypocrisies: polygamy, persecution, prostitution, murder, torture, and intolerance of other religions and of each other, a typical litany of Christian cruelties deployed by colonial authors. Christians practiced polygamy, *droit de seigneur*, and concubinage, and Ali strategically cited European authorities (Sep. 1895, 370–2). He historicized both Islam and Christianity, quoting Gibbon, among other English sources, to support his argument.[15] Referring to the 1857 mutiny, he touched British anxi-eties as he compared Muslim anger and revenge against traitorous fellow Muslims with English post-Mutiny anger and unchristian brutal revenge against those '*supposed* to have risen against constituted authority' (Sep. 1895, 369: italics mine).

But Ameer Ali also accepted some orientalizing assumptions: 'It is per-fectly true that Mohammedan countries are in a more or less backward state; that they have not advanced in material civilisation at the same rate as the European countries', due to historical events such as invasions by brutal hordes (Sep. 1895, 362). He adamantly transferred difference from a sign of *essential* traits to a sign of *historical* circumstances, embracing the fluctuations of all civilizations, Muslim or Christian. Evolutionary and cyclical models eliminated explanations by racial inferiority, innate Islamic backwardness, or inevitable Christian progress.

He argued that Muslim law was like English law, constantly evolving and adapting. He cited Orientalist scholars and histories, classical authors, and the Hedâya and Muslim civil law, which, he pointed out, the 'fanatical' MacColl 'Naturally . . . cannot be acquainted with' (363). Like many colonial authors he concluded with a veiled threat while identifying himself with British interests ('ours'): vicious attacks on Turkey, such as MacColl's, may drive the Turkish 'into the arms of any Power whose interests are not identical with *ours*' (Sep. 1895, 379; italics mine). Such threats played on Europeans' anxieties and competition, while appearing to identify with English anxiety over such alliances. He argued that the real threats were 'agitators [like MacColl] whose object is not the improvement of the Ottoman Empire, but its dismemberment', a greater threat to British alliances and to Turkey's reform (Sep. 1895, 380).

The editor of *Nineteenth Century*, James Knowles, also participated in this debate. Publishing MacColl's letters to Knowles (December 1895, with MacColl's permission) in which MacColl complained about Ali's reply, Knowles responded that MacColl began the attack and offended the periodical's Indian Muslim readers – the journal was 'much read in India' (1081) – through MacColl's harsh, ungentlemanly language in his attacks against Islam that 'transcends all proper limits of religious controversy'.[16] Knowles even cited MacColl's writings on Islam in *The Times* (1887) and *Contemporary Review* (1888) in his letters. In response, MacColl claimed that Gladstone himself described his essay as 'gentlemanlike and christianlike . . . effective, strong, smashing' (1077), and that Ameer Ali expressed 'scorn for the religion of his Queen', citing the contrary claims of national and religious identities for Muslims living in England (1079).

Knowles encouraged MacColl to respond to Ali's essay, and justified Ali's defending himself initially against a hostile anonymous reviewer. Knowles's letters, citing his editorial 'principle of full and free discussion' (1075), attacked MacColl for his denigration of Mohammed[17] but his main concern was MacColl's intemperate language that would 'only breed corresponding intemperateness in your opponents, and seems to me to be in every way deplorable, as I have often told you to your face'

(1076). Knowles's public disclosure of the letters was as intentionally sensational as it was defensive in protecting his Muslim readers' sensibility. Situated within the journal's coverage of empire, printing these letters was consistent with the periodical's often provocative titles and voyeuristic promises of views of native cultures, in titles like 'The Hindu Widow' (1886), 'A Muslim's View' (1897), 'Is the British Raj in Danger?' (1897), and 'The Attack on the Native States of India' (1889).

MacColl replied in lengthy letters. He mentioned that Knowles's quotes were in a book MacColl had published eighteen years before and which had been out of print for seventeen years, indicating that Knowles's choices were not random or current, but meant to sensationalize MacColl's arguments. MacColl pointed out that Knowles did not quote any of his evidence of Muslim abuse of Christian subjects abroad and that Ameer Ali attacked him personally. MacColl argued that if the correspondence were not published in *Nineteenth Century*, he claimed his right to publish it elsewhere (1079). Knowles in his counter-response claimed he was not censoring MacColl by insisting on a temperate language, since 'only the editor can thus prevent the clashings' such language would provoke, as in MacColl's writings in *The Times* and the *Contemporary Review* (1080–81). Knowles defined his position as a referee maintaining civility in contentious encounters, and argued that he only decided to publish their letters after reading MacColl's vituperative essay on Islam in the *Fortnightly* in response to Ali's first essay on MacColl's anonymous review (1082).[18]

Laurel Brake in her study of *Nineteenth Century* argues that the periodical intended to be a site of 'divergent positions on questions of philosophy, theology and science' and 'to exploit the revelations of signature' that underscored diversity and authority. Interestingly, the signatures of the 'Other' were just as authoritative as were the signatures of the British authors – pashas, rajahs, justices – making these authors a subset of the journal's British insiders.[19] The *Nineteenth Century* encouraged the oppositional and the critical in a period of doubt and change openly expressed in *Nineteenth Century* by such 'authorities as Gladstone and Tennyson'.[20] Islamic authors like Ameer Ali were fully in the discourse over British foreign policy in the last quarter of the century as it became dominated by doubt and hesitancy over the extent of British intervention in native customs, laws, and practices. These questions opened up a public space in this periodical for native authors to recommend changes in British rule or to counter-attack it, because they, like their British counterparts in *Nineteenth Century*, embodied political authority. But these encounters also crossed periodicals in this set of responses and counter-responses, appearing in the *Quarterly Review*, *Fortnightly Review*, and, thanks to Knowles's references, *The Times* and the *Contemporary Review* in 1887 and 1888, as well as in *Nineteenth Century*.

Woman, sign of civilisation

The subject of Islam was interwoven with the equally contentious subject of women's status under Islam. As Antoinette Burton notes, 'Oriental womanhood as a trope of sexual difference, primitive society, and colonial backwardness' and 'equated with helplessness and backwardness, was no less crucial to notions of British cultural superiority and to rationales for the British imperial presence in India'.[21] Muslim female emancipation, 'frequently undertaken in the name of Indian women',[22] gave British women an imperial role, although it was men who defended Islamic women against British charges that they were subordinate and oppressed.[23] In all cases, the silent native woman was a measure of a colony's progress or lack of it.

Annie Reichardt's article 'Mohammedan Women', in the June 1891 *Nineteenth Century*, expressed a fear that Islamic practices were invading 'free, Christian, hitherto happy England' which appeared to be succumbing to Islam's threat to 'any high and noble aim for her [woman] to reach after'.[24] Reichardt had lived in Damascus and Cairo and described cases of young girls subject to misery: 'no happy childhood, no pretty dolls, no merry games, no brightly-coloured pictures' for Islamic women whose marriages are planned from their infancy (943). They were punished for speaking, laughing, or playing, controlled by the men in their families, 'the natural outcome and fruit of that religion – that Koran – which is already beginning its baneful influences into England', in her view (944). She attacked polygamy and cited cases of domestic abuse: her servant's children suffered from polygamy and desertion, and one woman's husband killed his own two sons to punish her. One Englishwoman with her Islamic husband's complicity hid her daughter from his family to protect her from early marriage and subsequent abuse. Reichardt acknowledged that abuses existed in England but Christianity 'does *not* abet or permit it', which, she claimed, Islam did (946).

Reichardt focused on the harem, 'a world unto itself' whose women's 'strong wills and fierce passions, commanding intellects and unwearied energies', if 'rightly guided, might be of benefit to the world; but, being wholly without vent save among themselves, turn their little world into a perfect pandemonium' through jealousies and intrigues (949). Reichardt concluded that Islam enforced 'the selfishness of human nature that the strong shall triumph over the weak' by endorsing 'any and every exercise of power, however subtle or cruel it may be, as only the natural right and due given to man by God'. She contrasted this with Christ's words that what God joined 'let not man put asunder', insisting that these words 'have given woman her real status in this world . . . as a helpmeet' and that Christian men are admonished to love their wives 'as Christ also loved the Church' (952). Reichardt insisted that Christianity was a superior moralizing force in the Empire.

Syed Ameer Ali replied to Reichardt in 'The Real Status of Women in Islam', in *Nineteenth Century*, August 1891, 'real' resonating with his role as native informant.[25] He interpreted passages from the Koran and the history of Jewish and Christian treatment of women, tracing 'the existing aversion to Islam' to Pope Gregory and the Crusades (387). Ali demonstrated that Reichardt, 'neither logical nor historically correct' (388), ignored that the ancient Jews treated women like chattels, and that early Christians banned women in the clergy, described women as 'the devil's gateway' (Tertullian), and committed violence against women during the so-called 'chivalric' period. He described widespread polygamy among Christians, including the clergy and Charlemagne, in contrast to Mohammed's attempt to change deep-seated misogynist practices among Syrian Christians, Arabs, and Jews (391). Mohammed revised divorce laws, discouraged polygamy, argued against concubinage, and advocated property rights of married women.[26] Ali contrasted these attempts with the behaviour of Christian missionaries, hysterically and irrationally 'unhinging people's minds by announcing the immediate advent of the "Kingdom of Heaven"' (391). Here he orientalized Christianity against an enlightened Mohammed seeking to improve women's rights and status against centuries-old practices, as he condemned Reichardt as an hysteric, ignorant of the Koran.

Ameer Ali historicized Islam as a set of practices distinct from Islam as a theology, opening up options for change in defiance of the essentialized 'medievalism' projected onto Islam by Western Orientalists. Addressing purdah, he argued that originally it protected women from the moral laxity of an earlier period. He cited educated Islamic women, respected and appreciated, in contrast to Hypatia, the great scholar torn to pieces by a Christian mob. Ali concluded that Islamic women were as advanced as European ones; their marriages – which were civic, not religious – guaranteed their property rights under law and allowed them to keep money they earned, in contrast to the situation of English women before 1882. He placed responsibility for women's degradation on the thirteenth-century Tartars and exonerated Mohammed and Islam.[27]

Imperial policies, multiple positions

While British attacks on Islam or women's status seem not to have required much knowledge of colonial society, essays on imperial policy were written by experienced administrators. At least two encounters over imperial policies were three-way debates.[28] One such encounter was between Samuel Smith, MP; Grant Duff, former Under-Secretary of India and former Governor of Madras; and Dadabhai Naoroji, the first Indian elected to the House of Commons in 1892.[29] All three wrote two essays each, filled with technical data and tables on revenue and agricultural production. *Contemporary Review* published all the essays, first Smith's two essays, then Duff's two, and then Naoroji's two, giving him the last word in 1887.

The debates appeared to be among a British critic of the Raj (Smith) aligned with an Indian critic (Naoroji), both opposed to a British defender of imperial policies and administration (Duff). However, a close look at these authors' rhetorical performances reveals a much more diverse and divided encounter. Smith's first article was on the topics of British political and administrative reforms in India; his second focused on India's poverty, agricultural rents and peasant suffering.[30] His most devastating comparison was between British and Moghul rulers with whom the British always favourably compared themselves as more civilizing and beneficial to Indians, unlike ruthless and cruel Moghuls. For Smith, 'Asiatic rulers always demand much more than they get, but our scientific system squeezes out of the people all that is demanded' (II, 63). He recommended vast irrigation to prevent famines and a gradual development of railways to avoid draining Indian finances. He contrasted English and Indian views of food export, an 'unmixed source of wealth' to the English, but 'a dangerous depletion of the necessaries of life' to the 'Hindoo' (II, 65). Smith's Indians were Hindus, and he treated Muslims as interlopers. He attacked the application of political economy's concept of individual rights as inappropriate to the 'constitution of Hindoo society' in which individuals were submerged in family, caste, and village. Applying 'theories of our advanced political and commercial doctrinaires' was more harmful than 'the invasion of Tamerlane, or Nadir Shah, or the ruthless Moguls', despite 'a series of great [British] administrators' who adapted 'ancient Hindoo law to the modern needs of India . . . a country centuries behind us in social development' (II, 67).

Smith criticised the application of British jurisprudence to village life and ventriloquized the 'general complaint of the natives' against this jurisprudence, interposing his presumed authority to speak for Indians. Praising Lord Ripon's 'extension of municipal government' to encourage native participation and 'a spirit of enterprise', Smith also condemned 'extremists' who attacked British rule (II, 68). He still considered Indians backward 'children' for whom 'Government has to act as a kind but firm father' though he was optimistic about the 'rising into importance among the educated Hindoos'. British enlightenment would inevitably break up the 'ice of inveterate customs', and Indians' 'universal desire' to learn English and attend British School would civilise them (II, 72–3). Here he argued both for restoring Indian customs and for Anglicization, which certainly would eliminate many native customs.

What merged these contradictions was Smith's underlying argument for 'a permanent foothold for Christianity' to balance agnostic British science and philosophy in India. Christianity fitted the Indian character as Smith orientalized it – meek, 'naturally courteous' yet fearful of the 'swift penalty' and 'the prestige of the dominant race'. Condemning British racism, he still believed that only a Christian British rule could restore 'native industry' through technical schools and 'improved modern processes' (II, 74–5), while arguing that British rule depended on 'the good will of the natives', a common argument from the 1860s (II, 77). Smith hoped Muslims would also learn to appreciate British rule, as he assumed Hindus already did. His goal, he claimed, was to improve British administration through 'healthful criticism' (II, 79).

Sir Mountstuart Elphinstone (M. E.) Grant Duff attacked Smith's knowledge of India and his informants whom Duff dismissed as self-serving discontents.[31] Duff claimed to know 'the *real* native community . . . the steady-going, sensible people who are scattered over the land', distinct from Smith's 'pert scribblers in the native press, and the intriguers of the Presidency towns' (Jan. 1887, 9, 11, 12). Duff criticized Smith's data and income tables, drawing on his own experience as Governor of Madras (Jan. 1887, 12). Defending British educational efforts, Duff yet argued that the best-educated Indians were far inferior to the best-educated Britons. He concluded with a long, strident attack on Smith's informants, his 'chatterboxes', and on Smith's gullibility in contrast to Duff's knowledge and experience: 'I write as one who has talked the matter over again and again with Indian gentlemen' (Jan. 1887, 26).

The major issue for both authors, however, was poverty and the costs of running the Empire. Duff insisted that India was run cheaply and efficiently. The British soldier, 'in the words of an *Indian* orator . . . "is the backbone of your Indian army" ', making the costs worth it (though Duff used an Indian authority to underwrite his claim; Jan. 1887, 14; italics mine). Calling India 'only half-civilized' (15), a point upon which Smith appeared to agree, Duff described free trade as one of the greatest blessings England 'has poured out on' Indians whose 'ignorance . . . of the plainest truths of political economy is absolutely colossal' (17). He questioned British tolerance of free expression as something Indians would interpret as weakness: 'The ordinary native does not and cannot understand our system' (18). Smith was in agreement on this, but he advocated a rapprochement between British and Indian customs to help Indians approach modernization and British political knowledge. Regarding Indian customs, Duff treated corruption as a custom and commended British revision of land settlements. He insisted the British paid off India's debts 'out of our own pockets', sacrificing to help Indians (23). Duff defended administrations prior to Ripon as having improved India over time and condemned Smith's belief that educated Indians would become 'an intelligent body of electors,' though he supported increasing the numbers of Indians in the civil service and improving their pay (24, 27).

Both Duff and Smith agreed on several important points: India was backward, Britain was progressive, and India needed Britain for modernization. Both agreed that India was poor: Smith blamed England's economic and agricultural policies, and Duff denied poverty was as bad as Smith claimed. Naoroji's dilemma was to explain the seriousness of India's poverty and its causes in imperial policies. He also had to present a modernizable India to British readers to encourage them to identify with him as a fellow Enlightenment consciousness. His facts, figures, and government tables, and attack on Duff's *ad hominem* arguments, were strategies for bonding with British readers to make his central claim – British ideals were undermined by British officials, so the British public must aid India by insisting that the government fulfil its stated obligations (particularly policies of 1833 and 1858).

Naoroji reprinted tables of earnings per inhabitant of Europe, Australia and North America to argue that India's current poverty was not only serious and a 'perversion of the pledges' of 1833 and 1858, but also that 'the present system of administration is an obstacle to any material advancement of India'. Profits made in India were taken out of the country, leaving Indians with 'insufficient food'.[32] In his second article (Nov. 1887), he included tables on 'trade, bullion, population, drains, etc.', with their 'official facts and figures, which will enable the public to judge for themselves', as he compared the suffering of British India with the wealth of debt-free Native States, in one of which, Baroda, he served as Prime Minister (II: 694). The Native States (provinces ruled by maharajahs and 'indirectly' by the British) 'have exported so much more merchandise than they have imported' (II: 705). These tables, taken from 'statistical abstracts published among parliamentary returns', and thus from the British government, demonstrated how 'wretched' British India's trade was compared with Native States and the West (I: 233).[33] The details and pages of tables, especially in his second essay, established his authority as it also identified his native informant status as writing to help Britain by pointing out that India's poverty harmed Britain, since India was a poor customer for British goods and its poverty deprived Britain of revenue (II: 698). His third economic assertion was that India was not governed cheaply, as Duff claimed, because of burdens on Britain from India's poverty, making India a 'very paltry commercial benefit to England' (II: 702): 'British India cannot and does not make any capital, and must and does lose the profit of its resources to others' (II: 706).

Naoroji's data, in contrast to Duff's *ad hominem* arguments and anecdotes, presented Naoroji as enlightened and Duff as irrational and unscientific. Naoroji described himself as 'disappointed and grieved' at Duff's 'superficiality and levity of his treatment of questions of serious and melancholy importance to India' and the 'literary smartness of offhand reply . . . in the place of argument . . . mere sensational assertions . . . unworthy of a gentleman' (I: 221). Duff 'has allowed his feelings to get the better of his judgment' without any 'accurate knowledge of facts'. Naoroji singled out Duff's attack on educated Indians: 'It is the educated classes who realize and appreciate most the beneficence and good intention of the British nation' and thus become 'the powerful chain' through which 'India is becoming more and more firmly linked with Britain' (I: 221–2).

More seriously, Naoroji accused Duff of 'misleading the British public'. In the opposition between national ideals and government practice, Duff represented the latter. While 'it has been our good fortune to be placed under the British nation . . . the most advanced in civilization . . . in the advancement of humanity . . . the source and fountain-head of true liberty and of political progress in the world . . . all that is just, generous, and truly free' (I: 222), British bureaucracy 'subverts the avowed and pledged policy of the British nation, . . . against which I appeal to the British people' (I: 223). Duff exemplified this failure, 'an insult and an injustice to the British nation', and Naoroji appealed to his readers to fulfil 'these sacred and solemn promises' (I: 226). Deploying this dichotomy, he blamed India's dire material conditions on incompetent administrators' failures to fulfil British government promises. Describing Duff as callous and duplicitous, Naoroji sarcastically quoted 'Mr' Duff's remarks in 1870 (before he became 'Sir' Duff). The 1870 Duff was more sympathetic toward India's poverty and shared the liberal views of administrators Naoroji praised: Sir Evelyn Baring, Sir George Campbell, and Lord Lawrence (I: 228–9).

Naoroji concluded that without Britain, India would be 'able to supply all its own wants, would not remain handicapped, and would have a free field in competition with the foreign capitalists, with benefit to all concerned', a radical proposition based on the successes of the Native States (II: 706). He noted that so-called technological progress, such as railways, primarily served the British. He insisted that Duff's complaint about Indians' expenditures on funerals and weddings denied them a social life and reduced them to an animal existence (II: 708). Finally, like other colonial authors, he argued that unless Britain heard his argument, there would be disaster: 'I only hope and pray that Britain will see matters mended before disaster comes' (II: 707). As native informant, he appeared to help Britain to prevent another Mutiny/Rebellion, the disguised referent of 'disaster'. Naoroji cited 'good' Britons (Smith, George Birdwood, Ilbert, and Major Bell) to present British support for his arguments and praised Indian educated classes as mediators between British readers and impending disasters.

Conclusion

> It is in the emergence of the interstices – the overlap and displacement of domains of difference – that the intersubjective and collective experiences of *nationness*, community interest, or cultural value are negotiated. . . .   Homi K. Bhabha, *The Location of Culture*[34]

Periodical editors offered platforms for imperial debates to appeal to an expanding readership throughout the globe, including Muslims and Hindus abroad and at home. Debates even crossed from one periodical to another. Colonial authors recognised that English identity was interpellated through the periodical press, and they used the press to advocate uplift, reform, progress, and reason. These authors identified with these ideologies, discarding and attacking Oriental stereotypes and joining themselves to an English enlightenment-cum-native, un-Oriental and unsubaltern. Their historicizing of 'native' culture contrasted with their orientalizing of the English. They presented Hindus and Moslems as rational, explicable, historical, learned, and civilized by Europeans' own Enlightenment standards. They openly attacked bad policies and offered suggestions they expected readers to support; they threatened rebellion implicitly or explicitly if their suggestions were not taken seriously. They wrote as authorities who, existing in both worlds, knew the English character at its best and worst and could educate readers about the 'native' character which they portrayed as complex and fluid. They orientalized incompetent administrators, but treated readers as enlightened, educable, and empathetic. They strategically deployed both threats and cajoling, through displays of enlightenment ideals (factual evidence, argument, appeals of justice) and their dual knowledge of British and Indian religions, customs, and imperial attitudes.

As Lata Mani, Spivak, and Said have pointed out, textualization under colonial rule privileged writing as the force that 'produced consequences of domination'.[35] Colonized authors, thoroughly anglicized, participated to intervene in this textualisation as they also presented 'a subtle affiliation with the culture that colonialism had created', as Simon Gikandi argues.[36] Native informant essays were essays of agency. The press created a public domain in which colonial authors could intervene in a hegemonic imperial public space. Colonial authors addressed British readers empathetically to effect changes in imperial politicians and policies, stop famines, and end infant marriages and sati. The reader became a force for imperial administration as these authors wrote to help readers perceive the empire not as textual, which it was for most English readers, but as discursive, palpable, suffering, *and* civilized, educated, and reformist – post-Enlightenment, not medieval; rational, not superstitious; discursive, not inscrutably silent. To achieve these ends, they employed the press's character as public, discursive and mediating.

The press constituted a discursive Empire in which ideals of reform and progress could be passed between metropole and colony. Whatever the authors' views on Britain's 'civilizing' force, they readily appealed to it and its formation of English national identity to substantiate their re-textualizing of their own countries. Indian authors promised British readers that peaceful, gradual change was possible within the system, and that such change was a bulwark against more violent rebellion increasingly visible throughout the Empire. They identified their argumentative style and juridical logic as shared with their readers (although their native cultures had complex and nuanced legal systems, some presented positively in these articles). The press offered British and colonial antagonists a venue that was, as Ann Parry describes it, 'a complex process of collation and discontinuity'.[37] Colonial authors employed both arguments of collation and of discontinuity, distinguished practice from belief, custom from law, and history from orientalizing to empower British readers to inhabit an Englishness identified with political morality and justice that was both English and native.

Notes

1. *Art Bulletin*, 78 (June 1996), 205.
2. Between 1840 and 1900 there were over 100 articles by 60 authors from throughout the Middle East and Asia, and all well-educated, privileged, and prominent. In my essay, 'The Empire Writes Back: Native Informant Discourse in the Victorian Press', in *Imperial Co-Histories: National Identities and the British and Colonial Press*, ed. Julie F. Codell (Fairleigh Dickinson University Press, 2003), p 188–218, I focus on colonial authors, none of whom except one are examined here.
3. Spivak Gayatri, 'Criticism, Feminism and the Institution', *The Post-Colonial Critic: Interviews, Strategies, Dialogues*, ed. Sara Harasym (London: Routledge, 1990), 1.
4. Spivak Gayatri, 'The Rani of Sirmur: An Essay in Reading the Archives', *History and Theory*, 24 (1985), 251.
5. Sinha, *Colonial Masculinity* (Manchester: Manchester University Press, 1995), 1.
6. Pratap Chandra Mozoomdar (or Protap Chunder Mozumdar), 'Present-Day Progress in India', *Nineteenth Century*, 48 (December 1900), 998.
7. Some topics, like sati and child marriage, had been the subject of laws (1829 and 1891, respectively) that banned these practices and provoked resistance, public demonstrations, and writings.
8. Malcolm MacColl, 'Book Review – Art. X', *Quarterly Review* (July 1895), 231.
9. See also 243–9.
10. 'Islam and its Critic: A Rejoinder', *Fortnightly Review*, 58 n.s. (Oct. 1895), 621–40. This was a counter response to Ameer Ali's response to MacColl's anonymous review.
11. Syed Ameer Ali, 'Islam and its Critics', *Nineteenth Century*, 38 (Sept. 1895), 361–80, and 'Islam and Canon MacColl', *Nineteenth Century* 38 (Nov. 1895), 778–85. His book was entitled *Life and Teachings of Mohammed: The Spirit of Islam* (1891). Syed Ameer Ali, 1849–1928 (see *DNB*), an Indian jurist and Islamic leader born in Orissa, traced his descent from the Prophet Mohammed. He was educated at the Hooghly College, Chinsurah, and with scholarships graduated in arts and law at the University of Calcutta, the first

Moslem to take the M.A. degree. He was called to the bar in England in 1873 and practiced law in Calcutta. He held the Tagore law professorship at the University of Calcutta, 1884–5. In 1877 he founded the first Moslem political organization in India; in 1878 he became a member of the Bengal legislative council, and in 1883 was one of three Indian legislative members of the governor-general's council. From 1890 he was a judge of the high court of Calcutta for fourteen years. In 1904 he moved to England. In 1909 Lord Morley appointed him Indian judge to the Privy Council. He favoured reforms and founded the British Red Crescent. He considered Indian nationalism a cloak for Hindu domination. He refused a knighthood. See Rozina Visram, *Asians in Britain: 400 Years of History* (London: Pluto Press), 146–9.

12. 'Islam and its Critics', *Nineteenth Century,* 38 (Sept. 1895), 361–2.
13. 'Islam and Canon MacColl', *Nineteenth Century,* 38 (Nov. 1895), 783.
14. He had earlier referred to Turkish rulers 'whose friendship *we* are trying to retain and strengthen' (Sept. 1895, 362; italics mine).
15. E.g., Dozy, Draper, 366–7.
16. James Knowles, 'Canon MacColl on Islam. A Correspondence', *Nineteenth Century* (Dec. 1895), 1081.
17. In one letter, Knowles asked MacColl if he planned to reply to Ali. MacColl did not reply, so Knowles filled the space with their letters which, he argued, were not marked 'private' ('Canon MacColl on Islam', 1076).
18. The *Fortnightly* also had Indian authors writing about India (e.g., Romesh Chunder Dutt, the prominent nationalist, wrote 'Famines in India' for the August 1897 issue).
19. Laurel Brake, *Subjugated Knowledges: Journalism, Gender and Literature in the Nineteenth Century* (London: Macmillan, 1994), 51–2.
20. Ibid., 60–1.
21. Antoinette Burton, *Burdens of History: British Feminists, Indian Women, and Imperial Culture, 1865–1915* (Chapel Hill: University of North Carolina Press, 1994), 7. Dagmar Engels argues that 'In British India some of the most emotionally-charged conflicts between colonised and coloniser were about the control of female sexuality'; see Engels, 'The Age of Consent Act of 1891', *South Asia Research,* 3 (1983), 107.
22. Burton, 2.
23. Cornelia Sorabji was the only woman who wrote on behalf of women in the British periodical press.
24. Annie Reichardt, 'Mohammedan Women', *Nineteenth Century* (June 1891), 941.
25. Ameer Ali, 'The Real Status of Women in Islam', *Nineteenth Century,* 20 (Sept. 1891), 387–99.
26. 388–96.
27. Later he wrote 'The Influence of Women in India', *Nineteenth Century,* 45 (May 1899), 755–94.
28. *Fortnightly Review* participated in a three-way debate among Muhammed 'Abd al-Halim Pasha in *Nineteenth Century* (May, 1885) to which Julian Goldsmid (*Fortnightly,* 222 n.s [June 1885], 741–52) and Edward Dicey replied (*Nineteenth Century,* July 1885), after which Halim Pasha responded to their essays (*Nineteenth Century,* 18 (Sept. 1885), 485–92). The topic was the Khedivate of Egypt.

29. Dadabhai Naoroji, 1825–1917 (see *DNB*). Naoroji was the first Indian elected to the House of Commons. A Parsi born near Bombay, he studied at Elphinstone College where he taught, the first Indian professor, appointed to the chair of mathematics and natural philosophy (1854). He established a newspaper, *Rast Goftar*, 1851. A partner in Cama and Co., Naoroji opened an English branch in 1855, the first Indian firm established in England. He was professor of Gujarati at University College, London (1856–65) and a co-founder of the Indian National Congress (1885). An unsuccessful Liberal candidate for Holborn in 1886, Naoroji was adopted for Central Finsbury (1888). He was elected to the Commons by 2,961 votes to 2,956 in 1892. He lost his seat in 1895. In 1906 he stood for North Lambeth and lost. See Antoinette Burton, 'Tongues Untied: Lord Salisbury's "Black Man" and the Boundaries of Imperial Democracy', *Comparative Study of Society and History* (2000), 632–61; Rozina Visram, *Asians in Britain*, 126–39.
30. Samuel Smith, 'India Revisited, I', *Contemporary Review*, 49 (June 1886), 794–819, and 'India Revisited. II', *Contemporary Review*, (July 1886), 60–79. I refer to these essays as 'I' and 'II', respectively.
31. Grant Duff, 'India. A Reply to Mr. Samuel Smith, M. P., Part I', *Contemporary Review*, 51 (Jan. 1887), 8–31, and 'India: A Reply to Mr. Samuel Smith, M. P., Part II', *Contemporary Review*, 51 (Feb. 1887), 181–95. Also citations are from I, unless otherwise noted.
32. Naoroji, 'Sir M. E. Grant Duff's views about India', Part I, *Contemporary Review*, 52 (Aug. 1887), 221–35, and 'Sir M. E. Grant Duff's views about India', Part II, *Contemporary Review*, 52 (Nov. 1887), 694–711. This quote is from I, 233, 235.
33. These comparisons appear at the end of I, but are the bulk of II. He also refers to his papers 'Poverty of India' and 'Condition of India' (in II, 707), in which he demonstrates that India's per capita income is extremely low.
34. (London and New York: Routledge, 1994), 2.
35. Lata Mani, 'The Production of an Official Discourse on *Sati* in Early Nineteenth-Century Bengal', in *Europe and its Others*, ed. Francis Barker (Colchester: University of Essex, 1979) I, 122. See Edward Said, *Orientalism* (New York: Vintage Press, 1978).
36. Simon Gikandi, *Maps of Englishness* (New York: Columbia University Press, 1996), xiv.
37. Ann Parry, 'Theories of Formation: *Macmillan's Magazine*: Vol. 1, November 1859. Monthly. 1/0', *Victorian Periodicals Review*, 26 (1993), 101.

12

Government by Journalism and the Silence of the *Star*: Victorian Encounters 1885–90

Laurel Brake

The apparently overstated claim of the newspaper editor W. T. Stead in 1886 that journalism not Parliament best represented and served the people of Britain was not simply a boast of a solitary individual subject.[1] It was the outcome of a widely perceived growth of the power of the press throughout the century, spurred in 1855 by abolition of compulsory newspaper taxes, resulting in the development of cheap and numerous titles.[2] Stead's combative article was only its seal. That this first wave of the cocky new journalism was short-lived, a 'moment' before the advent of mass journalism germinated by the *Daily Mail* in 1896, will be shown by a comparison of two newspaper encounters with government produced towards the beginning and end of this six-year period. The first is Stead's series of articles in the *Pall Mall Gazette* in July 1885 entitled 'The Maiden Tribute of Modern Babylon'[3] and the second is the coverage of 'the Cleveland Street affair' in a number of papers in 1889–90.[4] The first story launched a political campaign to raise the age of consent, while the second was occasioned by the discovery of a male brothel in Cleveland Street in London. I will argue that the discourse of gender is the crucial factor in the respective strength and weakness of journalism in influencing government at these junctures.

However, the negotiation of power between journalism and government is one among a number of other encounters implicated in this historical moment. In 1885, the press and public were divided primarily over the mode and substance of Stead's campaign, rather than over raising the age of consent. While Stead insistently framed the encounter from beginning to end as one between journalism and government, commentators then and now turned their attention to the assault on conventions of 'public discourse' in Stead's story.[5] Reflecting the development of cultural studies in our own period, I want to highlight the exclusion of popular journalism from the definition of public discourse at the time. Journalistically, the encounter between Stead and the nineteenth-century public might rather be seen as Stead's introduction of popular journalism discourses (such as those in the police gazettes) into the predominant 'higher journalism' of the *Pall Mall Gazette*. For a culture marked by rigid categories of class, this transgression of borders – an encounter of diverse market niches – was bound to disturb its extant readers.

Other journalistic models of investigative journalism for 'The Maiden Tribute' are to be found in its earlier deployment in the *Pall Mall Gazette* by Stead and Frederick Greenwood. The paper actively sought out, investigated, and constructed 'news' which is naturalized in culture and unmarked as 'news'. The affiliation of investigative journalism with sensation is clear, both in its introduction by Greenwood into the early *Pall Mall Gazette* in 1866 in the midst of the decade of sensation fiction,[6] and in its appearance in the aggressive journalism of the United States,[7] of which Stead was a careful and early observer. Although investigative journalism is often singled out as characteristic of 'new journalism', its innovation is its high incidence rather than its creation. Clearly, it draws on the development of sociology and methods of social inquiry in a century that was well-known for its reports on social conditions in government 'blue books'. Greenwood in 1865 also had the model of Henry Mayhew's investigations into the London poor initiated in 1849, which appeared serially over a year to great acclaim in a London morning daily, the *Morning Chronicle*.[8] But while the blue books aspire to the burgeoning 'science' of economics and Mayhew's forays retain the air of Boz's 'sketches', the element of sensation tends to dominate in the new journalism versions.

Stead's focus on the encounter between journalism and government in the *Contemporary Review*[9] in 1886 is instructive, given his keen interest in the mores of journalism itself. However, with his astute sense of occasion and his eye on further Parliamentary reform, he turns his evangelical zeal to the defence of journalism as a fitting and triumphant alternative to government. The boldness of this hyperbole which proclaims the dignity of journalism may be gauged by noting that in this period literature itself was defending its 'dignity', not least against the upstart vulgarities of journalism.[10] Stead's representation of journalism, here and subsequently, is matched by the counter-insistence by literature of its superiority over 'journalism'.[11]

Stead's indebtedness to sensation fiction is not confined to his appropriation of sensation as a magnet to readers. His narration of 'The

Maiden Tribute' story itself appropriates additional aspects of the popular fiction of the day to construct his story. It is self-consciously literary. Part of Stead's strategy for his encounter with literature is not only to present journalism as a worthy alternative, but also to displace literature by incorporating it. Just as Daniel Defoe offered in the early novel an illusion of the more familiar pleasures of 'history' and truth, Stead's 'true' stories such as 'The Maiden Tribute', draw on the pleasures of fiction. This 'incorporation' model of Stead's is closely akin to his version of the encounter of journalism with government in 1886: in government *by* journalism he incorporates the former into the latter.

By 1889 and the 'Cleveland Street' story, the power of Stead and the *Pall Mall Gazette* appears much reduced. Whereas in 'The Maiden Tribute' Stead and his paper produced as well as conducted the campaign, in 1889 they are one of four main players, and the outcome of the encounter is quite different. The *Star*, a new Liberal daily, and *Truth*, a sensational weekly, leave the *Pall Mall Gazette* behind in coverage and tenacity. As in 1885, a journalist is imprisoned. However, whereas in 1885 the desired legislation was propelled by journalism into the Criminal Law Amendment Act (CLAA),[12] in 1889–90 journalism proved complicit with government in its uneven implementation of the new law. By permitting homophobic conventions of public discourse to prohibit disclosure in the first instance, it colluded with government attempts to hush up the case. Then, in framing the story as primarily one of party (and class) politics, it colluded in acting too late to hinder imprisonment of the underlings, or escape by the wealthy and culpable. Journalists' tardy allegations that the behaviour of both government *and* the monarchy conflicted with the new law seem to have had little effect.

The multiple titles involved in 1889 appear diverse – two national dailies, one new and radical, the other established and upmarket, and two weeklies, one upmarket and sensational, the other impoverished, fledgling, radical and local – with a wide social range of targeted readers. All four are, however, essentially in concert about their coverage and construction of the 1889 story. They attempt to mitigate legal liability by sharing it out among themselves through mutual quotation. This co-operation is explained by their common political affiliation. The diversity of the titles and readership significantly does not correspond to the political alliance of their editors, who are all 'radical' Liberals, so-called because of their support of Home Rule and the Gladstonians. The negotiation of discourses of gender by these diverse titles around an intractable topic indicates the power (and relative success) of government over the implementation of the law, and a press compromised and shackled.

The players

In May and November 1886, at the heady height of the proliferation of journalism in the UK, and in the dawning 'new journalism', W. T. Stead, editor of the London evening daily the *Pall Mall Gazette*, published two articles titled 'Government by Journalism' and 'The Future of Journalism' in the monthly *Contemporary Review*. In these pieces he acclaimed journalism as superior to government, by virtue of its power to represent the people directly. It was this association of the press with direct democracy and the right to govern that Matthew Arnold picked up a year later in his sneering definition of what he termed 'the new journalism'. He was perturbed by and directly addressed Stead's political ambitions for journalism, as may be seen in the context of his remarks: they appear as part of a review of the Parliamentary session 'Up to Easter' in the *Nineteenth Century*, the main rival of the *Contemporary*.

Raiding Arnold's characteristic model for England, classical Greece,[13] Stead deploys an image of an ancient Greek 'agora' into which the modern technology of the telegraph and the press have converted Britain: 'an assembly of the whole community in which the discussion of the affairs of state is carried on from day to day in the hearing of the whole people. . . . The secret of the power of the Press and of the Platform is the secret by which the Commons controlled the Peers, and the Peers in their turn controlled the King. They are nearer the people' (Stead [May 1886]: 654). He then goes on to place the press at the apex of the power structure he has outlined:

> Over the Platform the Press has great and arbitrary powers. It is within the *uncontrolled* discretion of every editor whether any speech delivered in the previous twenty-four hours shall or shall not come to the knowledge of his readers. . . . They decide what their readers shall know, or what they shall not know. This power of closure is enormous. . . . [W]ithin the range of his circulation – and readers, of course, are much more numerous than subscribers – he may be more potent than any other man.   (Stead [May 1886]: 662; my italics)

In his view, the press is now in a position to reverse the state's paradigm of the encounter between the state and the press, whereby the state, buttressed by numerous powers to hand, always succeeds in controlling the press. Stead also claims that the Press has both a missionary responsibility and a crucial educational function:

> It has been openly asserted not so long ago that a journalist is neither a missionary nor an apostle. . . . I cannot accept any such *belittling limitation* of the duties of a journalist. We have to write afresh from day to day the only Bible which millions read. The newspaper – too often the newspaper alone – lifts the minds of men . . . into a higher sphere of thought and action than the routine of the yard-stick. . . .   (Stead [May 1886]: 663; my italics)

What added fuel to Stead's claims for journalism was that this first article was published soon after he had left prison in January, to which he had been sentenced for three months for technical 'abduction' of a fourteen-year-old child. His consolation was that the resulting series of investigative (and sensational) articles, 'The Maiden Tribute of Modern Babylon', had proved successful in persuading Parliament within months to pass the Criminal Law Amendment Act (CLAA), which raised the age of consent for girls from 13 to 16.

During the high tide of the power of the press after 1885, a second campaign in 1889–90, around the 'Cleveland Street scandal', was regarded by Stead and other editors and MPs as a test of the new law. The principal editors in question are T. P. O'Connor, Henry Labouchère and Stead, and interestingly their respective papers, the *Star*, *Truth*, and the *Pall Mall Gazette*, are all relatively new. Postdating the repeal of the various newspaper taxes (1855–61), they constitute part of the first wave of the new journalism.

However, in 1889–90 the issue was *not* the 'protection of women', a hegemonic rhetoric underlying Stead's 1885 campaign that rendered the unspeakable existence of child prostitution just utterable in the public sphere, although not without widespread disapproval. The case in 1889 pertained to male homosexuals, the other target of the CLAA. This aspect of the Act was included through a last minute amendment in 1885. Known as the Labouchère amendment, it was named after its mover, the Radical MP Henry du Pré Labouchère.[14] In 1885–86, in 'The Maiden Tribute' campaign, the powerful element of 'child' prostitution carried related gender issues such as male concupiscence and the retrospective claim to 'government by journalism' along with its popular support, but in 1889 'government by journalism' was effectively scuppered by the 'unspeakable' (or unpublishable) nature of the male brothel at Cleveland Street.

Even the radical journalists whose campaigns I shall examine show themselves to be divided over aspects of the case identified in the contemporary press. These included (1) the disinterested and equitable implementation of the CLAA, specifically the Labouchère amendment, on which implementation Stead and Labouchère were very keen; (2) corruption and cronyism by the Tory government, specifically the Prime Minister, Lord Salisbury, and the Home Secretary, Henry Matthews, in protecting their friends, and ultimately the monarchy, although this last was only hinted at in the public prints at the time; (3) class issues around the trial and imprisonment of 'obscure', easily disregarded citizens, and a blind eye to escape for the rich or potentially damaging witness; (4) the right of an editor and journalists to protect their sources and maintain confidentiality; and (5) party politics, with these editors all Liberals, in opposition, and Lord Salisbury's government in power, Tory.

The issue of sexual orientation was the single factor on which all of the mainstream press of 1889–90 agreed; they were *univocal* in their anxious disapproval and hearty denunciation of homosexuality. The poverty of language available to public discourse for openly conducting the arguments in the press – for advocacy of heterosexual mores and the rejection of homosexual alternatives – is striking. However, proponents of the homosocial, including Walter Pater, J. A. Symonds, Charles Kains-Jackson, and Oscar Wilde among others, were simultaneously finding structures and nuanced language to put their alternative arguments in journals and books.

In these two encounters of the press with government, presented as encounters of the power of journalism over government (1885–86) and the corruption of government (1889–90), gender figured crucially if invisibly and ideologically. And even a cursory look at this period, with the long campaigns for married women's property and the repeal of the Contagious Diseases Acts that preceded 'The Maiden Tribute' articles, and the Parnell-Mrs O'Shea divorce case (whereby Parnell was forced to stand down as leader of the Radicals and Irish Home Rulers) that followed, reveals the saturation of politics by gender issues of the day. The element of gender is one of the defining variables in the claim of the press to the authority of governing. The tussle between the press and the state over Cleveland Street, then, shows the limits of the powers of the press, as opposed to the alleged strengths that emerged from 'The Maiden Tribute' in 1885–86.

In 1889 Labouchère even claimed in the capacious gossip department 'Entre Nous' which opened each weekly issue of *Truth*, that the government *deployed* the 'unsavoury', gendered nature of the Cleveland-street affair strategically:

> It is impossible to enter into it in the Press except indirectly. Government counted upon this and in their endeavour to hush up what they thought would tell against that portion of Society that they especially represent, they allowed two obscure men to be sent to prison for a few months, and took very good care that those most guilty should not be touched.   ('Entre Nous' [19 Dec. 1889]: 142)

But Labouchère and his fellow editors are complicit with government in this respect, rather than revelatory. Hardly anywhere in the press is the nature of the brothel explicitly stated. While some printed accounts refer to the 'unutterable', 'vicious' nature of the crime, 'the house', the clients, or the sex workers, only readers who understand this code would be privy to the occasion of the story. It is germane that the most explicit coverage is in *The Times'* long Parliamentary report on the occasion of Labouchère's intervention in February 1890, the Parliamentary reports being a gendered portion of the paper that most women who saw *The Times* would not read, disenfranchised as they were. The Parliamentary and court 'reports' however often included detailed information which was validated for inclusion in the paper only in this location, by the duty of fully reporting the high and serious deliberations of the authorities, government ministers, judges, barristers and solicitors. Unsurprisingly, these reports were also subject to editorial censorship through (de)selection, particularly when Parliamentary immunity protected MPs but not the press.

The context of this self-censorship of the newspaper press is instructive, particularly as the overwhelming majority of newspaper readers in this period were male. Was it apposite, or egregiously overdetermined? It was precisely in 1885 that George Moore was complaining about the gendered constraints on another mode of English discourse, fiction, in his pamphlet 'Literature at Nurse', constraints which he argued were confining the public discourse of fiction in English to what was deemed suitable for women *and children* to read. Then, in 1890, in dialogue with the reprise of the press campaign around the CLAA cited here, Moore's arguments were reiterated in a symposium in the monthly *New Review* called 'Candour in English Fiction'. It compared the English novel unfavourably with the French, with its laudable models of realism and naturalism. What we see in the simultaneous Cleveland Street newspaper discourse is precisely this tension about the constraints on discourse that constantly alludes to what is censored, and occasionally makes it visible, through negative emotion of denunciation, 'verbatim reporting', and vehement displacement.

But certainly, from the greater part of the reporting, casual or unworldly newspaper readers might mistake the case, and understand it to involve hegemonic, heterosexual brothels and female prostitution. This impression was reinforced by every aspect of the story, as I suspect *headlines* in the *Star* and *Pall Mall Gazette* often functioned as warnings to readers for whom this material might prove offensive, before they reached the substance of articles. Innovative for the period in these new journalism papers, headlines seem to have been deployed to *warn* an increasingly heterogeneous readership, as well as to break up the page and to attract readers' attention to itemised news. Stead set a precedent for this in 1885 in the case of 'The Maiden Tribute' where he published an entire leader of 'warning' the Saturday before the articles appeared. This was partly what it purported to be, an announcement of the unsuitability of the topic for young and women readers, but also a lascivious trailer for the revelations to come. As in 1885, the later headlines about Cleveland Street were sensational throughout the press, dually serving as warning and come-on.

Truth, a threepenny weekly whose ambivalent title invokes both authority and steamy revelation, was regarded generically as a scandal sheet largely due to its series of unheaded paragraphs which made up 'Entre Nous' each week. This department which encouraged readers to read the tit-bits successively was normally the first in each issue and occupied up to nine pages. In form these unheaded paragraphs resemble the 'Occasional Notes' which the *Pall Mall Gazette* pioneered from 1865, and which others had copied. However, in *Truth* their contents differed in the ubiquity of celebrity gossip in a mix that included diverse social campaigns and controversies, and party politics. Readers of *Truth* had no warnings from the format of 'Entre Nous', but then easily shocked men or women readers would not be perusing *Truth* in the first place. 'Gossip' was a category of information and entertainment legitimized by the new journalism for the 'new' readers that it targeted. So, while *Truth* was denounced as a scandal sheet by establishment papers, it was at the upper end of the market, and was by no means in price, appearance, or tone a cheap rag.[15] Like *Private Eye* in Britain today, it was full of insider knowledge and political and social gossip.

All of these serials were edited by Radicals, and all three titles pioneered and participated to varying degrees in the new journalism. The youngest, 'new journalism' evening paper, the *Star*, cost a ha'penny and aimed at a readership that reached far down into the middle classes, and in its earliest form, between 1888–90, into the literate working classes. The established evening daily, the *Pall Mall Gazette* cost a penny, and catered for the clubmen and the literary, and *Truth*, the 3d weekly gossip sheet, probably included many politicians and their wives, some other members of 'Society', and the politically aware of the middle classes more generally among its readership. This group of papers constituted a cultural formation stemming from a common politics, but one which crucially spanned the market from elite to popular.

Their editors were also professionally and personally interlocked. Labouchère, who like O'Connor, editor of the *Star*, had been elected in the Parliamentary elections of 1880, edited *Truth*. So, both Labouchère and O'Connor were Radical MPs *and* editors. This alliance between journalism and politics is noted as common in this period by Wilfrid Meynell. In 1880 Meynell cites politics as one of the few settings in which journalism was regarded as a positive stepping stone (to advancement) rather than a stigma,[16] and Stephen Koss notes that there were a significant number of journalist MPs in Parliament at this time. Labouchère and O'Connor were friends as well as fellow MPs, and when O'Connor's American wife suggested that her husband should become an editor, Labouchère set about finding Liberal backers for what emerged as O'Connor's *Star*. *Truth* and the *Star* were thus closer than their distinctive formats of upmarket weekly scandal sheet and radical daily suggested. O'Connor had also briefly worked for Stead and John Morley (also a Liberal MP), when they were editing the *Pall Mall Gazette* together in 1880: as a new MP, O'Connor wrote regular Parliamentary sketches for them until 1881. Stead, sole editor of the *Pall Mall Gazette* from 1883, had produced 'The Maiden Tribute' campaign, which resulted in the CLAA, to which Labouchère added his famous amendment.

Both men were broadly sympathetic with the notion of social purity, although Stead was far more evangelical on this count than Labouchère. Their differences are clear from the reservations expressed in *Truth* in 1889/90, about the vigilance societies that proliferated after the passage of the CLAA, in one of which Stead was a prominent member. While Stead published laudatory articles about the National Vigilance Association (NVA) at the time of Cleveland Street, Labouchère's position was more libertarian.[17] And *Truth* articulated the difference between vice and crime: Labouchère pursued a campaign highly critical of the NVA for permitting the sale of allegedly pornographic books by their own distributor. Despite these differences, close interpersonal relations among the editors – Stead with Labouchère through the Criminal Law Amendment Act, O'Connor and Labouchère in Parliament, and Stead and O'Connor as fellow Liberal editors of dailies – together with their respective personal circumstances, were to prove crucial to the treatment of Cleveland Street in the press.

Coverage

If through the Commons, national politics and party, and their profession, the three editors were close allies, it was not until quite late in the Cleveland Street proceedings, in November 1889, that the succession of events, originating in June, broke into the public sphere as an important story. It took the arrest of a journalist for alleged libel to make the case reportable, given that the *nature* of the brothel originally made editors reticent to cover it beyond the court arraignments. Events show that besides ideological prohibitions on the limits of public discourse, editorial discretion was governed by fear of the law. Once an editor published the *names* of putative clients of the brothel, the law was invoked, not by the government but by a Tory peer. This moved the Cleveland Street story into a number of publishable narratives, which duly *became* the story. A set of predictable moves on the part of both the press and the establishment enabled the story to be written: the publication of names by the press provoked a libel suit from a member of the aristocracy, to be tried in open court. For the press, coverage was a foreseeable risk but also an opportunity.

The decision of Lord Euston, one of the men named, to sue for libel thus spurred the story into widespread newspaper coverage, publicity which careful timing of hearings by government and the courts had effectively striven to avoid. By this strategy the attempt by government to restrict access to the hearings reinforced the reticence of the press to cover Cleveland Street. Several trials had already taken place with minimum publicity.

As for the risk of libel, it was well managed by the three editors. None of *them* was sued. Rather, the youthful editor of a small, local London weekly – the *North London Press* priced at $^{1}/_{2}$d – had borne the risk, published the names, and was summarily charged and held overnight. Ultimately Ernest Parke was tried, found guilty of libel, sentenced to prison for a year, due to his failure to name his sources, and freed in six months, after journalists presented a petition for compassionate release.[18] Parke, it emerges, was not the isolated editor of a local weekly that he appeared. He was simultaneously one of the original staff of the *Star*, which he was sub-editing at the time with H. W. Massingham, O'Connor's deputy. It is highly likely that, in ways now lost to view, Parke and his fledgling weekly had privileged access to information about Cleveland Street in circulation among the mainstream papers, and among the three radical Liberal editors. Between Labouchère's base in the Commons and his organizational advantage in gathering information as editor of a publication which traded in gossip, to say nothing of his special interest in the implementation of the CLAA, and Stead's and O'Connor's access to information as editors of dailies, the names were well-known in this network.[19] So it is significant both that Stead, in his established daily, broke the main story in the daily press in the *Pall Mall Gazette* (23 November) before the youthful and 'radical' *Star* (25 November), and that the local weekly *North London Press* beat them both (16 November).

Parke's silence about his sources suggests two possibilities: that Parke acted on what he came to know out of frustration with the reticence of the mainstream press, and particularly with O'Connor, Stead and Labouchère, *or* that he agreed to outright requests from them to publish the names, on the grounds that the obscurity of his weekly minimized the risk of libel charges that their mainstream titles would attract. The *North London Press* may have also benefited in other ways from the affiliation of its editor with the *Star*, financially and through the use of its presses, making it a sister paper, and thus more vulnerable to such a request.[20]

Irrespective of how the information made its way into public discourse, the libel case proved crucial in uniting the three editors and mainstream titles in commitment to coverage. The case was thoroughly investigated and publicised between November 1889 and March 1890 in the national press and in Parliament. The three papers constantly alluded to, and quoted, each other's coverage, in order to increase the sense of their critical mass and authority, but perhaps also for safety (quotation being an 'objective' form of reporting). However, they were also unwittingly aided by the status of *The Times*, which covered the case regularly in its lengthy and detailed court and parliamentary 'reports'. This form of allegedly objective reporting permits coverage without necessarily owning the story or commenting upon it. The ubiquitous use of such normalized narrative forms in covering Cleveland Street is indicative of the widespread cultural anxiety in the press about homosexuality.

A new phase of the story thus begins in the *North London Press* rather than the *Star*, when Parke undertook to publish the names of the (wealthy) clients of Cleveland Street, which no other paper had ventured to do. These silent papers, exercising precisely that power of 'closure' described above in Stead's 'Government by Journalism' (662), included the *Star* for which Parke worked daily. In this instance the silence of the press functioned as complicity with the government's strategies, which subsequently they criticise and identify as the nub of the 'scandal'. The press's silence includes the period in which Lord Arthur Somerset, a brothel client, and Charles Hammond, its owner, escaped,[21] and in which George Veck, the brothel manager, and Henry Newlove, a principal procurer, were charged and jailed.[22]

The *North London Press* story naming names appeared on 16 November 1889, and by 21 November the *Star* carried an advert for its sister paper's revelations in its next issue the following day. But the story did not appear elsewhere in the daily *Star*, until 25 November. Its main, front-page leader began with an explanation of its silence that corroborates Stead's delineation of the powers of the press, and Foucault's allegation of the omnipresence of sexuality in the Victorian period:

> *The Star* has always tried to be at once outspoken and clear. At much risk of being misunderstood, it has avoided those subjects which prurience in the name of purity delights to handle. Its conductors have never been able to convince themselves that the interests of society are advanced by *dragging* into light of day and into topics of ordinary converse the *foul, loathsome slimy things that are hidden out of sight*. For this reason there has not been admitted into the columns of *The Star* any allusion to a hideous subject, *which has been discussed in private for weeks, and even months, with a familiarity and a fulsomeness that make London conversation almost as horrible a thing as London vice*. . . . [T]hough some respected contemporaries have written on the subject, *The Star* has hitherto been silent. Silence is no longer possible. The trial has been begun, which must bring to the knowledge of the whole world the terrible scandal of which everybody has been talking. Concealment, *if desirable*, is no longer possible.[23]

The tissue of allusion and repression here constitutes the principal reference to the nature of the Cleveland Street house. The second paragraph begins 'Beside the unutterable and abominable crimes there is another topic in the some connection on which society speaks as frequently and as fiercely. The topic is the conduct of the authorities' (ibid.,

1). These authorities include 'the police', and 'Cabinet Councils'. This paragraph thus moves straight on to the transition to what may be seen as the displacement story, of political corruption, a common subject of public discourse. Even the *Star* accepts the delimiting of the press on this matter, without a murmur. However, this version of the story also is subject to self-censorship by the press, which in effect supports the rationale of government 'corruption' in this matter, and inhibits the force of the Liberal press's allegations of government misconduct. Both the government and the press agree to suppress the implication that the Duke of Clarence, Prince Eddy, the elder son of the Prince of Wales was among those who frequented Cleveland Street. The action on the part of the Home Secretary, Henry Matthews (who insisted that the Attorney General capitulate on this matter) to allow Lord Arthur Somerset to escape to the Continent may be explained by the knowledge that Somerset, a cavalry officer of 38, worked for the Prince of Wales as the overseer of his stables,[24] and was also a friend of Prince Eddy's.[25] Above all, the Prince of Wales and his family must be protected from association with Cleveland Street. The vulnerability of the government regarding the escape of Somerset and Hammond may be seen by its subsequent attempt to appear to implement the law even-handedly, as Labouchère had been demanding in *Truth*. In December 1890, months after Somerset fled, Arthur Newton, his family solicitor, who acted for Veck and Newlove, is arrested, charged with perverting the course of justice and briefly imprisoned.[26] Newton is yet another minion sacrificed to enhance the appearance that the government is serious in its implementation of the law.

The published story is essentially political: corruption in high places, interference with the police by government, victimization of ordinary people like the readers of the *Star*, and a challenge to the freedom of the press by the arrest of a journalist. These are all *manna* to a Liberal/Radical press constituency whose party is in opposition. The nature of the story is determined and truncated, if not remade, by the medium in which it is carried, and by the powerful limitations of hegemonic discourse. The abyss between the male world of intercourse between government and newspaper editors that cannot be deemed private but merely oral, and the world of public written discourse that inscribes both gender and class ideologies, is eminently visible in the *Star*'s leader. Moreover, this initial 'confession' is not full: it does not divulge Parke's connection with the *Star*, nor that of the *Star* with the *North London Press*. When a Defence Fund is mooted in the *Star* on 30 November, it is via an anonymous *letter*, signed 'ONE WHO ADMIRES

PLUCK AND FAIR PLAY',[27] which is almost certainly from Parkes' fellow journalists on the *Star*, whose anonymity obscures Parkes' connection with the daily. *Truth's* interventions in 'Entre Nous' tell the same displacement story in this respect. Ideally, neither women nor working class readers need know of the existence of male homosexual culture.

But Labouchère, with his upper class background and readers, is far more sceptical about backing Parke than the *Star*, whose radical readers would support both Parke's rights as a journalist not to divulge his sources, and his radical weekly, the *North London Press*, which closed soon after his trial, after the 25 January 1890 issue. Labouchère's case for supporting the Defence Fund for Parke is that in order for investigation of how *his* amendment to the CLAA has been implemented in the Cleveland Street affair, a connection he makes, the trial must take place; it should not fail for want of funds.[28] There is also a notable and repeated geographical error in the early articles in *Truth*, which may be an intentional ploy to avoid libel or personal identifications, whereby the story is associated with 'Cavendish-square' for several weeks. Labouchère, with his class connections, takes great pains to insist that there is no evidence that Lord Euston and the other members of the aristocracy rumoured to be clients are culpable. And later he strenuously denies that the Prince of Wales was in any way implicated in the machinations of the process of the cover up. So, Labouchère's class identification overrides his radical party and conservative gender politics, resulting in complicity with the aristocracy, with clients of a homosexual brothel, and with a Tory government's 'corruption' that allowed Somerset (and with him the monarchy) to escape exposure as well as the law.[29]

Nevertheless, as the story proceeds while Parliament is in recess, *Truth* begins to threaten to raise the question of *government* corruption and involvement in the case in the House. Both of the other radical papers gratefully quote these threats, whole paragraphs at a time. While reliance on ready copy from other sources is a standard technique of regional and metropolitan papers of the period, here selected quotations distance news and act as a substitute for serious coverage. Such inserts appear less transgressive, providing editors with a rationale for readers and proprietors who complain about the inclusion of the story at all.

But what about Stead, whose membership in the National Vigilance Association will be remembered and whose evangelical revulsion at vice of any kind seems by far the strongest of the three? Interestingly, he is the editor whose coverage of Cleveland Street is weakest. He appears to start well; the story is introduced as a main one on the news page of the *Pall Mall Gazette* in November, and *two* days before the *Star*, on the 23rd, under the heading 'The Cleveland-Street Scandals'.[30] However, set beside it is a less prominent article on a libel case against the *Star*, which the *Star* lost. This same story appears rather more quietly in the *Pall Mall Gazette* gossip column, 'Today's Tittle Tattle',[31] which identifies the libel case against the *Star* with the CLAA, a cause dear to Stead and one which provides a tacit context for the coverage of Cleveland Street on p. 4, which reminds us of the potential danger of publishing such material. But significantly the links of Cleveland Street with 'The Maiden Tribute' and the CLAA are not stated. Reticence rules.

By 25 November the Cleveland Street material commands a three-decker headline (characteristic of the new journalism) in the *Pall Mall Gazette* Court News on p. 5. There is no mention of the new element of the case against Parke, or the referent of the sobriquet 'Cleveland-Street', which are both left to the prior knowledge of the reader. This is in great contrast with the controversial explicitness of 'The Maiden Tribute' coverage in the *Pall Mall Gazette* four years before. However, further information is cautiously disseminated in the paper: 'Tittle Tattle' (p. 6) relates the circumstances of Parke's late-night arrest, and of his being held in the police station overnight because no magistrate was available to receive bail. For the following month, most of the *Pall Mall Gazette* coverage is of this order, muted, appearing in 'Tittle Tattle', far less foregrounded than on the 23rd and 25th, in small paragraphs which often report and quote other papers' stories, including *Truth*, the *Telegraph*,[32] and *The Times*, and a speech by Labouchère in Lincoln. On 28 November the nervousness of the reporting is indicated by inclusions of phrases such as 'it is said' and 'it is understood'.[33]

It is to Labouchère that the energy of the campaign is attributed in the *Pall Mall Gazette*, which uses a quotation from *Truth* to make the association between the CLAA and Cleveland Street:

> it is my particular business. Newlove and Veck were indicted under a clause in the CLAA that I moved and carried when the bill was in Committee. It is a clause that was specially designed to arm the police with powers in cases like this, and I am determined that my clause shall run against all, and not alone against the obscure.[34]

One unsympathetic contemporary of Stead claimed that this mincing coverage of Cleveland Street is the aftermath of his sensational coverage of 'The Maiden Tribute', and mainly a wish to avoid imprisonment again.

This brings us to a fifth element in these encounters between journalism and government, in addition to political affiliations, gender discourse, networks, and market niche. That is the professional circumstances of the respective editors. Such relations between editor and proprietor being potentially fraught, they are worth examining. What emerges is that two of these three editors of the mainstream Radical press were not in employment on their papers within months, by early 1890. Stead, who had been threatened with a reduced salary since September 1888 by Yates Thompson, a proprietor who held him responsible for the loss in circulation after publication of 'The Maiden Tribute', was out of his job by 1 January 1890. O'Connor had been having serious trouble with the Liberal backers found by Labouchère; complaining of the Radical tone of the paper with respect to the mainstream Liberal party, they ousted him circa February 1890.[35] Stead had been watched carefully by his assistant, E. T. Cook, as was O'Connor by Massingham. So, in the first part of the Cleveland Street case between June and December 1889, when issues important to the Radical press were raised, including the rights of journalists to confidentiality, and government corruption, two of the three editors were insecure in their jobs; in the new year they were off the case.

Conclusion

These individual professional circumstances of Stead and O'Connor with respect to their proprietors – along with conventions of gendered discourse in the public sphere, the danger of attracting libel charges, and a complicity with government to protect the monarchy – contributed to the silence, late investigation, and half-hearted intervention of the Radical *Star* and *Pall Mall Gazette*, into the series of events around Cleveland Street. Sharing hegemonic orientation toward gender and the monarchy, the radical Liberal press and the Tory government agreed sufficiently to render the ire of the papers rhetorical. In this encounter, the government did its worst while the press watched in silence. Even when the libel case granted the story a newspaper life, the journalist messenger was bullied and jailed, with the only concession by the Government to the press being Parke's early release.

Five years before Cleveland Street, and from jail, Stead was able to look back with satisfaction on an effective, mainstream press campaign which, though it had pushed the limits of acceptable public discourse, resulted in national legislation. Its widespread support from bishops and clerics across religious divisions, MPs, disenfranchised women and the poor, derived above all from the extent to which the cause – 'child' prostitution – fitted into extant gender categories of heterosexuality: female helplessness, childhood innocence, and male concupiscence and violence, particularly in the underworld and underclasses. Hegemonic values were also exploited in other lexicons employed by Stead in his 1885 campaign – those of Christianity (and 'Paganism') for example, melodrama, and slavery, which had been outlawed on British territory since 1807. These in turn contributed to the overweening presence of the discourse of imperialism, into which Stead's 'traffic', 'white slavery', and 'kidnapping' of child victims for importation to the iniquities of the Continent, outside British jurisdiction, easily fitted. So, despite Stead's dubious (even illegal) methods of investigative journalism in 1885, considerable and sufficient public support was forthcoming.

None of this could be mustered around Cleveland Street with its unpublishable sexuality, its consenting male 'victims', its aristocratic clients, and its involvement with the monarchy, despite the undeniable illegality of the acts under the new legislation. Moreover, Stead lacked a secure institutional base to stage a robust encounter with the government's undermining of the CLAA, even had he been willing to risk the outing of a flourishing homosexual culture. Stead's silence, his recourse to late exposure, his problem with his proprietor, and the sharing of professional responsibility and legal liability with his rival editors indicate the limitations of the power of journalism over government, at least with respect to ideological issues such as homosexuality.

Five years later, the existence of the homosexual and homosexual communities and events similar to Cleveland Street were to break through hegemonic prohibitions into the public sphere, through the press and court reporting of the trials of Oscar Wilde. Once again on the issue of sexual orientation, the mainstream press, the courts, and the government were in general agreement. This breakthrough may be in part attributable to the focus of the case on an individual, which served both the government and the press, with its newly acquired taste for 'personality'. In 1889 the Cleveland Street case, as it was constructed, focussed on an institution rather than on any individual. Although the press searched for personalities beyond 'the house' in 1889, the culpable had fled, the government admitted nothing, and the jailed were regarded within a class framework as too lowly to be newsworthy. In the context of 'Wilde' in 1895, such figures were swept into view by the magnet of the larger spectacle.

It is also clear that in 1889 even the press was ambivalent and in difficulties about publication of what such a personality might say. Like the government, it had reasons to prefer silent, absent witnesses. This may be seen in the failure of the press to grasp the opportunity of the one figure in 1889 who talked well and authoritatively, and with some style. This was Jack (or John) Saul, putative author of the pornographic novel *The Sins of the Cities of the Plain* (1881). Saul, whose evidence to the court in the libel trial was relatively frank and very informative about gay culture in the West End, is a real candidate for the 'personality' of Cleveland Street. The magisterial dismissal by the judge of Saul's testimony in favour of the monosyllabic responses of Euston seems to be based entirely on the premise of class as the measure of credibility; there was no contest for the judge between a Lord and a self-confessed homosexual. Tellingly, the Crown did not charge Saul under the Act, just as his colourful testimony failed to attract much attention in the press. Material ripe for dissemination as sensational by a later press appeared in most detail in the court report in *The Times* on 16 January, in an abbreviated, openly censored form: 'The witness then proceeded to give evidence of a character unfit for publication'.[36]

In 1890 only Labouchère, his own proprietor, wealthy, *sui generis*, secure in his paper and in the House, was in a position to pursue the matter in the House as he had threatened, well after Parke was committed to prison. It is undoubtedly in the weekly *Truth*, in court, and in the House of Commons where Labouchère had Parliamentary immunity that the story evolved in the greatest detail. At a point late in the history of the story, when his intervention would not harm Hammond, or save Somerset or Hammond's minions Veck and Newlove, Labouchère's limited object in raising the matter in the House can only have been party political – to associate the government with corruption and to expose their failure to implement the new CLAA fairly. It is unlikely that he had in view Parke, who was currently serving his jail sentence.

The court reports of the libel trial were to the satisfaction of *The Times*, which concurred wholeheartedly with the class discrimination of the proceedings. No further, parallel comment was thus required in that paper at the time beyond the verbatim reports (*The Times*, 16, 17 January 1890: 6a–d, 6c–d). The later Parliamentary debate in February was also duly circulated by *The Times*, consisting of verbatim passages edited to exclude offensive matter.[37] Unable to shape Labouchère's charges to their satisfaction, *The Times* resorted unusually to leaders to put their readers straight, and to contest his allegations of government corruption. The case was *not* 'a great public scandal'. It did not warrant Labouchère's language, 'the unsavoury subject of which is known as the Cleveland-street case', 'the disgusting imputations and insinuations out of which the Separatists of the baser sort have been trying to manufacture political capital for many months past' (*The Times*, 1 March 1890: 11a–c).

The construction of 'Cleveland Street' as a story and its representation in this group of papers edited by Radical editors illustrate the ways ideology works in discourse, the ubiquitous and powerful gender dimensions of government by journalism, and the ways that individual professional circumstances of individual editors can seriously effect, in this case mute, the investigation and representation of news. The phenomenon of 'Cleveland Street' also eloquently shows how formations such as the press and government are alike embedded in discourse of a common culture; they are spoken by it, subjugated to it as well as journalists and politicians, and active in its development. What appear as 'encounters' between separate estates of journalism and government in 1885 and 1889–90 may also be viewed then as conversations between parties that share not only a common *langue*, but also a *parole* determined by gender ideology.

Stead's analysis of the power of journalism only four years before seems, in retrospect, blind to the contingencies of journalistic practice and the extent to which even insightful, committed, and radical editors can be, like politicians, silenced and subjugated by language, capital, and gender. In 1885 heterosexuality and its many discourses were on his side, though he didn't know it. The homosexual culture of Cleveland Street defeated him and his fellow editors, as it did in some respects the government. *Both* formations were prompted to compromising actions that resulted in silence: the government acted illegally to undermine the implementation of its own law, and the Liberal press sat on a story whose language was unavailable to them for use in public discourse, until it was translated into a story whose language they could deploy.

The silence about Cleveland Street is replicated in twentieth-century biography, history, and obituaries of the four protagonists and their papers.[38] It is hardly mentioned until after 1967, the year that the Labouchère amendment was rescinded. Two full-length books on Cleveland Street finally appeared in 1976. Like our ancestors, we remain historical speaking subjects, our principal encounters being those hardest to see, with history, culture, gender, ethnicity, and language.

Notes

1. W. T. Stead (1849–1912) edited a London, upmarket, evening daily (the *Pall Mall Gazette*) from 1883–90. A crusading and investigative journalist, Stead was notorious by 1886 for having instigated the sale and abduction of an underage girl for sex and having been jailed for his pains. A moral reformer, Stead aimed to raise the legal age of consent *and* to publish a serialized and salacious account of the proceedings in his daily. Stead's success, on both counts, was criticized by rival journalists for the sensationalist copy and distribution tactics, and by generations of women critics for his lascivious prose and mixed motives. For Stead, see Frederic Whyte, *The Life of W. T. Stead* (2 vols; London: Jonathan Cape, 1925) and Raymond L. Schults, *Crusader in Babylon: W. T. Stead and the Pall Mall Gazette* (Lincoln, Nebraska: University of Nebraska Press, 1972); for feminist critique see Judith R. Walkowitz, *City of Dreadful Delight* (London: Virago, 1992) and Lucy Bland, *Banishing the Beast* (Harmondsworth: Penguin, 1995).

2. For a conspectus of the 'new journalism', see Joel H. Wiener, *Papers for the Millions: The New Journalism in Britain, 1850 to 1914* (Westport, CT: Greenwood, 1988).

3. For the 'The Maiden Tribute' and its reception see J. W. Scott Robertson, *The Story of the Pall Mall Gazette* (London: Oxford University Press, 1950); Shults, 1972, Chapter 5; Walkowitz, 1992; Bland, 1995, 7–9, 58–60; and Toni Johnson-Woods, 'A Media's Tribute to Modern Babylon', unpublished paper delivered at the Australian Victorian Studies Association conference, Perth, 2000.

4. For the first twentieth-century full accounts of the trials and the personages of Cleveland Street, see H. Montgomery Hyde, *The Cleveland Street Scandal* (London: W. H. Allen, 1976) and Lewis Chester, David Leitch and Colin Simpson, *The Cleveland Street Affair* (London: Weidenfeld and Nicolson, 1976). While these rely heavily on newspaper coverage to help piece together the facts of the affair, their aim is a comprehensive history of the event rather than an analysis of the power of the press. Chester, Leitch and Simpson do not use the *Star* or even mention it, while Hyde (valuably) concentrates on the trials, quoting transcripts at length. For the latest commentary on Cleveland Street, see Harry Cocks, *Homosexual Desire in the Nineteenth Century* (London: I. B. Tauris, 2003) and Matt Cook, *London and the Culture of Homosexuality, 1885–1914* (Cambridge: Cambridge University Press, 2003).

5. The *Standard*'s early onslaught on Stead's story is informative about the general vehemence of the response, and the shock at his methods as well as the material. The long leader begins 'We venture to say that no other capital in Europe would tolerate for an hour the spectacle presented in the main thoroughfares of London at the present moment of men, women, and children offering to men, women and children copies of a newspaper containing the most offensive, highly-coloured and disgusting details concerning the vicious ways of a small section of the population' (*Standard* [17 July 1885]; quoted in Schults, 1972, 51).

6. Early in January 1866 Greenwood published a series of three articles on 'A Night in the Workhouse' by 'An Amateur Casual' (his brother James), who had disguised himself as a vagrant or 'casual' and stayed overnight in a work-

house ward designated as a shelter. See An Amateur Casual [James Greenwood], 'A Night in the Workhouse', *Pall Mall Gazette* (1 Jan. 1866), 1. Schults makes little of this investigative story (Schults, 1972, 15), but see Whyte, 1925, I. 68.

7. For a good general account of American journalism up to this period, see William E. Huntzicker, *The Popular Press, 1833–1865* (Westport, CT: Greenwood, 1999). Also see James L. Crouthamel, *Bennett's* New York Herald *and the Rise of the Popular Press* (Syracuse: Syracuse University Press, 1989), which focuses on Bennett and the *Herald*.

8. For Mayhew and earlier reports, see Anne Humpherys, *Travels into the Poor Man's Country: The Work of Henry Mayhew* (Athens, GA; Firle, Sussex: University of Georgia Press; Caliban, 1977).

9. See W. T. Stead, 'Government by Journalism', *Contemporary Review*, 49 (May 1886), 653–74. The *Contemporary Review* was an upmarket, intellectual, and respected monthly that was particularly interested in articles which explored current events, publications, and issues from a Christian, evangelical point of view. Stead's self-styled alliance of the press with morality was evident from his earliest journalism. The prominence of this claim in respect to 'The Maiden Tribute' and no doubt his notoriety/newsworthiness made publication of his riposte to his critics particularly alluring to the *Contemporary*. For more on the *Contemporary Review* see Laurel Brake, *Subjugated Knowledges* (Basingstoke: Macmillan, 1994), 51–62, John Griffin, *British Literary Magazines*, ed. Alvin Sullivan (Westport, CT: Greenwood Press, 1984), III: 77–82, and *Wellesley*, I: 210–13.

10. The notion of 'the dignity of literature' was introduced by Thackeray in a letter of 12 January 1850 published in the *Morning Chronicle*. It was written in response to an attack on *Pendennis* by John Forster, a close friend of Dickens. The phrase also figured in exchanges between Dickens and Thackeray when Dickens and Bulwer attempted to organise authors into a Guild to protect themselves as a profession through copyright. Forster's replies to Thackeray appeared in the *Examiner*, 19 January 1850 and 12 July 1851. These differences of opinion between Thackeray and Dickens/Forster survived long after the original exchanges in 1850–51. See Gordon Ray, *Thackeray: The Age of Wisdom* (London: Oxford University Press, 1958), 36–8, 150–3.

11. See Terry Eagleton, *The Function of Criticism* (London: Verso, 1984), especially chapters 1–3, and Laurel Brake, 'Writing, Cultural Production and the Periodical Press in the Nineteenth Century' in *Writing and Victorianism*, ed. J. B. Bullen (London and New York: Longman, 1997), 62–3, and Brake, *Print in Transition* (Basingstoke: Palgrave, 2001), 248–9.

12. The CLAA (1885) was the outcome of Stead's 'Maiden Tribute' campaign to lower the female age of consent to sex. A late addition extended the criminal liability of sexual acts between consenting male adults from sodomy in public to all sexual acts in public or private. Known as the Labouchère amendment, it was prompted by Stead, and functioned as a 'blackmailer's charter'. Under it Wilde was charged with 'gross indecency' a decade later.

13. Arnold's championing of a classical model spans his work, from his 1853 'Preface' to *Poems* through 'The Function of Criticism' (1864), *Culture and Anarchy* (1869), to 'The Study of Poetry' (1880).

14. Labouchère's grandparents were bankers from Amsterdam to which their French Huguenot ancestors had emigrated.

15. Such derision of rival periodicals, particularly those from a different cultural zone, was not uncommon. The *Saturday Review*, known jocularly as 'The Saturday Reviler' often shored up its own dignity by denunciation of other titles. See for example, its ridicule of the *Star* in an article called 'Parnellium Sidus' (*Saturday Review* [21 Jan. 1888], 71).

16. Qtd. in Stephen Koss, *The Rise and Fall of the Political Press in Britain*, 2 vols (London: Hamish Hamilton, 1981), 216–17.

17. See Frederic Whyte, I (1925): 177.

18. Parke's trial took place 15–16 January 1891, and he was released in early July.

19. The initial leader in the *Star* on Cleveland Street confirms this: 'a hideous subject which has been discussed in private for weeks, and even months' (*Star*, 25 Nov. 1889, 1).

20. Parke was registered as owner and proprietor of the paper. The Colindale catalogue shows that for four numbers (513–16; 18 May–8 June 1889) in its short life it revealed the link between the *Star* and itself in its title, the *North London Press and Star*. Before that (30 March–11 May 1889) its title was the *North and East London Star*, and afterwards, for the duration of its existence including the Cleveland Street period (15 June 1889–25 Jan 1890), the *North London Press*.

21. In October and July, respectively. See Hyde 1976: 26.

22. In August/September.

23. 'WHAT WE THINK. A Word on the Scandals', *Star* (25 Nov. 1889), 1; my italics.

24. He was Superintendent and Extra-Equerry to the Prince of Wales.

25. See Theo Aronson, *Prince Eddy and the Homosexual Underground* (London: John Murray, 1994), and James Lees-Milne, *The Enigmatic Edwardian* (London: Sidgwick and Jackson, 1986), 4.

26. Newton's trial was held very late on in the proceedings, 16–20 May 1891. If the CLAA links the Cleveland Street prosecutions to the Wilde trials, so does Newton who acted in 1895 for Alfred Taylor, Wilde's co-defendant.

27. *Star* (30 Nov. 1889), 2e.

28. *Truth* (5 Dec. 1889), 1039.

29. Chester Leitch, and Simpson's subtle analysis of Labouchère's conflicting loyalties and public positions in *Truth* and Parliament repays reading. See Chapter 9 especially.

30. *PMG* (23 Nov. 1889), 4.

31. 'Today's Tittle Tattle', *PMG* (23 Nov. 1889), 5.

32. *PMG* (4 Dec. 1889), 6a.

33. 'Today's Tittle Tattle', *PMG* (28 Nov. 1889), 4.

34. *Truth*, quoted *PMG* (4 Dec. 1889), 6c.

35. See John Goodbody, 'The *Star*' in Joel M. Wiener, ed. *Papers for the Millions: The New Journalism in Britain, 1850 to 1914* (Westport CT, London: Greenwood, 1988), 143–63.

36. *The Times* (16 Jan. 1890), 6c. The whole of the transcript of the libel trial may be read in the Public Record Office in the files relating to Cleveland Street at DPP 1/95/4.

37. *The Times* (1 Mar. 1890), 8e–10d.

38. The omission of all mention of Cleveland Street from Ernest Parke's obitu-
    ary in *The Times* (23 June 1944: 7e) is particularly notable, since he had been
    imprisoned. Parke went on to succeed O'Connor as the editor of the *Star*
    (1891–1908), to found and edit the *Morning Leader* from 1892, become vice-
    chairman of a county council, a JP and a member of the National Liberal
    Club. Nor is Parke's defence of his sources at the *North London Press* men-
    tioned more recently in Dennis Griffiths's entry on Parke (Dennis Griffiths,
    The Encyclopaedia of the British Press [New York: St Martin's Press (now
    Palgrave Macmillan), 1992], 455).

Bibliography

Archives

British Library, Department of Western Manuscripts, Escott Papers
Library of Congress, Manuscripts Division, Pennell-Whistler Collection
Pearson Papers, Special Collections, University College London
Whistler Archive, Glasgow University Library, Glasgow, Scotland

Victorian periodicals cited

Athenaeum, 1830–1921
Birmingham Daily Post, 1857–1918
Birmingham Journal, 1859–69
Britannia, 1839–43, 1869
Contemporary Review 1866–74; 1876–1990
Critic, 1820
Edinburgh Review, 1813–1929
Eliza Cook's Journal, 1851–52
Englishwoman's Domestic Magazine, 1859–74
Era, 1838–1939
Foreign Quarterly Review, 1827–47
Fortnightly Review, 1865–1934
Hansard, 1829–91
Illustrated London News, 1842–1990
Lloyd's Weekly Newspaper, 1849–1902
London Telegraph, 1824–25, 1848, 1865, 1916
Longman's Magazine, 1882–1905
Merry England: An Illustrated Magazine, 1883–95
Mitchell's Newspaper Press Directory, 1846–1907
Monthly Packet of Evening Reading, 1851–99
New Review, 1889–97
News of the World, 1843–present
Nineteenth Century, 1877–1900 (thereafter *Nineteenth Century and After*)
North American Review, 1877–1907
North London Press, 1889–90
Northern Star, 1837–52
Pall Mall Gazette, 1865–1923
Pearson's Magazine, 1896–1939
Punch, 1841–2002
Quarterly Review, 1809–1967
Review of Reviews, 1890–1904
Reynolds's Miscellany, 1846–69
Reynolds's Weekly Newspaper, 1850–51

Saturday Review, 1855–68
Sketch, 1893–1959
Star, 1888–1915
Sunday Citizen, 1960–67
Sunday Times, 1822–present
The Times, 1788–present
Truth, 1877–1957
Universal Review, 1888–90
Weekly Dispatch, 1801–1928
Woman at Home, 1893–1920
Woman's Signal, 1894–99
Woman's World, 1887–90
Women's Penny Paper, 1888–90
Westminster Review, 1824–1914
World: A Journal for Men and Women, 1874–1922
Yellow Book, 1894–97

Secondary sources

Adams, W. E. *Memoirs of a Social Atom*. 1903. 2 vols; reprinted in one volume. Intro. John Saville. New York: A. M. Kelley, 1968.

Adorno, Theodore, and Max Horkheimer. *Dialectic of Enlightenment*. London: Verso, 1979.

Altick, Richard D. *The English Common Reader: A Social History of the Mass Reading Public, 1800–1900*. Chicago: University of Chicago Press, 1957.

Anderson, Patricia. *The Printed Image and the Transformation of Popular Culture 1790–1860*. Oxford: Oxford University Press, 1991.

Andrews, Alexander. *The History of British Journalism*. 2 vols. London: Bentley, 1859.

Anon. *The Progress of British Newspapers*, London: Simpkin, Marshall, Hamilton, Kent and Co, n. d. [1901].

Armstrong, Alan. *Farmworkers in England and Wales: A Social and Economic History 1770–1980*. Ames: Iowa State University Press, 1988.

Arnold, Dana. *Re-presenting the Metropolis: Architecture, Urban Experience and Social Life in London 1800–1840*. Aldershot: Ashgate, 2000.

Aronson, Theo. *Prince Eddy and the Homosexual Underground*. London: John Murray, 1994.

Bakhtin, Mikhail. *The Dialogic Imagination*, ed. Michael Holquist. Austin: University of Texas Press, 1981.

Baron, Wendy. *Walter Sickert*. New York and London: Phaidon, 1973.

Baudelaire, Charles. *Selected Writings on Art and Literature*, trans. P. E. Charvet. London: Penguin, 1992.

Beckson, Karl. *London in the 1890s: A Cultural History*. London and New York: W. W. Norton, 1992.

Beetham, Margaret. *A Magazine of her Own? Domesticity and Desire in the Woman's Magazine, 1800–1914*. London: Routledge, 1996.

Beetham, Margaret. 'Towards a Theory of the Periodical as a Publishing Genre', in *Investigating Victorian Journalism*, ed. Laurel Brake, Aled Jones, and Lionel Madden. Basingstoke: Macmillan, 1990, 19–32.

Belchem, John. *'Orator' Hunt: Henry Hunt and English Working-Class Radicalism.* Oxford: Clarendon, 1985.

Benjamin, Walter. *Illuminations.* London: Fontana, 1977.

Benjamin, Walter. *Charles Baudelaire: A Lyric Poet in the Era of High Capitalism,* trans. Harry Zohn. London and New York: Verso, 1997.

Benn, Tony. *Arguments for Socialism.* London: Verso, 1979.

Bennett, Scott. 'Revolutions in Thought: Serial Publication and the Mass Market for Reading', in *The Victorian Periodical Press: Samplings and Soundings,* ed. Joanne Shattock and Michael Wolff. Leicester: Leicester University Press, 1982, 225–57.

Berridge, Virginia. 'Popular Journalism and Working-Class Attitudes 1854–1886: A Study of *Reynolds's Newspaper, Lloyd's Weekly Newspaper* and the *Weekly Times'.* Ph.D., 2 vols, University of London, 1976.

Bhabha, Homi K. *The Location of Culture.* London: Routledge, 1994.

Biagini, Eugenio F. *Liberty, Retrenchment and Reform: Popular Liberalism in the Age , of Gladstone, 1860–1880.* Cambridge: Cambridge University Press, 1992.

Bladgen, Cyprian. *'Longman's Magazine'. Review of English Literature,* 4 (1963), 9–22.

Bland, Lucy. *Banishing the Beast: Sexuality and the Early Feminists.* New York: New Press, 1995.

Bleiler, E. F. Introduction and Bibliography to George W. M. Reynolds, *Wagner the Wehr-wolf.* New York: Dover, 1975.

Boos, Florence. 'A History of Their Own: Mona Caird, Frances Swiney, and *fin de siècle* Feminist Family History', in *Contesting the Master Narrative,* ed. Jeffrey Cox and Shelton Stromquist: Iowa City: University of Iowa Press, 1999.

Bourne, H. R. Fox. *English Newspapers: Chapters in the History of Journalism.* 2 vols. London: Chatto and Windus, 1887.

Brake, Laurel. *Print in Transition.* Basingstoke: Palgrave, 2001.

Brake, Laurel. *Subjugated Knowledges.* London: Macmillan, 1994.

Brake, Laurel. 'Writing, Cultural Production and the Periodical Press in the Nineteenth Century', in *Writing and Victorianism,* ed. J. B. Bullen. London and New York: Longman, 1997, 54–72.

Brooks, Chris, ed. *The Albert Memorial.* New Haven: Yale University Press, 2000.

Brooks, Peter. *The Melodramatic Imagination: Balzac, Henry James, Melodrama, and the Mode of Excess.* New Haven and London: Yale University Press, 1995.

Bud, Robert, and Gerrylynn K. Roberts. *Science vs. Practice: Chemistry in Victorian Britain.* Manchester: Manchester University Press, 1984.

Burton, Antoinette. *Burdens of History.* Chapel Hill: University of North Carolina Press, 1994.

Burton, Antoinette. 'Tongues Untied: Lord Salisbury's "Black Man" and the Boundaries of Imperial Democracy'. *Comparative Study of Society and History* (2000), 632–61.

Caird, Mona. *The Morality of Marriage and Other Essays on the Status and Destiny of Women.* London: Redway, 1897.

Cannadine, David. 'The Context, Performance and Meaning of Ritual: The British Monarchy and the "Invention of Tradition", c.1820–1977', in *The Invention of Tradition,* ed. E. Hobsbawm and T. Ranger. Cambridge: Cambridge University Press, 1983, 101–64.

Chamberlain, Joseph. *A Political Memoir, 1880–92*. Westport, CT: Greenwood, 1975.

Chapman, Elizabeth Rachel. *Marriage Questions in Modern Fiction, and Other Essays on Kindred Subjects*. London and New York: John Lane, 1897.

Chester, Lewis, David Leitch, and Colin Simpson. *The Cleveland Street Affair*. London: Weidenfeld and Nicolson, 1976.

Clapperton, Jane Hume. *Scientific Meliorism and the Evolution of Happiness*. London: John Lane, 1885.

Cocks, Harry. *Homosexual Desire in the Nineteenth Century*. London: I. B. Tauris, 2003, 188–218.

Codell, Julie F. 'The Empire Writes Back: Native Informant Discourse in the Victorian Press', in *Imperial Co-Histories*, ed. Julie F. Codell. Fairleigh: Dickinson University Press, 2003.

Cook, Matt. *London and the Culture of Homosexuality, 1885–1914*. Cambridge: Cambridge University Press, 2003.

Corbett, David Peters. *Walter Sickert*. London: Tate Publishing, 2001.

Crouthamel, James L. *Bennett's New York Herald and the Rise of the Popular Press*. Syracuse: Syracuse University Press, 1989.

Cunningham, Hugh. 'The Language of Patriotism', in *Patriotism: The Making and Unmaking of British National Identity. Volume 1: History and Politics*, ed. Raphael Samuel. London: Routledge, 1989.

Curran, James, and Jean Seaton. *Power without Responsibility: The Press and Broadcasting in Britain*. London and New York: Routledge, 1997.

Dolin, Tim. 'Hardy and the Decline of Victorian Liberalism, 1880–1900'. Unpublished paper. http://www.newcastle.edu.au/department/el/pages/dolin.htm.

Drazin, Yaffa Claire, ed. *'My Other Self.' The Letters of Olive Schreiner and Havelock Ellis, 1884–1920*. New York: Peter Lang, 1992.

Dyos, J. and M. Woolf, eds. *The Victorian City*. 2 vols. London and Boston: Routledge and Kegan Paul, 1973.

Eagleton, Terry. *The Function of Criticism*. London: Verso, 1984.

Ebbatson, Roger. *Hardy: The Margin of the Unexpressed*. Sheffield: Sheffield Academic Press, 1993.

Edwards, Peter D. *Dickens's 'Young Men': George Augustus Sala, Edmund Yates, and the World of Victorian Journalism*. Brookfield, VT: Scolar, 1997.

Ellegard, Alvar. 'The Readership of the Periodical Press in Mid-Victorian Britain'. *Victorian Periodicals Newsletter*, 13 (1971), 3–22.

Elliott, Bridget J. 'Sights of Pleasure: Beardsley's Images of Actresses and the New Journalism of the Nineties', in *Reconsidering Aubrey Beardsley*, ed. Robert Langenfeld. Ann Arbor and London: UMI Research Press, 1989, 71–101.

Ellis, Henry Havelock. *My Life*. London: Heinemann, 1940.

Ellis, Henry Havelock. *Women and Marriage, or, Evolution in Sex, Illustrating the Changing Status of Women*. London: William Reeves, 1888.

Engels, Dagmar. 'The Age of Consent Act of 1891: Colonial Ideology in Bengal', *South Asia Research*, 3 (1983), 107–34.

Engels, Frederick. *The Condition of the Working Class in England*. London: Grafton, 1984.

Epstein, James. *Radical Expression: Political Language, Ritual and Symbol in England, 1790–1830*. Oxford: Oxford University Press, 1994.

Fanon, Frantz. *Black Skin, White Masks*. New York: Grove, 1982.

Farwell, Marilyn. 'Heterosexual Plots and Lesbian Subtexts: Toward a Theory of Lesbian Narrative Space', in *Lesbian Texts and Contexts: Radical Revisions*, ed. Karla Jay and Joanne Glasgow. London: Onlywomen, 1992, 91–103.

Felstiner, John. *The Lies of Art: Max Beerbohm's Parody and Caricature*. London: Victor Gollancz, 1973.

Finn, Margot. *After Chartism: Class and Nation in English Radical Politics 1848–1874*. Cambridge: Cambridge University Press, 1993.

Flint, Kate. *The Woman Reader 1837–1914*. Oxford: Clarendon, 1993.

Foucault, Michel. *Discipline and Punish: The Birth of the Clinic*, trans. Alan Sheridan. Harmondsworth: Penguin, 1977.

Foucault, Michel. The Foucault Reader, ed. Paul Rabinow. Harmondsworth: Penguin, 1984.

Fox, Celina and Michael Wolff. 'Pictures from the Magazines', in *The Victorian City*, ed. J. Dyos and M. Woolf. 2 vols. London and Boston: Routledge and Kegan Paul, 1973, 2: 559–82.

Gagnier, Regenia. *Idylls of the Marketplace: Oscar Wilde and the Victorian Public*. Berkeley: University of California Press, 1986.

Gallagher, Catherine. *The Industrial Reformation of English Fiction: Social Discourse and Narrative Form 1832–1867*. Chicago: University of Chicago Press, 1985.

Geertz, Clifford. *The Interpretation of Cultures*. London: Hutchinson, 1975.

Gikandi, Simon. *Maps of Englishness*. New York: Columbia University Press, 1996.

Gill, Conrad. and C. G. Robinson. *A Short History of Birmingham*. Birmingham: Corporation of the City of Birmingham, 1938.

Gilmartin, Kevin. *Print Politics: The Press and Radical Opposition in Early Nineteenth-Century England*. Cambridge: Cambridge University Press, 1996.

Gleadle, Kathryn. *The Early Feminists: Radical Unitarians and the Emergence of the Women's Rights Movement, 1831–51*. New York: St. Martin's, 1995.

Griffin, John. 'The *Contemporary Review*', in *British Literary Magazines*, ed. Alvin Sullivan, vol. III. Westport, CT: Greenwood Press, 1984.

Griffiths, Dennis. *The Encyclopedia of the British Press*. New York and Bath: St Martin's, 1992.

Habermas, Jürgen. *The Structural Transformation of the Public Sphere: An Inquiry into a Category of Bourgeois Society*. London: Polity, 1989.

Hadley, Elaine. *Melodramatic Tactics: Theatricalized Dissent in the English Marketplace 1800–1885*. Stanford: Stanford University Press, 1995.

Haight, Gordon. *George Eliot and John Chapman, with Chapman's Diaries*. Hamden, CT: Archon, 1969.

Hall, Catherine. *White, Male and Middle-Class: Explorations in Feminism and History*. Cambridge: Polity, 1992.

Hamlin, Christopher. 'Providence and Putrefaction: Victorian Sanitarians and the Natural Theology of Health and Disease', in *Energy & Entropy: Science and Culture in Victorian Britain*, ed. Patrick Brantlinger. Bloomington: Indiana University Press, 1989, 93–123.

Hardy, Thomas. 'Author's Preface', *Far From the Madding Crowd*. New York: Penguin, 1978.

Hardy, Thomas. *The Collected Letters of Thomas Hardy*, ed. Richard Little Purdy and Michael Millgate. Vol. I: 1840–1892. Oxford: Clarendon, 1981.

Hassan, John. *A History of Water in Modern England and Wales*. Manchester: Manchester University Press, 1998.

Hatton, Joseph. *Journalistic London, Being a Series of Sketches of Famous Pens and Papers of the Day*. London: Sampson Low, Marston, Searle and Rivington, 1882.

Hayes, William A. *The Background and Passage of the Third Reform Act*. New York: Garland, 1982.

Heilmann, Ann. 'Mona Caird (1854–1932)', *Women's History Review*, 15 (1996), 67–95.

Hobsbawm, Eric, and George Rudé. *Captain Swing*. New York, Pantheon, 1968.

Holdenby, Christopher. *Folk of the Furrow*. London: Smith, Elder, 1913.

Hollis, Patricia. *The Pauper Press: A Study in Working-Class Radicalism of the 1830s*. Oxford: Oxford University Press, 1970.

Homans, Margaret. *Royal Representations: Queen Victoria and British Culture 1837–67*. Chicago: Chicago University Press, 1998.

Horn, Pamela. *Labouring Life in the Victorian Countryside*. Dublin: Gill and Macmillan, 1976.

Howitt, Mary. *An Autobiography*, ed. Margaret Howitt. 2 vols. London: William Isbister, 1889.

Howkins, Alun. 'The Discovery of Rural England', in *Englishness: Politics and Culture, 1880–1920*, ed. Robert Colls and Philip Dodd. London: Dover, NH: Croom Helm, 1986, 62–88.

Howkins, Alun. *Reshaping Rural England: A Social History, 1850–1925*. London: Harper Collins, 1991.

Humpherys, Anne. 'G. W. M. Reynolds: Popular Literature and Popular Politics'. *Victorian Periodicals Review*, 16 (1983), 78–89.

Humpherys, Anne. 'Generic Strands and Urban Twists: The Victorian Mysteries Novel'. *Victorian Studies*, 34 (1991), 463–72.

Humpherys, Anne. 'Popular Narrative and Political Discourse in *Reynolds's Weekly Newspaper*', in *Investigating Victorian Journalism*, ed. Laurel Brake, Aled Jones and Lionel Madden. Basingstoke: Macmillan, 1990, 33–47.

Humpherys, Anne. *Travels into the Poor Man's Country: The Work of Henry Mayhew*. Athens, GA and Firle, Sussex: University of Georgia Press and Caliban, 1977.

Humphrey, Mary and Seitz, Don C. 'The Story of Sheridan Ford – International Critic', *Detroit Free Press*, 30 Apr. 1922, 8.

Huntzicker, William E. *The Popular Press, 1833–1865*. Westport, CT: Greenwood, 1999.

Hyde, H. Montgomery. *The Cleveland Street Scandal*. London: W. H. Allen, 1976.

Jackson, Holbrook. *The Eighteen Nineties: A Review of Art and Ideas at the Close of the Nineteenth Century*. London: Grant Richards, 1913.

James, Louis. *Fiction for the Working Man 1830–1850: A Study of the Literature Produced for the Working Classes in Early Victorian Urban England*. London: Penguin University Books, 1973.

James, Louis, and John Saville. 'G. W. M. Reynolds', in *Dictionary of Labour Biography*, ed. Joyce Bellamy and John Saville, Vol. 3. London: Macmillan, 1976.

Jay, Karla, and Joanne Glasgow, eds. *Lesbian Texts and Contexts: Radical Revisions*. London: Onlywomen, 1992.

Jefferies, Richard. *Landscape and Labour*, ed. John Pearson. Wiltshire: Moonraker, 1979.

Jefferies, Richard. *Hodge and His Masters*. Gloucestershire: Alan Sutton, 1992 [1880].

Jenkins, Mick. *The General Strike of 1842*. London: Lawrence and Wishart, 1980.

Jenkins, T. A. *The Liberal Ascendancy, 1830–1886*. New York: St. Martin's, 1994.

Johnson-Woods, Toni. 'A Media's Tribute to Modern Babylon'. Unpublished paper delivered at the Australian Victorian Studies Association conference, Perth, 2000.

Jones, Aled. *Power of the Press: Newspapers, Power and the Public in Nineteenth-Century England*. Aldershot: Ashgate, 1996.

Jones, Andrew. *The Politics of Reform, 1884*. Cambridge: Cambridge University Press, 1972.

Jopling, Louise. *Twenty Years of My Life*. London: John Lane, 1925.

Joyce, Patrick. 'The constitution and narrative structure of Victorian politics', in *Re-reading the Constitution: New Narratives in the Political History of England's Long Nineteenth Century*, ed. James Vernon. Cambridge: Cambridge University Press, 1996, 179–203.

Joyce, Patrick. *Democratic Subjects: The Self and the Social in Nineteenth-Century England*. Cambridge: Cambridge University Press, 1994.

Joyce, Patrick. *Visions of the People: Industrial England and the Question of Class, c. 1848–1914*. Cambridge: Cambridge University Press, 1991.

Kapp, Yvonne. *Eleanor Marx*. 2 vols. London: Virago, 1979.

Keith, W. J. *Regions of the Imagination: The Development of British Rural Fiction*. Toronto: University of Toronto Press, 1988.

Keith, W. J. *The Rural Tradition: William Cobbett, Gilbert White, and Other Non-Fiction Prose Writers of the English Countryside*. Toronto: University of Toronto Press, 1975.

Kestner, Joseph. *Protest and Reform: The British Social Narrative by Women 1827–1867*. London: Methuen, 1985.

Klancher, Jon P. *The Making of English Reading Audiences, 1790–1832*. Madison: University of Wisconsin Press, 1987.

Koss, Stephen. *The Rise and Fall of the Political Press in Britain. Volume 1: The Nineteenth Century*. London: Hamish Hamilton, 1981.

Langland, Elizabeth. *Nobody's Angels: Middle-Class Women and Domestic Ideology in Victorian Culture*. Ithaca: Cornell University Press, 1995.

Law, Graham, ed. *The Illustrated London News (1842–1901) The Graphic (1869–1901) Indexes to Fiction*. Queensland: University of Queensland, 2001.

Law, Graham. 'New Woman Novels in Newspapers', *Media History*, 7 (2001), 17–32.

Law, Graham. *Serializing Fiction in the Victorian Press*. Basingstoke: Palgrave, 2000.

Le Gallienne, Richard. *The Romantic '90s*. London: Robin Clark, 1993.

Leach, Joseph. *Bright Particular Star: The Life Times of Charlotte Cushman*. New Haven: Yale University Press, 1970.

Lee, Alan J. *The Origins of the Popular Press in England 1855–1914*. London: Croom Helm, 1976.

Lees-Milne, James. *The Enigmatic Edwardian: The Life of Reginald Brett, 2nd Viscount Esher*. London: Sidgwick and Jackson, 1986.

Levy, Anita. *Other Women: The Writing of Class, Race, and Gender, 1832–1898*. Princeton: Princeton University Press, 1991.

Lewis, W. G. *The Cook: Plain and Practical Directions for Cooking and Housekeeping; With Upwards of 700 recipes*. Rev. ed. London: Houslton and Stoneman, 1849.

Liebig, Justus, M. D. *Researches on the Chemistry of Food*, ed. William Gregory. London: Taylor and Walton, 1847.

Lightman, Bernard. ' "The Voices of Nature": Popularizing Victorian Science', in *Victorian Science in Context*, ed. B. Lightman. Chicago: University of Chicago Press, 1997, 187–211.

Lown, Judy. *Women and Industrialization: Gender at Work in Nineteenth-Century England*. Cambridge: Polity, 1990.

Lyotard, Jean-Francois. *The Differend: Phrases in Dispute*, trans. Georges Van Den Abbeele. Manchester: Manchester University Press, 1988.

Maccoby, Simon. *English Radicalism 1853–1886*. 3 vols. London: George Allen and Unwin, 1938.

Mackenzie, John. *Propaganda and Empire: The Manipulation of British Public Opinion 1880–1960*. Manchester: Manchester University Press, 1985.

Mahon, Derek. *The Yellow Book*. Loughcrew, Ireland: Gallery, 1997.

Maidment, Brian E. 'Magazines of Popular Progress and the Artisans', *Victorian Periodicals Review*, 17 (1984), 83–93.

Maidment, Brian. *Into the 1830s: Some Origins of Victorian Illustrated Journalism*. Manchester: Manchester Polytechnic Library, 1992.

Maidment, B. E. *Reading Popular Prints, 1790–1870*. Manchester: Manchester University Press, 2001.

Mani, Lata. 'The Production of an Official Discourse on *Sati* in Early Nineteenth-Century Bengal', in *Europe and its Others*, ed. F. Barker. Colchester: University of Essex, 1979, 107–27.

Marks, Patricia. ' "Love, Larks & Lotion": A Descriptive Bibliography of E. J. Milliken's "Arry" Poems in *Punch*', *Victorian Periodicals Review*, 26 (1993), 67–75.

Marsh, Jan. *Back to the Land: The Pastoral Impulse from 1880 to 1914*. London: Quartet, 1982.

Marx, Karl. *The Eighteenth Brumaire of Louis Napoleon. Marx and Engels: Basic Writings on Politics and Philosophy*, ed. Lewis S. Feuer. London: Fontana, 1974.

McCalman, Iain. *Radical Underworld: Prophets, Revolutionaries and Pornographers in London, 1795–1840*. Cambridge: Cambridge University Press, 1988.

McKenzie, D. F. *Making Meaning*. Amherst and Boston, MA: University of Massachusetts Press, 2002.

McWilliam, Rohan. 'The Mysteries of George W. M. Reynolds: Radicalism and Melodrama in Victorian Britain', in *Living and Learning: Essays in Honour of J. F. C. Harrison*, ed. Malcolm Chase and Ian Dyck. Aldershot: Ashgate, 1996, 182–98.

Mee, John. ' "Examples of Safe Printing": Censorship and Popular Radical Literature in the 1790s', in *Literature and Censorship*, ed. Nigel Smith. London: English Association, 1993, 81–95.

Merrill, Linda. *A Pot of Paint: Aesthetics on Trial in Whistler v Ruskin*. Washington, DC: Smithsonian Institution Press, 1992.

Merrill, Lisa. *When Romeo was a Woman: Charlotte Cushman and her Circle of Female Spectators*. Ann Arbor: University of Michigan Press, 1999.

Miller, Florence Fenwick. *Harriet Martineau*. London: W. H. Allen, 1884.

Miller, George, and Hugoe Matthews. *Richard Jefferies: A Bibliographical Study*. Brookfield, VT: Scolar, 1993.

Millgate, Michael. *Thomas Hardy: A Biography*. Oxford: Oxford University Press, 1985.

Mitchell, Charles, ed. *The Newspaper Press Directory*. London: Charles Mitchell, 1846.

Mitchell, Charles, ed. *The Newspaper Press Directory*. London: Charles Mitchell, 1851.

Mitchell, Sally. *The Fallen Angel: Chastity, Class and Women's Reading, 1835–1880*. Bowling Green, OH: Bowling Green University Popular Press, 1981.

Mix, Katherine Lyon. *A Study in Yellow: The Yellow Book and its Contributors*. Lawrence, KS: University of Kansas Press; London: Constable, 1960.

Morgan, Kenneth O. *Wales 1880–1980: Rebirth of a Nation*. Oxford: Oxford University Press, 1981.

Morison, Stanley. *The English Newspaper: Some Account of the Physical Development of Journals Printed in London between 1622 and the Present Day*. Cambridge: Cambridge University Press, 1932.

Munt, Sally R. *Heroic Desire: Lesbian Identity and Cultural Space*. London: Cassell, 1998.

Myers, Greg. 'Science for Women and Children: The Dialogue of Popular Science in the Nineteenth Century', in *Nature Transfigured: Science and Literature, 1700–1900*, ed. John Christie and Sally Shuttleworth. Manchester: Manchester University Press, 1989.

Nelson, James G. *The Early Nineties: A View from the Bodley Head*. Cambridge: Harvard University Press, 1971.

Nestor, Pauline A. 'A New Departure in Women's Publishing: *The English Woman's Journal* and *The Victoria Magazine*'. *Victorian Periodicals Review*, 15 (1982), 93–106.

North, John S. *The Waterloo Directory of English Newspapers and Periodicals 1800–1900*. Waterloo: North Waterlook Academic Press, 1997.

Notable Women of Our Own Times. London: Ward Lock, 1883.

Nowell-Smith, Simon. *The House of Cassell 1848–1958*. London: Cassell, 1958.

O'Hanlon, Rosalind. 'Recovering the Subject: Subaltern Studies and Histories of Resistance in Colonial South Asia', *Modern Asian Studies*, 22 (1988), 189–224.

Olney, R. J. 'The Politics of Land', in *The Victorian Countryside*, ed. G. E. Mingay. 2 vols. London: Routledge and Kegan Paul, 1981, I: 58–70.

Orel, Harold, ed. *Thomas Hardy's Personal Writings*. Lawrence, KA: University of Kansas Press, 1966.

Parry, Ann. 'Theories of Formation: *Macmillan's Magazine*: Vol. 1, November 1859. Monthly. 1/0'. *Victorian Periodicals Review*, 26 (1993), 100–4.

Parsons, Deborah. *Streetwalking the Metropolis: Women, the City and Modernity*. Oxford and New York: Oxford University Press, 2000.

Patten, Robert L. *Charles Dickens and his Publishers*. Oxford: Clarendon, 1978.

Pearson, Karl. *The Ethic of Free Thought: A Selection of Essays and Lectures*. London: T. Fisher Unwin, 1888.

Pelling, Margaret. *Cholera, Fever and English Medicine 1825–1865*. Oxford: Oxford University Press, 1978.

Pickering, Paul. *Chartism and the Chartists in Manchester and Salford*. Basingstoke: Macmillan, 1995.

Plunkett, John. *Queen Victoria – First Media Monarch*. Oxford: Oxford University Press, 2003.

Porter, Roy. 'Seeing the Past', *Past and Present* (1988), 186–205.

Price, W. T. *A Life of Charlotte Cushman*. New York: Brentano's, 1894.

Prochaska, Frank. *Royal Bounty: The Making of a Welfare Monarchy*. New Haven: Yale University Press, 1995.

Prothero, Iowerth. *Radical Artisans in England and France, 1830–1870*. Cambridge: Cambridge University Press, 1997.

Queffélec, Lise. *Le roman-feuilleton français au XIXe siècle*. Paris: Presses Universitaires de France, 1989.

Quilter, Harry. *Opinions on Men, Women and Things*, ed. Mary Quilter. London: Swan Sonnenschein, 1909.

Quilter, Henry, ed. *Is Marriage a Failure? The Most Important Letters on the Subject in the Daily Telegraph, a Paper on the Philosophy of Marriage by Mrs Lynn Linton*. London: Swan Sonnenschein, 1888.

Randall, Tim. 'Towards a Cultural Democracy: Chartist Literature 1837–1860'. M. Litt., University of Birmingham, 1994.

Ray, Gordon. *Thackeray: The Age of Wisdom. 1847–1863*. London: Oxford University Press, 1958.

Read, Donald. *Peterloo: The 'Massacre' and Its Background*. Manchester: Manchester University Press, 1958.

A Return of the Number of Newspaper Stamps, 1837–50. House of Commons Papers, 28:42, 1852.

A Return of the Number of Newspaper Stamps, 1851–53. House of Commons Papers, 39:117, 1854.

Rive, Richard, ed. *Olive Schreiner Letters 1871–1899*. Oxford: Oxford University Press, 1988.

Robertson, J. W. Scott. *The Story of the Pall Mall Gazette*. London: Oxford University Press, 1950.

Rogers, Helen. 'From "Monster Meetings" to "Fire-side Virtues"? Radical women and "the People" in the 1840s'. *Journal of Victorian Culture*, 4 (1999), 52–75.

Rosenberg, Sheila. 'The Financing of Radical Opinion: John Chapman and the *Westminster Review*', in *The Victorian Periodical Press*, ed. J. Shattock and M. Wolff. Leicester and Toronto: Leicester University Press, Toronto University Press, 1982, 167–92.

Rosenman, Ellen Bayuk. 'Spectacular Women: *The Mysteries of London* and the Female Body', *Victorian Studies*, 40 (1996), 31–64.

Rupp, Leila. 'Finding the Lesbians in Lesbian History: Reflections on Female Same Sex Sexuality in the Western World', in *The New Lesbian Studies: Into the Twentieth Century*, ed. Bonnie Zimmerman and Tony McNaron. New York: Feminist, 1996, 153–9.

Ruskin, John. *Arrows of the Chace* (1880), in *The Works of John Ruskin*, ed. E. T. Cook and Alexander Wedderburn. 39 vols. London: George Allen, 1903–12, 34: 470–1.

Said, Edward W. *Orientalism*. New York: Vintage, 1978.

[Saul, Jack.] *The Sins of the Cities of the Plain; or, The Recollections of a MaryAnn*. 2 vols. London: privately printed, 1881.

Schlor, Joachim. *Nights in the Big City: Paris, Berlin, London 1840–1930*, trans. Pierre Gottfried Imhof and Dafydd Rees Roberts. London: Reaktion, 1998.

Schults, Raymond L. *Crusader in Babylon: W. T. Stead and the Pall Mall Gazette*. Lincoln, Nebraska: University of Nebraska Press, 1972.

Shattock, J. and M. Wolff. *The Victorian Periodical Press: Samplings and Soundings*. Leicester and Toronto: University of Leicester Press, 1982.

Shirley, Mike. 'On Wings of Everlasting Power: G. W. M. Reynolds and *Reynolds's Newspaper* 1848–1876.' Ph.D., University of Illinois, 1997.

Shteir, Ann B. *Cultivating Women, Cultivating Science: Flora's Daughters and Botany in England 1760–1860*. Baltimore: Johns Hopkins University Press, 1996.

Sinha, Mrinalini. *Colonial Masculinity*. Manchester: Manchester University Press, 1995.

Sinnema, Peter W. *Dynamics of the Pictured Page: Representing the Nation in the 'Illustrated London News'*. Aldershot: Ashgate, 1998.

Snell, K. D. M. *Annals of the Labouring Poor: Social Change and Agrarian England 1660–1900*. Cambridge: Cambridge University Press, 1985.

Stanton, Elizabeth Cady. *Eighty Years and More (1815–1897)*. London: T. Fisher Unwin, 1898.

Stanton, Theodore. *The Woman Question in Europe: With an Introduction by Frances Power Cobbe*. London: Sampson Low, 1884.

Stanton, Theodore and Harriot Stanton Blatch, eds. *Elizabeth Cady Stanton as Revealed in her Letters, Diary and Reminiscences*. New York and London: Harper and Bros., 1922.

Stetz, Margaret and Mark Samuels Lasner. *The Yellow Book: A Centenary Exhibition*. Cambridge, MA: Houghton Library, 1994.

Sullivan, Alvin. *British Literary Magazines*. Westport, CT: Greenwood Press, 1983–6.

Taylor, Anthony. '*Reynolds's Newspaper*, Opposition to Monarchy and the Radical Anti-Jubilee: Britain's Anti-Monarchist Tradition Reconsidered'. *Historical Research*, 68 (1995), 318–37.

Taylor, Anthony. 'Commemoration, Memorialisation and Political Memory in Post-Chartist Radicalism: The 1885 Halifax Chartist Reunion in Context', in *The Chartist Legacy*, ed. Owen Ashton, Robert Fyson and Stephen Roberts. Woodbridge, Suffolk: Merlin, 1999, 255–85.

Thomas, Trefor. 'Introduction' to George W. M. Reynolds, *The Mysteries of London*. Keele, Staffordshire: Keele University Press, 1996.

Thomas, Trefor. 'Rereading George W. M. Reynolds's *The Mysteries of London*', in *Rereading Victorian Fiction*, ed. Alice Jenkins and Juliet John. Basingstoke: Palgrave Macmillan, 2000, 59–80.

Thompson, Dorothy. *The Chartists: Popular Politics in the Industrial Revolution*. Aldershot: Wildwood House, 1984.

Thompson, E. P. *The Making of the English Working Class*. Harmondsworth: Penguin, 1977.

Thompson, F. M. L., ed. *The Cambridge Social History of Britain, 1750–1950*. 3 vols. Cambridge: Cambridge University Press, 1990.

Thompson, John. *The Media and Modernity*. Cambridge: Polity, 1995.

Thompson, Nicola. *Reviewing Sex: Gender and the Reception of Victorian Novels*. London: Macmillan, 1996.

Tickner, Lisa. *Modern Life and Modern Subjects: British Art in the Early Twentieth Century*. New Haven: Yale University Press, 2000.

Turner, Mark W. *Backward Glances: Cruising the Queer Streets of New York and London*. London: Reaktion, 2003.

Tylor, E. B. *Primitive Culture: Researches into the Development of Mythology, Philosophy, Religion, Language, Art and Custom*. 2 vols. New York: Henry Holt, 1889.

Van Arsdel, Rosemary T. 'Mrs. Florence Fenwick Miller and the *Woman's Signal*, 1895–1899'. *Victorian Periodicals Review*, 15 (1982), 107–18.

Van Arsdel, Rosemary T. *Florence Fenwick Miller: Victorian Feminist, Journalist, and Educator*. Aldershot: Ashgate, 2001.

Van Den Abbeele, Georges. 'Introduction' to *Community at Loose Ends*, ed. Miami Theory Collective. Minneapolis: University of Minnesota Press, 1991, ix–xxxvi.

Vernon, James. *Politics and the People: A Study in English Political Culture, c. 1815–1867*. Cambridge: Cambridge University Press, 1993.

Vernon, James, ed. *Re-Reading the Constitution: New Narratives in the Political History of England's Long Nineteenth-Century*. Cambridge: Cambridge University Press, 1995.

Vernon, Peter. *Politics and the People: A Study in English Political Culture c. 1815–1867*. Cambridge: Cambridge University Press, 1993.

Vicinus, Martha. 'Lesbian History: All Theory and No Facts or All Facts and No Theory?' *Radical History Review*, 60 (1994), 57–75.

Vincent, David. *Literacy and Popular Culture: England 1750–1914*. Cambridge: Cambridge University Press, 1989.

Visram, Rozina. *Asians in Britain: 400 Years of History*. London: Pluto, 2002.

Walkowitz, Judith R. *City of Dreadful Delight*. London: Virago, 1992.

Weber, Gary. 'Henry Labouchère, *Truth* and the New Journalism of Late Victorian Britain'. *Victorian Periodicals Review*, 26 (1993), 36–43.

The Wellesley Index to Victorian Periodicals, ed. Walter E. Houghton (vols 1–2); Walter E. and Esther Rhoads Houghton (vol. 3); Walter E. Houghton, Esther Rhoads Houghton and Jean Slingerland (vol. 4); Jean Slingerland (vol. 5). 5 vols, Toronto: University of Toronto, 1966–89.

Whistler, James McNeill. *The Gentle Art of Making Enemies*. London: Heinemann, 1929 [1892].

Whyte, Frederic. *The Life of W. T. Stead*. 2 vols. London: Jonathan Cape, 1925.

Widdowson, Peter. *Hardy in History: A Case-Study in the Sociology of Literature*. London: New York: Routledge, 1989.

Wiener, Joel H. *Papers for the Millions: The New Journalism in Britain, 1850 to 1914*. Westport, CT, London: Greenwood, 1988.

Wiener, Joel. *The War of the Unstamped: The Movement to Repeal the British Newspaper Tax, 1830–1836*. Ithaca and London: Cornell University Press, 1969.

Williams, Merryn. *Thomas Hardy and Rural England*. New York: Columbia University Press, 1972.

Williams, Raymond. 'Radical and/or Respectable', in *The Press We Deserve*, ed. Richard Boston. London: Routledge and Kegan Paul, 1970, 14–26.

Williams, Raymond. *The Country and the City*. New York: Oxford University Press, 1973.

Williams, Raymond. 'The Press and Popular Culture: An Historical Perspective', in *Newspaper History from the Seventeenth Century to the Present Day*, ed. George Boyce, James Curran and Pauline Wingate. London: Constable, 1978, 41–50.

Williams, Richard, *The Contentious Crown: Public Discussion of the British Monarchy in the Reign of Queen Victoria*. Aldershot: Ashgate, 1997.

Wilson, Elizabeth. 'The Invisible *Flâneur*'. *New Left Review*, 195 (1992), 90–110.

Wolff, Janet. 'The Invisible *Flâneuse*: Women and the Literature of Modernity'. *Theory, Culture and Society*, 11 (1985), 37–46.

Wolff, Michael. 'The British Controversialist and Imperial Inquirer, 1850–1872: A Pearl from the Golden Stream', in *The Victorian Periodical Press: Samplings and*

Soundings, ed. J. Shattock and M. Wolff. Leicester and Toronto: University of Leicester Press, 1982, 367–92.

Wolff, Michael. 'Charting the Golden Stream: Thoughts on a Directory of Victorian Periodicals'. *Victorian Periodicals Newsletter*, 13 (1971), 23–38.

Wood, Marcus. *Radical Satire and Print Culture 1790–1822*. Oxford: Clarendon, 1994.

Woodring, Carl. *Victorian Samplers: William and Mary Howitt*. Lawrence: University of Kansas Press, 1952.

Yates, Edmund. Preface, *Celebrities at Home*. 3 vols. London: Office of 'The World', 1877–9.

Yates, Edmund. *Edmund Yates: His Recollections and Experiences*. 2 vols. London: Bentley, 1884.

Yeo, Eileen. 'Culture and Constraint in Working-Class Movements, 1830–1855', in *Popular Culture and Class Conflict 1590–1914: Explorations in the History of Labour and Leisure*, ed. Eileen Yeo and Stephen Yeo. Brighton: Harvester, 1981, 155–86.

Zatlin, Linda Gertner. *Aubrey Beardsley and Victorian Sexual Politics*. Oxford: Clarendon, 1990.

Zimmerman, Bonnie. '"The Dark Eye Beaming": Female Friendship in George Eliot's Fiction', in *Lesbian Texts and Contexts: Radical Revisions*, ed. Karla Jay and Joanne Glasgow. London: Onlywomen, 1992, 126–42.

Index